IMPRESSIONIST SUBJECTS

TAMAR KATZ

Impressionist Subjects

GENDER, INTERIORITY, AND

MODERNIST FICTION IN ENGLAND

UNIVERSITY OF ILLINOIS PRESS

URBANA AND CHICAGO

Library of Congress Cataloging-in-Publication Data
Katz, Tamar.
Impressionist subjects : gender, interiority, and modernist
fiction in England / Tamar Katz.
p.   cm.
Includes bibliographical references and index.
ISBN 0-252-02584-9 (alk. paper)
1. English fiction—20th century—History and criticism.
2. Modernism (Literature)—Great Britain. 3. Gender
identity in literature. 4. Impressionism in literature.
5. Subjectivity in literature. 6. Masculinity in literature.
7. Femininity in literature. 8. Sex role in literature.
9. Women in literature. 10. Self in literature. 11. Men in
literature. I. Title.
PR888.M63K38   2000
823'.9109112—dc21   99-050859

C 5 4 3 2 1

In memory of Shlomo Katz

and Rebecca Samuels Katz

and for Edward Hardy

Contents

Acknowledgments

Many people are needed to make a book possible. I thank Sandra Siegel, Molly Hite, Paul Sawyer, Satya Mohanty, Matt Morris, Julie Vandivere, Alison Sainsbury, Saundra Morris, and Wendy Jones at Cornell for their comments on this project at an early stage and since.

Bob Scholes, Nancy Armstrong, Daniel Kim, Beth Bryan, Ellen Rooney, Laurie Teal, Mark Gaipa, Jennifer Fleissner, and John Marx have been valuable interlocutors at Brown, as have the students in my courses on modernism, as well as my reading group colleagues, Carolyn Dean, Elizabeth Francis, and Gretchen Schultz.

I am pleasurably indebted—through e-mail, letters, and conferences—to Jane Garrity and Irene Tucker for their generous comments, and to Meredith Tucker for special assistance. Ann Lowry at the University of Illinois Press helped speed this book on its way.

Finally, Jim Egan and Francesca Sawaya have read this book repeatedly in its many stages and have helped it (and me) in more ways than I can ever detail.

This project has benefited from the financial support of several institutions: I am grateful to Cornell University for a Mellon fellowship that assisted with the earlier stages of this project, and to Brown University's English department for a Bronson fellowship, which greatly helped with its completion.

A version of chapter 1 was published as "'In the House and Garden of His Dream': Pater's Domestic Subject" in *Modern Language Quarterly* 56 (1995): 167–88. A version of the material on *The Waves* in chapter 6 appeared as "Modernism, Subjectivity and Narrative Form: Abstraction in *The Waves*" in *Narrative* 3 (1995): 232–51.

Introduction

The sensibility of the female young is indubitably, for early youth, the greater, and my plan would call, on the part of my protagonist, for "no end" of sensibility.
—Henry James, Preface to *What Maisie Knew*

The essential characteristic of wom[a]n is egoism. . . . Because she is one with life, past, present, and future are together in her, unbroken.

"Bang, bang, bang, on they go, these men's books, like an L.C.C. tram."
—Dorothy Richardson, "Women and the Future," *Pilgrimage*

It has been with considerable shaking in my shoes, and a feeling of treading upon a carpet of eggs, that I have taken the cow by the horns in this chapter, and broached the subject of the part that the feminine mind has played—and minds as well, deeply feminized, not technically on the distaff side—in the erection of our present criteria.
—Wyndham Lewis, *Men without Art*

How do we read the centrality of the feminine subject to modernism? The passages I have quoted suggest the connection, even as they offer the oddly mixed set of assumptions through which we must record it. For surely what we notice first is dissonance. What kinds of commonalities might join James's professionally detached plan to capitalize on female sensibility with Richardson's utopian vision of woman as an enigma who disrupts the mechanical time of conventional, mas-

culine fiction? What might either have to do with Lewis's notorious di-
atribe against what he viewed as the suffocating state of modern literature? Yet opposed as they are, all three passages associate new or modernist writing with the patterns of feminine subjectivity. This is the case
even with Lewis, whose larger point is a familiar contrast between the
damaging feminization of contemporary literature and a better—harder
and more masculine—modernism. For we should note that his "feminine
mind" refers obliquely to Woolf, Wilde, Proust, and Strachey—refers, that
is, to figures literary history has cast as modernist themselves, if in a
different way. And his comment links femininity in particular to those
modernist literary experiments that were anchored in subjectivity and
focused on an inwardness he saw as decadently passive.[1] Indeed all these
passages suggest that modernist understandings of subjectivity are themselves indebted to contemporary ideas about femininity, whether in the
form of the young girl's infinite "sensibility," woman's confounding "egoism," or the "feminine mind" more generally.

Critical readings of the last twenty years have responded in a variety of ways to the problems of gender in modernism signaled by the evident differences among these quotations. Feminist critiques have shown
how often male-authored literary production in the period cast the figure of woman as "modernism's other," to use Andreas Huyssen's influential phrase (44).[2] Such analyses have revealed the way avant-garde texts
often asserted high cultural authority by opposing themselves to practices and spaces disparaged as feminine—from mass culture to middle-
class convention to realist representation (Huyssen 44–62; Gilbert and
Gubar, *War*; Tickner). As part of this reassessment of modernism, feminist readings have also illuminated the work of insufficiently recognized
female modernists—as writers, painters, performers, editors, and activists. Such an expansion of the modernist canon may register women's
participation in a modernist aesthetic of disruption; it may also register
the way women's activity in modernism can resist masculinist arguments
about the virility of art. Bridget Elliott and Jo-Ann Wallace articulate the
premise of many such studies when they suggest that critics should examine the positions of female writers in order to reveal the breaks in
dominant modernist ideology, in order to show how modernist regula-
tory "discourses [may be] disrupted and complicated" by the analysis of
women in modernism (16). In all these varied strands of feminist analysis, recent critics have challenged the traditional exclusions that shaped
literary and academic canons, and have begun to trace the historical discourses shaping modernism and its canonization, not least the claim

threaded through much modernist work that great literature rises above such historical particularities as gender.[3]

Such readings, however, risk producing a divide within modernism, and I have opened with the resemblances among these passages in order to begin to unsettle that division. In arguing that the feminine subject is central to modernism, and in stressing—as I will—the continuity between positions as apparently varied as those of James and Richardson, Ford and Woolf, I wish to shift our critical gaze from what has become an overly familiar opposition. Here the obsessive modernist attention to women divides between a canonical and conservative masculinist modernism which imagines woman as its debased specular object or its disruptive "other" and the oppositional traditions of primarily female writers for whom feminine subjectivity enables a radical freedom, dissolving conventional hierarchies and narratives.[4] While I will attend to the crucial political differences that this divide names, I will be arguing for a different reading of modernism, one which registers the far more problematic mixing of authority and subversion within literary and historical texts and which charts the highly ambiguous work of gender in shaping the terms of that mixture. I will trace the importance of femininity in simultaneously establishing and complicating modernist cultural authority. My account will thus read across the work of male and female writers in order to examine the function of gender in the mingled conservative and radical politics of modernism.[5] Most importantly, I will argue that the category of femininity is itself pivotal for assessing the way modernist texts aspired to both anarchy and order, to stable meanings and a vertiginous, fluid refusal of reference, to both political commitments and claims for the autonomy of high culture.

I have chosen to read across modernism's conservative and subversive impulses and across male- and female-authored texts for two related reasons. The first is that these conceptual divides obscure how far women function as modernism's characteristic *subjects,* rather than as its objects or others.[6] Many writers, both male and female, saw modern fiction and modern ideas of the subject as based productively—if also problematically—in feminine subjectivity. Writers attempting to chart an explicitly masculine literary authority, for instance, found it tied—both enablingly and discomfortingly—to the patterns they saw in the modern female mind and took as the basis for narrative experiment. The troubled accounts of modern art they produced thus owe a great deal to the definitions of feminine subjectivity sketched there. And these same difficulties and definitions, this cultural logic, were often shared by female, feminist writers who turned to women's consciousness as the basis for an alternative social and literary order. Thus Henry James's heroines and Ford Madox Ford's secretive female and feminized characters, for instance, no less than Dorothy Richardson's enigmatic protagonist or Virginia Woolf's mobile female consciousnesses, suggest that modernist narrative method is shaped to an idea of the "feminine mind."

But still more crucially, reading the centrality of the feminine subject in this way demands that we reimagine what feminine subjectivity means and how it works at this cultural moment. Much productive critical work has shown how often the category of the "feminine" appears as a disruptive underside of order or logic in this period (DeKoven; Kofman; Jardine; Lyon, "Women").[7] Here femininity names a space that unravels literary authority—whether it is disparaged for its failures or lauded for its resistant potential—a space that disturbs the cultural terms in which modernism traditionally claims power: psychological interiority and the aesthetic sphere's autonomy from history. But while such readings of femininity as disruption point toward an important gendering of modern discourse, I argue that they underestimate the ways femininity has simultaneously been linked to these same privileged terms of modern culture and modernist art—linked, that is, to interiority and literary autonomy (N. Armstrong; Psomiades). To address fully the interconnections between gender and modernism we need to read both resonances of femininity and we need to confront their peculiar—historically weighted—contradiction. In reading the centrality of the feminine subject then, I want to consider the way this subject both establishes and disrupts modernist models of literary authority.

Indeed I will argue that such paradoxical doubleness is precisely the quality that makes feminine subjectivity important for this cultural movement, and makes a reading of that subject crucial for understanding modernism's ideas and its politics. The female subject is central because she frames a series of contradictions central to modernism. She at once represents a decentered subject and the most securely enclosed interiority; the most thorough construction by historically specific places as well as the ability to transcend history. In this way she offers a figure for modernism's contradictory aesthetic self-definition, its troubled attempt to manage a relation to the history that produces it. Modern woman emphasizes both art's inevitable historical implication, its social specificity, and art's most emphatic claim to autonomy, its claim to escape the shaping force of the world into a realm of universality and abstraction. And as a figure for paradox itself, she also frames modernism's

claim to move between these positions, its claim to stand apart from place, freed by this very ambiguity.

In *Impressionist Subjects* I consider modernism's dependence upon this gendered subject as a problem simultaneously historical and formal. I address this issue by examining key examples of modernist fiction, reading such fiction as part of a network of historical discourses which shaped its narrative experiments and its conceptions of subjectivity, as well as its attempts to define a cultural role for literature. But the book also reads, reciprocally, the way modernist formal innovation shapes our characteristic cultural understandings of identity. To explore these connections, I focus on a strand of modernist writing centered on subjectivity—on those "strategies of inwardness" Fredric Jameson terms "the most influential formal impulses of canonical modernism" (*Fables* 2). I focus, that is, on literary impressionism, in particular as it was produced in England.

Literary impressionism—as it was first rendered influential by Walter Pater, and as it was critically elaborated by Ford Madox Ford, among others—articulated a sense of social instability and change in the late nineteenth and early twentieth centuries. Often interpreted by nineteenth-century critics as "the first misstep down the slippery slope of Decadence," such impressionism voiced the idea that existing conventions of representation were inadequate to capture the world's complexity (Matz 434). Like visual impressionism—a related cultural development which is outside the scope of this book's argument—impressionist fiction delivered this critique by suggesting a rift between conventions of realist representation and the subject's perceptions, as well as between realist conventions and the simultaneity of the object world. Often speaking in the name of a greater, more mimetic realism, theories of impressionism like the one Ford Madox Ford began to spell out in "On Impressionism, I" turned to alternate sources of authority, including the authority of a character's perceptions—stressing the technique's power to render the fundamental "expression of an ego" (167) and "to render those queer effects of real life that are like so many views seen through bright glass" (174).[8]

In thus focusing modernist fiction on the perceptual processes of the subject, impressionism draws attention to the problematic nature of subjectivity. Presuming that we can know the world only from the impress of sensations upon us, such fiction uses the parameters and processes of the impressionable subject to create a range of characteristically modernist experiments in reorganizing narrative—from the use of a central consciousness through unreliable first-person and stream-of-consciousness narration.[9] But impressionism also illuminates modernism's gendered patterns, for as Wyndham Lewis begins to suggest, it was frequently associated with femininity. Impressionist texts were often fascinated by female character and anchored their narrative methods and claims to truth on a complex mixture of dependence on women—as exemplary perceiving subjects—and strategies of distance from them. They thus reveal how far modernist debates about the shape of the subject are anchored in the contradictions of contemporary ideas about female subjectivity.

Impressionist fiction's attention to feminine subjectivity arises from a range of historical and literary pressures, focused in large part through the nineteenth-century novel, with its traditional interest in women's plots and sensibilities. But impressionism is particularly keyed to the register of femininity at the turn of the century because of the way social changes in this period brought women ever more acutely to the center of a debate always vital to questions of modern subjectivity: the question of woman's public or private nature. From the late nineteenth through the early twentieth centuries, middle-class women moved with increasing visibility into the public sphere—as activists, consumers, and professionals—and literary texts at the time both shape and reveal what that transition means (Ardis; Bowlby, *Just Looking;* Vicinus). As the image of the private, unworldly domestic woman gave way to that of a modern woman who traveled far more freely in public yet still often claimed to stand apart from the world's corruption, feminine subjectivity offered a powerful arena for questions about the status of the subject in general. And it offered an arena for the question of literature's relation to the public sphere as well—its claim to distinguish itself from historical pressures and remain similarly unworldly.

It is important to recognize how thoroughly this intersection of ideas about woman, literary authority, and subjectivity is formed—like modernism itself—by the broad, continuing historical horizon of modernity (Calinescu; Felski; Nicholls 5–23). The social shifts critics have noted at the turn of the century—among them middle-class women's new public presence, vigorous debates about the nature of psychology, and radical alterations in literary form—emerge in the context of longer-range historical pressures: the rise of the commodity form and the literary marketplace under capitalism, and the related rise of a bourgeois, individualized subject. To register this view means modifying a familiar account of literature and culture in late-nineteenth- and early-twentieth-century England—the history that casts this period as one of radical disjunction, both in narrative methods and in the understandings of subjectivity and gender with which they are enmeshed. This story, favored by many modernists themselves, sees a clear break between modernism and the Victorian period which preceded it.[10]

I will be arguing that such a narrative of rupture deserves a degree of skepticism. In part this is because the story has shaped literary history itself as a gender divide for so long—cast it as the revolt of a masculinized experimental modernism against feminized Victorian fiction (Douglas). More recently and more productively, from the perspective of a history of women's writing, this break has been read as marking dramatically different stages in women's social position: the before and after of women's increasing freedom to work, vote, and circulate publicly (Ardis). But while these accounts draw our attention to historically crucial shifts—from the increasing professionalization of literature to suffrage and the New Woman movement—the story of rupture may obscure cultural continuities important to understanding the form such changes took. Further, by borrowing a language of liberation from modernism, this story may obscure the ideological complexities of modernist cultural movements, which neither jettisoned the weight of the cultural past in order to fly free of it nor remained stuck in an unchanging, repetitive history. To consider fully the connection between ideas about women and those about subjectivity and literary authority requires that we refigure this narrative and read the continuities between the Victorian and the modernist as such continuities shape cultural change. In particular, we must read this period as one in which familiarly conservative Victorian structures like domestic ideology reach forward to take new forms, while literary experiments build on older conceptual bases. The newly mobile, feminized impressionist subject draws upon long-standing problems of modern subjectivity as it reforms them.

Modernism's understanding of the links between subjectivity and gender was shaped by the complexities of the Victorian culture that preceded it. In the past decade, much critical work analyzing the nineteenth century has shown how the figure of the middle-class woman helped form the idea of a normative, interiorized subject—a subject that would be crucial to modernist experiment. The domestic ideology of separate spheres produced an ideal of woman and the home as ruled by the emotions, thus forging an equation between the private sphere and the privatized subject. In doing so it helped recast a world seen through explicitly political conflicts into one that could be understood in depoliticized, psychological terms (N. Armstrong; Poovey; Gallagher; Psomiades). The bourgeois subject thus imagined was defined by her interiority, by the possession of psychological depths and by qualities purely internal. This private subject offered the novel that described her a form of cultural authority. Narrating matters of the mind and the heart, the novel might claim to address itself to a set of universal truths which shape, order, and may ultimately subsume the force of historical contingency. But this female subject is also a contradictory one. Not only might she promise interiority and separation from historical pressures or a public market-place; at the same time she signaled quite opposed qualities. Women might equally seem historically limited: tied to local and embodied per-ceptions (Poovey 125; Schor; S. Smith). Unable to move beyond their particular place to attain the authority of ostensibly wider and more gen-eral truths, women could be seen as limiting the novel's claim to social transcendence even as they had come to seem necessary to it.

As I have begun to suggest, the middle-class woman who might rep-resent both an interiorized separation from history and politics and an immersion in specific historical places is an important figure for mod-ernism. For modernist writers were notoriously troubled in their attempts to imagine their relationship to history. Indeed when critics have tried to assess the politics of this cluster of movements they have most often done so by asking whether such work acknowledges its formation by historical contexts or instead claims to be autonomous from them. Does modernism make a conservative claim to the timelessness of the artwork, to uncovering the universal depths of human character? Or do modern-ist texts instead recognize and comment on the historical conditions of their own and the subject's making?

The debate has long rested on modernism's understanding of subjec-tivity. Diagnoses of the subject's isolation, for instance, have grounded critiques of modernism since the early twentieth century, perhaps most acutely in a Marxist tradition. Georg Lukács objected that modernist lit-erature's exaltation of subjectivity—embodying capitalist reification—falsely isolates the individual from historical forces and prevents the modernist novel from diagnosing and thus helping to change social con-ditions ("Narrate"). More recently, in *The Political Unconscious* Fredric Jameson has described point-of-view narration as a prime modernist "con-tainment strategy" (221) for "derealizing" (214) and displacing the his-torical content of literary texts.[11] At the same time, the methods of mod-ernism have also seemed to exemplify an opposed trend, one embodied in the period's much-discussed "crisis of the subject." In this reading modernist narrative experiment instead decenters traditional realist no-tions of autonomous or coherent character and unravels the depoliticiz-ing effects of the bourgeois individual and its plots—often through asso-ciation with a radically disruptive femininity. Marianne DeKoven, for instance, citing Benjamin, Adorno, and Marcuse as well as feminist critics from Rachel Blau DuPlessis to Julia Kristeva, traces a "promodern-ist" critical tradition which claims that the fragmented subject produced by such experiments undermines any illusion of individual autonomy and thus disrupts the social systems that produce it (6–10). And Michael Trat-ner has recently argued that modernism can best be read as the rejection of individualism; it participates instead in a range of early-twentieth-century theories of collectivism. Modernist authors, he notes, wrote "from and to . . . the mass unconscious" (47).

I will be arguing here that the feminine subject and the literary im-pressionism that depended upon her belong at the center of this debate over modernism—not because they support one reading of modernist politics over another, but because their very doubleness, their contribu-tion to both readings of modernism, helps generate modernism's critical and political contradictions themselves. Reading the historical and for-mal shape of the connection between impressionism and feminine sub-jectivity thus tells us a great deal about the terms of both modernism and its criticism. And such a reading may illuminate how accounts of mod-ernist subjectivity, and thus of modernist politics, may be so divided.

We can locate the contradiction within the very premises of impres-sionism, which far from simply claiming inwardness or refusing it—as critics have in turn suggested—instead both offers and retracts it. Thus in impressionism the idea that we know the world only from the sensa-tions that press in upon us points toward two different views of charac-ter. On the one hand impressionism seems to suggest that the subject is indeed isolated, its only contact with the world a stream of unreliable perceptions. In this view we appear as autonomous selves, constructing fictions about the shape of a world that is outside us. But impressionism equally posits a subject who is thoroughly permeated by sensation and is thus so formed by its specific setting that it lacks any autonomy; rather it is wholly constructed from without. Constituted by the world's cate-gories, this subject is woven and rewoven; it is the place where histori-cal structures make their mark.[12]

Walter Pater's familiar aestheticist version of this contradiction may stand as a brief if resonant example here, one I will analyze at greater length in chapter 1. For the moment, we might note the tension between juxtaposed claims in his "Conclusion" to *The Renaissance.* "Experience," he writes in a famous passage, "is ringed round for each one of us by that thick wall of personality through which no real voice has ever pierced on its way to us" (187). Yet, immediately afterward he proposes a very different subject, one whose "physical life, is a perpetual motion . . . the modification of the tissues of the brain under every ray of light and sound"

(187). Pater's aesthetic subject, immersed in its impressions, is thus walled off from a world beyond it and yet in the next clause seems to have no existence that is not formed by the very matter and impulses of the world. Impressionist fiction reorganizes narrative around these concerns, and thus centers literary experiment on one of the main tensions structuring the modern "subject," a tension famously visible in the term itself as Althusser framed it in his influential essay "Ideology and Ideological State Apparatuses": that if we are subject to, subjected by, the ideological structures of the world, their prime effect is to make us see ourselves as autonomous individuals.[13]

Like the accounts of feminine subjectivity with which it is so often entwined, impressionism insists on both aspects of the modern subject at once, and moves between them. It installs an open, impressionable, socially constructed subject at the center of fiction, even as it works through strategies by which this figure may be effectively reenclosed. The genre thus presents an insistent ambiguity, a contradiction, and part of my purpose in this study is to reconsider how such a contradiction in modernism may be read. DeKoven, in *Rich and Strange: Gender, History, Modernism,* has suggested that the contradiction at the center of modernist literary experiment renders such texts instances of deconstructive self-erasure, in which certainties are dissolved and texts made unstable (20). This powerful critical account registers the doubleness of modernist texts and their critique of ideological figures like the autonomous subject; feminist narratological work has similarly argued for the subversive power of contradictory and ambiguous stories (Mezei).

But there are reasons to hesitate before aligning such contradictory literary works wholly with instability and the undermining of ideological certitude. For at the same time that we read the force of critique in these texts, we must also take seriously the way that modernism in particular often used contradiction, ambiguity, and uncertainty instead as the signs of a privileged textual difficulty, and as the signs of that privileged sensibility which can hold contraries together in the mind. The force of this claim persists in part because modernism has played such an important role in giving it institutional effect in the twentieth-century, helping to shape the academic criteria that value texts for their complexity. Ambiguity, that is, may itself generate a form of high cultural authority for modernist literature rather than disabling it (White).[14] Indeed, as a movement that often aligned forms of high cultural stratification with an oppositional social stance, modernism is particularly interesting for the thoroughness with which it entwines aesthetic strategies that anchor critique with those that constitute new forms of cultural authority. The difficulty of disentangling such impulses is particularly acute for impressionist subjectivity, which will remake the open subject as the center of a new definition of literary authority, and in doing so effectively reenclose it.

I have suggested that impressionism's doubleness draws upon the divided pattern of feminine subjectivity in the period. To take account of this intermingling of critique and authority, we must trace narrative impressionism and the ambiguities of its subject back to particular turn-of-the-century discourses in which women are crucial figures. Critics have called our attention to the links between the New Woman movement of the 1890s and the rise of new fictional strategies; impressionism offers a key instance of this convergence (Ardis; DuPlessis; Bjorhovde; Gilbert and Gubar, *War*). We can mark the connection through the emergence of particular authors, noting that at least one critic has called George Egerton's New Woman fiction of the 1890s the first example of impressionist technique in English (Harris), and that Henry James's much-noted narrative experiments often center on the perceptions of rebellious young women.

But to read these literary events adequately we need to examine more closely the broader contemporary debates over women's changing place and the patterns of female subjectivity from which impressionism emerges. For in the late nineteenth century, as middle-class women began to move out of the home, advocates of these New Women deliberately described them as possessing a kind of culturally important doubleness. Advocates cast modern women as figures who could render the public and the private self compatible—as subjects who could bridge a radical openness to the world and an enclosure from it. As critics have noted, the New Woman explicitly rejects the Victorian angel's domestic seclusion; she travels in the world and is imagined as fully immersed in it (Ardis). And yet we must register too that such immersion hardly cancels the powerful notion of the New Woman's interiority. Indeed modern woman can promise to reform her society precisely because she remains unspoiled by the corruption she sees around her. She thus exemplifies the way a subject's immersion in the world's messy details might be reconceived as a form of cultural virtue; and she transfigures and extends the unworldliness that was so central to the earlier domestic woman. Paradoxically then, the newly mobile woman of the 1890s used the conventions of a conservative domestic ideology and its ideal of an untouched subject to anchor her more radical social work as well as her critique of the domestic sphere itself. And as a center for literary experiment, this figure's complex relation to domestic interiority begins to suggest the way that modernism

itself might draw upon a domesticity—and a Victorian cultural tradition—it seems to disdain. The New Woman, that is, offers a precursor
and a model for modernism's claim to absorb and stand apart from a commodified world.

Both immersed in the world and removed from it, modern woman
could appear as a powerful enigma in these discussions. For this reason
she was particularly central to those turn-of-the-century debates about
the mysterious nature of subjectivity that informed modernist literary
experiment.[15] It is as an enigma that cannot be pinned down or conclusively placed that the modern woman provided a figure for modernism's
experiments and its privileging of ambiguity. She offered a spur to new
narrative techniques that both created and exploited her contradictions,
anchoring a new literary movement in her cultural possibilities.

As a result, the modern woman's imagined contradictions had a divided effect. In part they provided the New Woman herself with a form
of social authority, by suggesting that she might exceed the restrictions
of conventional social rules, and by suggesting that she had the power to
reform the nation while remaining unsullied. But these same contradictions placed her in an unstable relation to the writers who drew on her
complexity. Focusing on this complexity, and developing new narrative
forms to elaborate its effects, modernist writers might affiliate themselves
with modern women as an exemplary subjects. However they also, in the
same gesture, defined for themselves a professional expertise and cultural
authority that could distance them from women. They defined the mastery of narrative form as a specialized artistic skill that could exploit
woman's nature while standing above it.

This turn-of-the-century vision of modern woman's contradictions
thus opened a way for modernist literature to establish new terms of
cultural authority through its difficulty and its innovation. For woman's
ability to reconcile the idea of a subject immersed in the world with the
notion of a subject securely self-enclosed provided a useful figure for
modernist texts managing their own relation to history—as a figure
whose mysterious mind could limit the implications of her historical
immersion. But modern woman, like her Victorian counterpart, also presented difficulties for literary authority, and particularly for the ideal of
ahistorical disinterest on which it had been propped. For despite the potential of their mystery, women were also persistently associated with
the local and the particular, with an immersion in the petty social details of everyday life. Feminine subjectivity thus raised acutely for modernism the problem of how historically specified, how located, the literature focused on women might be.

The problem was intensified by impressionist presumptions. For when impressionism imagined the subject as formed by its perceptions, it not only opened subjectivity, it also tied character to the local contexts that permeated it. If Walter Pater's exemplary domestic child is formed by the sensations that enter him at an early age, is he not shaped by the very specific historical space of the home and its meanings? If Virginia Woolf's characters unfold in and absorb the post–World War I urban landscape, are they not defined and limited by it? The anchoring of impressionism in a feminized subject intensifies strategic dilemmas facing modernism more generally: how to write femininity without seeming limited to it, how to engage with historical specificity while signaling the transcendence of historical place, how to stand above the local and claim a more general truth. The problem will center modernist notions of character and literary authority. Attempting to move between a subject permeated by the world and one enclosed from it, modernist impressionism also tries to move rhetorically between a subject imagined as socially specified, formed by particular places, and the possibilities of a subject that might seem to be above place, to be universal.

This last move is perhaps impressionism's—indeed modernism's—most characteristic and most culturally powerful, as well as its most troubling. I trace throughout this study a rhetorical shift which critic Charles Altieri has noted as central to modernist poetry, a rhetoric I argue is marked by impressionism's complex and uneasy dependence upon the cultural patterns of feminine subjectivity. Impressionist fiction attempts to convert the social specificity of its subjects into something more abstract; attempts to generalize or universalize the subject, an impulse that continues despite the movement's persistent criticisms of abstraction and universality.[16] We might think here of the passages I have already cited from Pater's "Conclusion," describing a mind or a soul suspended in space, occupying no particular location. Or we might consider the narrator of Ford's *The Good Soldier*, with his insistence that he is not a feminized American cuckold but rather a bewildered everyman; what could happen to him, he suggests, could happen to anyone. We might note the epiphanies of Dorothy Richardson's *Pilgrimage*, which move the protagonist into a register of "reality" insistently placeless and abstracted, or the possibility in Woolf's *To the Lighthouse* that mother and child can be adequately depicted by the painting of a purple triangle. While all these texts critique the impulse to abstraction and all offer alternate accounts of the subject's formation by historically specific contexts and ideologies, all nonetheless use abstraction as a path to narrative and cultural authority—to validate a speaker, to distance the author, or to stake out a claim for the text's own wider view. In this they attempt to resolve a difficulty intensified by impressionism's reliance on the feminine subject: she at once offers a model for imagining how historically specific context may be evaded and subsumed, and provides the feminized subject matter such literature is culturally pressed to transcend.

In impressionism the rhetorical movement into abstraction intervenes in the problem of subjectivity at the genre's core. Abstraction powerfully reencloses the subject, reestablishes that dream of autonomy which impressionism begins by denying. In the course of doing so, such fiction makes an explicit claim about the social work of the literary text. Abstraction seems to signal that literary work, and particularly literary experiment, offers a privileged arena in which universality can be wrought from social detail, autonomy from immersion, a generalized subject from a gendered one. In the course of this movement, modernist impressionism may powerfully efface the historical and gendered context which it is also committed to sketching, and which sets the debate's terms.

Of course my own analysis here—like all analytic work—itself encounters the unavoidable problems of abstraction and generalization. In particular this study often faces the difficulty of using one particular generalization: that of the "feminine subject." For while my aim is to analyze the extent to which writers of an earlier period imaginatively constructed subjects as feminine in historically specific ways, the category of femininity never simply refers to historical particularities without grouping them; in doing so the term itself can efface or override a range of other details. But if my own shaping of texts and categories through the rubric of femininity cannot fully avoid this problem, we might productively reflect upon this as a sign of the continuing importance of modernism itself for feminist criticism. Indeed we might read it as signaling the important historical interconnections between modernity and Western feminism that modernism so distinctly embodies. For just as modernism could evoke the ostensibly unmarked category of feminine subjectivity as a vital part of its abstracting strategy, so too Western feminism, as Denise Riley has shown, has a long history of claiming and contesting the general category of "women." Indeed the contradiction between specificity and generality, between difference and abstraction, Joan Scott suggests, is intrinsic to feminism—which is built on the fault lines of enlightenment ideas about the universal subject as much as it reveals them. The connection is especially pronounced in American feminist literary criticism, where the work of a modernist like Woolf has been so influential. The debates Woolf played out between attention to historical detail and a turn to generalization recur in the development of feminist literary canons and reading strategies, which early on often risked unselfconsciously generalizing the model of white, middle-class women's texts, and overemphasizing the resemblances among women from very different global, class, or racialized places at the expense of their different historical specificities. My argument in this book suggests that it is not only the history of feminism which teaches us to be self-conscious about such problems but that the complexity of modernism may do so too.

In *Impressionist Subjects* I seek to read the literary texts of impressionism as part of the networks of historically specific discourses (about gender, about the subject, about the status of the literary) that give them meaning. I also seek to register the discursive specificity of modernist impressionism—not only in its particular formal and narrative methods but in the claims, themselves historical, for what experimental narrative can do. Through this reading I locate in impressionism's connection with feminine subjectivity a self-conscious set of questions about the subject and history, about social specificity and universality, that are central to modernism as a whole. Writers such as T. S. Eliot and James Joyce, it has long been acknowledged, explicitly defined modernist art in terms of the problematic desire to merge the temporal and the timeless, to transfigure the material of a historical moment into monuments in the "ideal order" of universal art (Eliot 44).[17] Critics, however, have often ascribed this interest to a high modernism they distinguish from impressionism through its attention to myth, to objectivity rather than subjectivity, through its commitment to "words set free," in Hugh Kenner's resonant phrase (*Pound Era* 121).[18] Indeed it is through these methods that canonical writers such as Joyce and Eliot were long understood as the central exemplars of modernism. My reading here suggests not only that impressionism also participates in these modernist concerns but that its self-consciousness illuminates modernist questions especially clearly and lets us recast them. Impressionism can be most acute in this analysis, I argue, precisely because its account of history and subjectivity acknowledges and foregrounds modernism's complex relation to the feminine subject. Reading this relation may allow us to trace the interconnections of gender and generalization, historical specificity and universalism, both in modernism and in our own critical work.[19]

As my discussion has begun to suggest, if I am tracing here a trajectory within modernist fiction of the way abstraction may erase the marks of fiction's historically specific conditions of possibility, I am also tracing a movement that shapes the span of critical approaches to reading modernism. To read the way modernism both registers its own historical nature and attempts to generalize it away is thus to participate in the ongoing critical project of historicizing modernism and revealing its political implications. But I am also suggesting that such analysis must let us see the way the double strands of modernism inform our own critical projects. This commonality with modernism has most often been visible upon in criticism that presents literary texts as shut off from the world, or in the rhetorical pressure of abstraction, but it appears too, I would argue, in those critical priorities we too quickly oppose to modernism—in the contemporary concern to trace the importance of location, of cultural specificity (C. Kaplan). While modernism's belief in the power of art either to resolve or to occlude such problems may seem far less certain than it did early in the century, the broader dynamic of questions this belief addressed cannot be dismissed. The movement from nineteenth- to twentieth-century culture suggests that there are no clear breaks from the past, that we still occupy a social terrain shaped by modernism, as modernists occupied one shaped by Victorians. It also suggests that such continuities may nonetheless yield change rather than repetition. We can be more self-conscious about our cultural and rhetorical embedding only if we learn to read the complexity and self-consciousness already present there. Reading and crediting the difficult politics of modernism, with its interest in both specificity and abstraction, requires that we register the complexity of its relation to the feminine subject who holds these terms apart as well as fuses them together.

This book makes its argument through close readings of a series of central impressionist texts and debates. I begin my account of the cultural and gender politics of impressionism's methods by examining aestheticism—an important influence in formulating the idea of the sensitive spirit finely tuned to its sensations. Walter Pater's "Conclusion" to *The Renaissance,* from which I have already quoted, has long seemed an ideal illustration of the dilemmas of impressionist subjectivity. Both wholly enclosed and yet also formed by a web of sensations, the Paterian aesthete illustrates in a condensed manner the problems of the modernist subject. Yet it is important to read the way this rather disembodied figure is shaped by the more explicitly social spaces of Victorian culture. And while Pater has most often been critically placed in relation to the masculine, high-cultural sphere of nineteenth-century Oxford, with its elaborated language of homoeroticism and classicism, I frame him here instead in relation to figures of Victorian femininity and feminine space— figures that recur through his work in the image of the "House Beautiful" or the redemptive Christian household of *Marius the Epicurean*. In particular, I turn to one of Pater's central essays on developing consciousness—"The Child in the House"—to read his model of the impressionable subject in the context of Victorian domestic ideology. This ideology, which maps national health and security onto the image of a world split between safe interiors and risky exteriors, sets the cultural stakes of imagining what it would mean to have an interior or to fail to have one, and thus frames the question of subjectivity for modernism.

For Pater, this domestic context is enabling; it allows him to cast his eccentric aesthete as that compelling object of Victorian attention, the vulnerable, feminized child, and to unite a meditation on sensation with a haunting image of home and its failures. But the domestic setting also renders the essay's authority precarious; while it gives its speaker a form of cultural centrality, it also threatens to place him in too limited a context, restricts his ability as a narrator to range across experience and summarize it. In short, feminized domesticity makes the speaker vulnerable. Pater's essay shows in an exemplary manner how a subject so densely enmeshed in social contexts may, in response, be translated into one that is ostensibly generic or universal. It offers a model, for my studies in this book, of how abstraction may touch even sensation itself—converting fears about the eminently social world of the home into a glorious aesthetic play of color and light. It also provides a model of how abstraction is implicated in the questions of narrative distance that will be so crucial to later fictional experiments. As Pater's text will suggest, abstraction modifies the impressionable subject's relation to femininity; by rendering the impressionable subject a closed one, it allows him to range through domestic spaces without ever being fully situated in or by them.

However, the Victorian notion of home, and of a female or feminized subject whose mobility is limited by its sphere, changes at the end of the nineteenth century. Indeed one of the shaping forces behind modernist narrative revision is the rejection of the domestic marriage plot that powerfully formed Victorian novels, and a concomitant recasting of the borders between public and private offered in the ideal of home. In chapter 2 I consider how middle-class women's entrance into the public sphere altered notions of subjectivity and narrative in the 1890s. To do so I examine some of the decade's central discussions of female knowledge and interiority as they appear in debates over degeneration and New Woman fiction, over venereal disease and the sexual knowledge of young girls. I read these debates together with fiction by three writers of the 1890s whose work takes a range of different positions on the issues of New Woman debates, from sexuality to marriage, and whose cultural terrain spans the popular and the highbrow: George Egerton, Sarah Grand, and Henry James. Taken together, however, their texts sketch a coherent cultural vision of this new female subject.

Examining Egerton's eroticized female characters, Grand's heroine crusading for male chastity, and James's complex female consciousness in the context of such contemporary debates, I analyze the enigmatic and permeable female subject central to fin-de-siècle literature and culture. This new young woman, defying or denied the conventional security of home, is exposed to the world rather than cloistered from it. But I argue that this figure for subjective openness—to brutal facts or to impressions—in fact offers a new form of enclosure and social authority. Merging an encounter with the forces of the public world and an immunity from its corruption, she becomes a figure for a privileged and enigmatic doubleness. It is this doubleness which establishes the mysterious quality of her interiority. A cluster of related narrative strategies—including limited point-of-view narration and the use of a central consciousness—convey and construct this mystery, as narrators both enter the minds of young women and preserve the sense that these minds are inviolately remote from our access. And in the course of fitting narrative to this new figure, writers generate many of the characteristic arguments of modernist literary authority, by claiming modern women's power for their own formal experiments. Such texts thus transfer the ideological basis of Victorian domesticity—the claim to be a discrete social space above the debased public realm—into an account of how this newly mobile subject and a new experimental literature may transcend convention more generally.

The newly mobile woman thus offers literature a subject both public and private, vulnerable and interiorized. The balance of this book examines the way the central texts of impressionist fiction in England are shaped by this figure and find in her characteristically modernist definitions—and problems—for literary authority. One of the clearest problems this figure poses is how to ground masculine literary authority. Male-authored modernism has long been known for its ambivalence about inheriting what was seen as the feminized literary tradition of the novel. I argue here that masculine literary authority develops its characteristically modernist strategies of narrative distance from an engagement with this mobile female subject. And rather than founding such authority on a simple denial of femininity and its cultural terms, male narrators and masculinized narrative strategies derive their authority from a resemblance to feminine subjects and stories.

Thus in chapters 3 and 4 I focus on modernist attempts to shape forms of masculine narrating authority and to relate them to dangerously proximate models of female subjectivity. I begin by sketching in chapter 3 some cultural anxieties about masculine agency and British imperial decline at the turn of the century. To do so, I turn to texts that helped shape definitions of masculinity and literariness in the period, texts that also have centered our critical accounts of this culture: Joseph Conrad's *Lord Jim* and the handbook of the scouting movement, Lord Baden-Powell's *Scouting for Boys*. While these two works occupy quite different cultural spaces—with Conrad's novel constructing the terms of a new, self-consciously modern literature and Baden-Powell's Scouting movement one of the most influential practical shapers of imperial youth—both texts claim the broad social purpose of linking "character" to masculinity and connecting questions of empire to those of consciousness. Thus Conrad's novel proposes a model of imperial masculinity that can ground high-cultural narrative innovation and Baden-Powell's handbook attempts to train a version of boyish character that will exceed the particular setting of empire to provide a general norm of citizenship.

Both texts share a concern with the unraveling of masculine interiority that links literary impressionism with the contemporary cultural attention to masculine citizenship. Both attempt to construct a form of what we might term impressionist imperial agency by reimagining manly character as able to absorb impressions and consolidate them into an authoritative subject. For Conrad's novel, such consolidation works through the figure of its narrator and through its narrative method, which recasts a multiplicity of stories about the failure of the traditional imperial hero into the drama of a new existential heroism: the difficulty of braving an abstract and unknowable universe. But this text must attempt—with great difficulty—to disentangle the value of such masculine uncertainty from its feminized incarnation in the novel. To do so it sets the narrator Marlow's characteristically modernist interpretive stance against the alternate, historically particular account offered by a female character explicitly tied to colonial and romance plots. In doubling masculine abstraction with feminized specificity, blurring the authority of male uncertainty into a female lack of knowledge, *Lord Jim* raises questions about the relation of masculinized modernism to the feminine spaces it claims to surmount.

Chapter 4 returns to the work of narrative uncertainty and to the problematic closeness between masculine narration and feminine subjectivity. Here I turn to one of the classic examples of modernist unreliable narration, Ford Madox Ford's *The Good Soldier*, as a place to consider how a feminized unreliability helped shape modernist ideas about narrative distance and continued to shape critical responses to modernism through the twentieth century. The chapter considers the way Ford's use of an unreliable narrator in *The Good Soldier* uneasily bases male narration on a feminine model, while trying to disentangle modernist literary authority from the association. Indeed, for Ford's text, the association is inevitable; modernity itself appears here as a feminizing social decline that has reshaped subjectivity. In the modern world subjects are both secretively, solipsistically enclosed and violently breached by the desire to tell their secret stories—problems which are attributed to female character. Ford's central strategy of unreliable narration makes explicit the difficulty of this link for a modern fictional project itself founded on knowing and narrating interiority. Both the text's embodied narrator and Ford's authorial persona respond to this feminization of subjectivity and storytelling with a series of distancing abstractions: they turn to the stance of impersonal everyman to cope with the feminine terms in which they have defined modern narration. As Ford's essays on modern fiction in the *English Review* show, such distance—a form of abstracting narrative impersonality—is deeply implicated in the desire to imagine a modern novel with no debt to a feminized Victorian literary past, and to imagine modern authorship as truly general and disinterested. For critics since Ford, this narrative structure has continued to extend the paradigm of the universalized narrator, and to associate it with the claims of modernism, while effacing the historical relationship between epistemology and femininity that Ford's texts reveal.

Where chapters 3 and 4 read the project of generating an impersonal or universalized masculine narrating subject against a vision of female subjectivity that seems discomfortingly central, the final two chapters of the book examine feminist versions of impressionist paradigms to consider how literary feminism both adopts and refigures the question of the modern subject's relation to interiority and abstraction. In particular, I consider the forms impressionist premises took from two female modernists, Dorothy Richardson and Virginia Woolf, who explicitly anchored aesthetic experiment in visions of a modern female subject. I focus on the work of these two writers because as innovators in impressionism and as feminists of very different sorts, they have centered much recent critical work on the relation between feminine subjectivity and modernism; in particular both writers have been important to recent attempts to imagine an alternate, feminist modernism which might oppose the claims of universalism, of interiority, and of literary autonomy associated with a canonical masculinist modernism.

I argue however that the mobile feminine subject both Richardson and Woolf use to anchor narrative experiment and literary authority has a doubled political valence that explains why such texts produce characteristically modernist accounts of autonomy and interiority despite their argument with these terms. Indeed, as the trajectory of my argument thus far has suggested, the very doubleness linking femininity to literary experiment produces such a contradiction. In this sense the work of female modernists should be seen as paradigmatically modernist, rather than at modernism's margins—especially to the extent that it centers on the figure of the modern woman. For modern woman—imagined as a figure able to roam through different, public, social spaces—evokes in these texts all of the ambiguities of mobility—its association with enclosure as well as openness, with abstraction as well as local contexts. The work of Richardson and Woolf not only finds in mobility a basis for feminist critique but uses the subject's movement to generate the forms of narrative and subjective distance and abstraction we have seen emerge in the work of male writers. It thus begins to suggest the way that turn-of-the-century literary feminism, with its claims for feminine leverage on social and political problems, itself was shaped by impressionism, even as it adapted this rhetorical form to varieties of feminist response.

For Dorothy Richardson, for instance, feminine subjectivity provides the modern novel's experimental strategies and its access to the real, but the female subject she imagines in *Pilgrimage* provokes familiar dilemmas about historical specificity, narrative distance, and the ability of art to transcend social location. Richardson's extended impressionist experiment claims for female subjectivity both an endlessly destabilizing immersion in specific contexts—as its protagonist moves from place to place and impression to impression—and the power to stand apart from context in placeless, sublime moments of permanent truth. *Pilgrimage* figures this conflict as the privileged double stance of modern women and connects it to women's new movement out of a single, limiting domestic context and into circulation between public spaces and confining social categories. Female mobility, imagined here as women's perpetual if limited foreignness from their culture, thus joins location and abstraction, English national identity and modernist internationalism, political embeddedness and the ideal of transcendence.

Virginia Woolf's work has long been exemplary for readings of the intersection between feminism and modernism. The final chapter of this book discusses an ongoing tension in her work between the use of explicitly gendered subjects for posing a feminist social critique and the authority of formalist literary abstraction in her fiction. While these two strands of Woolf's writing have often been read as stark opposites, I consider here the way that these positions are linked in her novels as they have been in the cultural history to which she responds. Reading *Mrs. Dalloway* in relation to *Pilgrimage* as a text imagining the aesthetic effects of a woman's mobility through urban spaces, I examine the dual construction of its protagonist as both a limited, socially specified character and as a potentially exemplary subject. I further read this tension through Woolf's own doubled aesthetic, which compresses social critique together with the potentially abstracting unities of metaphor, by turning to *The Waves* as an illuminating high point of modernist abstraction—at once dependent on its methods and a critical comment upon them. Reading the text's models of the decentered subject alongside its formal tensions, I consider how the feminine consciousness central to modernism both prompts a transformation into the impersonal voices of *The Waves* and remains to signal a resistant social reference. As a preeminent text in which gender both matters and seems to disappear, and in which the details of daily interwar urban life both anchor and are subsumed into a high-cultural aesthetic artifact, *The Waves* reveals the complexity of the connection between modernism and feminine subjectivity—a connection measured as much in gender's apparent disappearance as in its persistent marks.

In concluding with an account of one of modernist fiction's most self-consciously abstract texts, I wish to emphasize the trajectory and the project of this book, which connects the historically specific details of nineteenth- and twentieth-century English culture with a literary modernism too often defined simply as the refusal of such details. In historicizing the notions of subjectivity, of formal experiment, and of literary abstraction that shape modernist impressionism, this project argues for more than the simple priority of terms imagined as historical over those imagined as sheerly formal. My goal, that is, is not to substitute gender as a discretely historical category for abstraction as an ahistorical or formal one. Instead I consider throughout this study the way that historical and formal terms cannot be separated but instead intersect with and shape each other. Thus the historical category of femininity at the turn of the century is—as I discuss here at length—as much a formal model as a historical one, just as modernism's interest in abstraction can more familiarly be seen as historical as well as formal. The connection between formal and historical structures is not unique to the categories of femininity and modernism which interest me here. However it is part of my aim in this book to show the way that gender in this period does embody a particularly charged site of connection and slippage, in which the claims of history and those of form are set at odds as well as brought together. Tracing the rhetoric through which impressionist modernism uses these disjunctions, feminizing and abstracting them, is the project of my remaining pages.

1 Pater's Domestic Subject

The work of Walter Pater has long provided a logical starting place for accounts of subjectivity and modernism. Pater wrote frequently about the subject's troubled relation to the external world, and these meditations—on whether the subject is solipsistically enclosed and interiorized or instead radically permeable to the point of dissolution—point toward modernist narrative experiment, which raises similar questions when it organizes fiction around subjects formed by their impressions (Levenson, *Genealogy*; McGrath; Meisel, *Absent Father, Myth*). Pater's aestheticism has also been important for inquiries into modernist literary production because of the questions he posed about art and the commodity, the private and the public spheres—issues that signal modernism's fundamental continuity with Victorian and aestheticist culture (Freedman 47–71). When Pater's texts ask about the subject's formation by the world and about art's relation to its historical location, they thus reflect on a central contradiction of high culture in modernity more broadly: its simultaneous circulation as a commodity and its claim to stand apart from the public realm of politics and exchange. Pater attempts to manage this tension through his formulations of subjectivity and in doing so he offers powerful rhetorical strategies that modernists will take up and adapt.

It is important to register, however, how fully such questions took shape in a cultural field marked by gender, and marked in ways that framed for Pater and for modernists—both female and male—a complex relation among subjectivity, artistic authority, and femininity. While accounts of modernism have often aligned its ideas of cultural authority

with an endorsement of masculinity, and readings of Pater have productively begun to highlight his revisions of Victorian masculinity (Adams;
Dellamora, *Masculine Desire;* Dowling, *Hellenism;* Matz; Sussman), I
will argue here that Pater's location within nineteenth-century discourses
on the subject demands that we complicate this gendering. For as recent
criticism has noted, when Victorian artists tried to think through the
contradictions in their worldly and artistic status they frequently turned
to the ideologically central figure of woman to represent their relation
to the public world (N. Armstrong; Poovey; Psomiades). This iconic figure, embodying a domestic sphere ostensibly removed from politics, exchange, and history, helped male artists imagine a privileged place for
their art and themselves away from the marketplace. Domestic ideology similarly shaped notions of subjectivity by its offer of private space,
and we must read Pater's influential formulations of the subject, of its
interiority or openness to the world, as mapped by domesticity's vigorously posited but supremely unstable divisions of the world into public
and private. And we must begin to reread modernism accordingly.

Walter Pater's work has not often been linked critically to domestic
ideology. His interest in juxtaposing high cultural philosophical categories such as Hellenism, hedonism, and asceticism, his attention to the
cultivation of rarefied taste, his lack of interest in female characters and
his erotically charged writing on masculine beauty, the learned formality of his writing—all these qualities have seemed to separate his work
from the realm of middle-class culture and popular literary forms such
as the novel to which domesticity is sometimes confined. The domestic
sphere is nonetheless an important frame in much of Pater's writing;
however critics have tended to read through it as a transhistorical metaphor for more abstract ideals.[1] In the postscript to the essays collected in
Appreciations, for instance, Pater turns to the traditional image of the
"House Beautiful" as the ideal form which can reconcile the apparent
aesthetic divisions between classical and romantic art (241). His extended exploration of competing religions and philosophies in *Marius the
Epicurean* similarly finds the most powerful symbol of Christianity's
value in the secluded domestic space of the church in Cecilia's house.
Most compellingly for my argument here, however, Pater turns to Victorian domestic space as a shaping context when he speculates about the
aesthetic subject's development. In an essay he once termed "the germi-
nating, original, source, specimen of all my *imaginative* work"—"The
Child in the House"—Pater explicitly casts the aesthetic subject as a
Victorian child.[2] In doing so he links the shape of the child's mind to the

qualities of the home that forms and encloses it. A reading of this essay thus clarifies the close connections between Pater's notion of subjectivity and a domestic ideology which organizes many of the concerns of the nineteenth century, in popular culture and high culture alike.

In reading Pater's relation to Victorian domesticity as it emerges in his ideas about subjectivity—and particularly through his central formulation of the subject as a child—I thus trace an important identification between aesthetic subjectivity and femininity that will shape modernist impressionist fiction. This link anchors aestheticism as well as modernism, however much it is also elided or refused. Indeed only by registering the close connection in Pater's work between aesthetic subjectivity and femininity may we read the cultural problems of locating the aesthetic subject too firmly in feminized terrain, and see the terms in which femininity may be elided.[3] For male artists faced distinct difficulties in appropriating feminized space as the basis for literary authority amid a web of cultural discourses in which the feminine signaled not only seclusion from the public world but a problematic immersion in it as well. Thus while the domestic sphere promised distance from a compromised public realm, it equally threatened to constrain the aesthetic subject in a space limited and specified as female. Domesticity, that is, might appear so localized that it immersed the subject in a specific, historical location, rather than positioning him above history entirely. I will be arguing that the task Pater encountered in fashioning an authoritative aesthetic subject was to incorporate domesticity's promise—to remove the subject from the vicissitudes of the public world—while avoiding the domestic sphere's definition as specific and as female. Pater would try to preserve his subject's ability to stand for the domestic and for something more general. In short, he attempted to link the aesthete with the feminine while rendering him more and thus other than merely feminine—a paradigmatic and universal subject.

In this double movement of identifying with and refusing domesticity, Pater frames a dilemma central for modernism and reveals the complexity of its gendered associations: how to imagine the literary text's authority in relation to historical location and specificity. I will be exploring throughout this chapter one of Pater's central strategies for resolving this dilemma, a strategy that will become crucial for modernist impressionist fiction: abstraction. In trying to incorporate the authority of the domestic subject while at the same time avoiding its feminization, Pater turns to forms of rhetorical generalization to universalize the subject he writes about. Such generalization will in turn offer modernist

impressionism a way to use the powerful contradictions of feminine subjectivity, to embrace them, enfold them, and in the process of doing so try to exceed them.

Before turning to read Pater's engagement with the structures of Victorian domesticity more explicitly, I wish to pause to explore briefly the way the strategy of generalization works. For the rhetorical gesture of claiming generic or universal status for the aesthetic subject—marking it as a "model" subject—has important effects on the boundaries of subjectivity, on the question of its removal from or immersion in the world, and variations on this strategy will shape the way impressionist fiction dealt with the question of gender. We can see this strategy at work in a well-known passage from Pater's "Conclusion" to *The Renaissance* that has been central to critical readings of Paterian subjectivity. Here Pater depicts a subject faced, famously, with two extreme and opposed predicaments.[4] On the one hand, it seems radically isolated, bounded by its own walls, any contact with an outside world, or any certainty of that world's existence, impossible: "Experience," he writes, "is ringed round for each one of us by that thick wall of personality through which no real voice has ever pierced on its way to us, or from us to that which we can only conjecture to be without" (187).[5] However in the essay's other concurrent presentation of subjectivity, the outside world so permeates and constructs us that we cannot speak of a discretely bounded self at all: "Our physical life," he comments, "is a perpetual motion . . . the modification of the tissues of the brain under every ray of light and sound" (187).

Critical readings have long attempted to account for the sources of this contradiction in the "Conclusion" or to resolve its tensions as part of a larger, coherent proposition about subjectivity.[6] Here I wish to point instead to an aspect of the passage that plays a vital role in both the essay's contradictions and their potential reconciliation: its immoderate language. The claims of the "Conclusion" seem irreconcilable in part because the terms in which Pater asserts them are so absolute; they are universalizing or generic.[7] That is, each attributes a generic nature to subjectivity by defining the condition of all human perception, rather than by describing specific instances. Thus, if the subject is isolated, it is because "experience" in general is "ringed round for each one of us." And if we are in contrast absolutely permeated by the world around us, it is because general scientific laws governing the universe of sound and light as well as self dictate that any and all influences, "every ray of light and sound," modify "the tissues of the brain" (187). Such moments in the "Conclusion," then, create a generic category called "the subject" by describing a model that might apply to any individual in any circumstance.

But it is evident that this category of the generic subject itself reshapes the boundaries of subjectivity and complicates the particular claims each model makes about the subject. We can see this effect at work most clearly with the notion of subjectivity as permeable. For in the "Conclusion," the subject's openness to sensation becomes a susceptibility to sensations imagined as abstract qualities. Because it is absolute here, our susceptibility does not enable us to distinguish between specific impressions, since reflection reveals that each impression is merely an undifferentiable instance of a continuous, abstracted, stream. So Pater notes that although "at first sight experience seems to bury us under a flood of external objects . . . when reflexion begins to play upon those objects they are dissipated under its influence . . . each object is loosed into a group of impressions—*colour, odour, texture*" (187, my emphasis). And paradoxically, this same reflection that reveals objects dissolved into abstract qualities goes on to show that the subject is in fact fundamentally enclosed, that "experience, already reduced to a group of impressions, is ringed round for each one of us by [a] thick wall of personality" (187). Thus the "Conclusion" reinstates, on the very grounds of the subject's permeability to the world around it, an impenetrable boundary between subjectivity—abstracted, generically defined, and essentially stable—and any specific influence that might enter and form it.

The strategic use of generalization in the "Conclusion" raises a number of questions especially central to Pater's writings, given the persistently foregrounded tension between the general and the particular in his work and his oft-stated allegiance to the specific, the embodied, the historically particular.[8] Why does Pater invoke the universal or generic when he wishes to imagine subjectivity? How does abstraction function at such moments? In order to consider these questions, however, we must reposition Pater's vision of subjectivity within the structure of nineteenth-century domestic ideology that, in aligning interiority with an idealized private sphere, provides its logic. Pater's essay "The Child in the House" allows us to see the way a paradigmatic instance of subjectivity—a child susceptible to and constituted by sensations—takes form as part of discourses on the middle-class home, and to see how Pater uses that notion of home to shape a metaphor and model for the child's mind. In using this figure to construct a subject that resembles the aesthete and yet may stand for all subjects, Pater clarifies aestheticism's implication in domestic ideology—in its complex interconnections of subjectivity and the marketplace, of gender and urban unrest. He will clarify too the logic according to which his aesthetic proto-modernism must abstract the domestic subject to ensure its own cultural authority.

———————

When Walter Pater turned to a domestic setting as the most appropriate place in which to examine the nature of the subject, to examine "that process of brainbuilding by which we are, each one of us, what we are," he joined a central nineteenth-century tradition ("Child" 1). As historians and literary critics have recently discussed, ideals of home shaped the discussion of a broad range of issues in Victorian culture, from religion to materialism, from the proper place of women to the regeneration of the slum and the nation. Most compellingly for Pater, as for the modernists who would draw upon him, contemporary attempts to define subjectivity too were entwined with ideas about domesticity, often invoking the home as the Victorian self's strongest support or shaping influence.[9] These mingled discussions of home and subject framed a range of questions about enclosure and permeability familiar from Pater's "Conclusion." The questions were urgent ones, and their pressing nature becomes the more understandable when we consider that the domestic sphere claimed social and spiritual authority on the basis of a complete seclusion from the world outside. We might turn to John Ruskin's famous account of domesticity in "Of Queens' Gardens" for an illustration. Ruskin writes that:

> Within [the home] . . . need enter no danger, no temptation, no cause of error or offence. This is the true nature of home—it is the place of peace; the shelter, not only from all injury, but from all terror, doubt, and division. In so far as it is not this, it is not home; so far as the anxieties of the outer life penetrate into it, and the inconsistently-minded, unknown, unloved, or hostile society of the outer world is allowed by either husband or wife to cross the threshold, it ceases to be home; it is then only a part of that outer world which you have roofed over and lighted a fire in. (84–85)

Enshrined in novels and parodied in *Punch*'s cartoons, the dream of home's enclosure found expression in architectural trends like the Queen Anne style and the design of family wings for large country houses; most importantly, it anchored the ideology of a growing middle-class and their movement into suburbia, which advocates proposed as the epitome of domestic seclusion (Hall; Girouard, *Country House*, *Sweetness*; Jahn; Dyos and Reeder). This enclosure of the domestic sphere, we might further note, helped shape ideals of national identity. Removed from the political and economic turmoil of the public realm, the idealized home promised a solid anchor for English cultural values and social stability. It allowed Englishness too to be imagined as stable or transcendent, removed, like home, from the dangers of revolution and the social dissolution that threatened to follow rampant materialism.[10]

In these varied accounts, home signaled transcendence, access to a universal realm of value that might unify an entire nation. However, joined to this description was a rather different one: the domestic sphere was also portrayed as a specific, isolated space with qualities that were limited, if benevolent, in their opposition to the public world. Home stood for self-sacrifice instead of competitiveness, emotion instead of rationality, the feminine instead of the masculine. The authority of the domestic sphere and of the feminine subject within it thus derived from a peculiarly double position, both as particular entities and as the embodiments of universal, transcendent value.

This overlap and its enormous cultural weight arose from the origins of domestic ideology in interrelated economic and social movements of the eighteenth and early nineteenth centuries that marked the rise of middle-class power: the gradual separation of middle-class homes from a visible place in an expanding market economy and the evangelical revival. As the production of goods was industrialized and centralized, and as goods and labor were increasingly exchanged outside the home and through the mediation of money, the household began to appear—indeed was strategically redefined—as a place separate from both the function and the values of the economic, public world (Davidoff and Hall 272–315, 364–69). At the same time, new and renewed religious doctrines invested this apparently limited, feminine sphere with enormous transcendent value, by describing it as the site of religious training and inspiration, and as the model on earth of a heavenly home. According to such doctrines, home became a center of religious authority, instilling piety into the children who were shaped there and spiritually renewing the men who daily entered a materialist public arena incompatible with Christian principles (Davidoff and Hall 108–18). The domestic sphere's apparent isolation from worldly ambitions thus formed the basis for its claim to transcendent moral authority.

As we trace the connection between ideals of home and self, we can see how the rhetoric of home's spiritual authority and seclusion is linked to analogous claims for the seclusion of the subjects sheltered there. For the home promised to exert a moral and political influence precisely by molding its residents so that they could remain unswayed by unsavory public forces. This admirable aspect of the domestic subject appears most explicitly in claims made for women's authority during the period (Helsinger, Sheets, and Veeder ix). Sarah Lewis, for instance, argues for woman's "boundless" (13) influence on the world from the home, by using the very boundedness of that home to claim woman's moral, rational, and even—paradoxically—political authority: "The beneficial influence of woman is nullified if once her motives, or her personal character, come to be the subject of attack; and this fact alone ought to induce her patiently to acquiesce in the plan of seclusion from public affairs. . . . Removed from the actual collision of political contests, and screened from the passions which such engender, she brings party questions to the test of the unalterable principles of reason and religion" (52–53, 66). Here woman's enclosure in the private space of the home both secludes her and gives her a universal authority. Only by restricting her worldly sphere can she reach those transcendent, "unalterable" principles of "reason and religion" that offer truths badly needed, and fully applicable, in the public world.

But the construction of an idealized private sphere was accompanied by, indeed it depended upon, imagined threats to that seclusion. The various problems of modern England—urban poverty, working-class unrest, the disruptions of industrialism—appeared in this light as challenges to home's enclosure, which was thus defined as perpetually under siege. We might note that Ruskin, for instance, in praising domesticity, dwells far more vividly on the dangers of the "outer life" than on the "place of peace" itself. He paints the outside world as a place of unremitting danger, as a society utterly "unknown, unloved, or hostile." And significantly, the world is most threatening when it endangers the subject's integrity: the world offers "temptation[s]"; it is the arena of the "inconsistently-minded," of "terror, doubt, and division." If home is imagined as a space immune to these disruptions—fortifying the individual against the public realm's temptations—it thus performs an important, and indeed a necessarily ceaseless, social function, constantly warding off the pollution, temptation, and disorder that threaten home and subject even as they reciprocally constitute them.

This interconnection between home and subject and that which endangered them—dangers as fascinating as they were fearful—shaped and in turn depended upon a cultural map of the city elaborated by Victorian reformers (Stallybrass and White 125–48). Apparently securely divided into suburb and slum, respectable and disreputable, the city became the place where Victorians most often imagined that such divisions threatened to break down, amidst the jostling of public spaces and the contagious immorality and corruption attributed to slums and slum-dwellers. The respectable private home, defined by its separation from the city it dreaded, was thus also tied to the city as its imagined opposite, perpetually endangered by the city's fascinating lack of all "architectural barriers or protections of decency," by the city's embodiment of contagion and vagrancy (E. Chadwick, cited in Stallybrass and White 126). It is this potential transgression of home's borders, as Stallybrass and White suggest, that in turn provided a language for subjectivity. The fear of and desire for breached boundaries equally frame the Victorian home and the Victorian subject; they render both the home and the subject's defining dilemma as one of permeability.

———

Amid this contemporary preoccupation with inviolate homes and enclosed domestic subjects, Pater's essay "The Child in the House" may seem somewhat incongruous. Pater's prototypical child Florian unashamedly celebrates his susceptibility to the impressions that permeate him; he would appear to have little of the anxiety about the outside world that fuels domestic ideology. This child and the essay's narrator have, it seems, no interest in the subject's enclosure. The essay revels in Florian's openness to the impress of the outside world, indeed his constitution by it, and it proposes a happy subjection to what Pater terms the "tyranny of the senses" as essential to Florian's nature (9).

Further, the essay claims such susceptibility for more than the aesthetic child Florian; it proposes that such openness characterizes the relationship of all subjects to the outside world. For as Pater puts it, the soul is wholly penetrated by the world by "law," so that neither can be divided from the other:

> In that half-spiritualised house he [Florian] could watch the better, over again, the gradual expansion of the soul which had come to be there—of which indeed, through the law which makes the material objects about them so large an element in children's lives, it had actually become a part; inward and outward being woven through and through each other into one inextricable texture—half, tint and trace and accident of homely colour and form, from the wood and the bricks; half, mere soul-stuff, floated thither from who knows how far. (2)

There can be no question here of protecting subjectivity from the threat of outside influences; "inward and outward" are thoroughly "inextricable," as they were in the comparable moment in *The Renaissance* examined earlier. Pater's characteristic syntax reinforces this sense; the distance of pronoun reference making it hard to distinguish whether the "half-spiritualised house" or "the soul" provides the antecedent for "it." The essay makes it difficult to decide, that is, which element has "actually become a part" of the other.

The fundamental image with which "The Child in the House" figures the idea of the subject's openness is that of the mind as *tabula rasa*. When impressions from the outer world penetrate the child, they inscribe themselves on the child's mind, which is blank and impressible like white paper or a waxen tablet: "How insignificant, at the moment, seem the influences of the sensible things which are tossed and fall and lie about us, so, or so, in the environment of early childhood. How indelibly, as we afterwards discover, they affect us; with what capricious attractions and associations they figure themselves on the white paper, the smooth wax, of our ingenuous souls, as 'with lead in the rock for ever,' giving form and feature . . . to early experiences of feeling and thought" (4). This passage, like the preceding one, asserts the child's openness to the external, sensible world, and it does this so thoroughly that the differences between human child and material world themselves begin to unravel. Perhaps the undermining of such distinctions here may sound the first, albeit tentative, note of alarm charging the essay. The child now becomes inanimate material—"white paper," "smooth wax"—and the world around him not only possesses all agency but introduces the only mention of human features: "form and feature" come from without, from the "influences of . . . sensible things." Even these attributes are granted to "early experiences of feeling and thought" rather than to the child.

The essay suggests a more extreme concern at the prospect of a child so wholly marked by his impressions in those moments when it retreats from the intermingling of inward and outward and begins, like the "Conclusion," to envision a contradictory and more familiar notion of enclosed subjectivity. And it is here that we may begin to see the structuring of domestic ideology on the subject in Pater's essay. For these moments anchor the subject more explicitly in the contemporary domestic ideal, with that ideal's view of the home as an insulating haven. Here both the child and the house are enclosed with a kind of anxious iteration: "the sense of security could hardly have been deeper, the quiet of the child's soul being one with the quiet of its home, a place 'inclosed' and 'sealed'" (6). The child's soul is thus not only protected by the literal enclosure of the home but made impermeable too by the proposed analogy between them—between the "assured place" (6) and "the child's assured soul . . . [that] resemble[s] it" (6). And in fact, Pater's essay has evoked English domesticity quite explicitly earlier. Florian's singular "good fortune . . . [is] that the special character of his home was in itself so essentially homelike . . . the sort of house that I have described . . . is for Englishmen at least typically homelife [*sic*]" (5).[11] Indeed, the house described does sound like a suburban embodiment of domesticity—with its "proportions of red-brick and green" (5) and its location near a "great city, which sent up heavenwards, over the twisting weather-vanes . . . its beds of rolling cloud and smoke" (3). Enclosed soul, enclosed home, home's security and Englishness—all suggest that Pater's contradictory formulations of subjectivity in the essay, his concern with the seductive *tabula rasa* of the child's mind, are anchored in the familiar divisions and anxieties of domestic ideology.

Pater maintains his central, quintessentially aestheticist, vision of the child's openness in "The Child in the House," despite such moments of enclosure. This insistence on the power of the sensory impression is what makes Pater's work influential for modernism; it is also what makes his relation to domestic ideology interesting here. For his essay shows us how the notion of subjective openness may itself draw upon the Victorian domestic ideal, and on its structuring anxieties about the ability of home to exclude a threatening external world. Such cultural concerns emerge throughout the essay's meditations—on the power of place, on the charms of decadent sensibility, on the workings of language. We may see these anxieties, for instance, in the double structure of the influence of the house on the child. If in the first description of permeability we examined, the house becomes part of the child's mind as a specific content and sensation (as wood and bricks, color and form), in the essay as a whole, the house shapes the child's mind by supplying a metaphor for its structure.[12] And this house is a notably vulnerable one, poised on the edge of a city whose "gloom and rumours" (3), like the "rumours of the greater world without [the house, threaten to] steal in through the wall of custom about us" (4). The essay uses this vulnerability—the potential failure of the house to keep out that which it should exclude—as both a cause and a figure for the child's openness to sensations. Sensations enter the child because the house's walls have failed to exclude them, but also because the essay imagines the child's mind as vulnerable by analogy. While sensations, therefore, by definition form the child, at the same time they threaten him as well; in entering, they transgress a border.

Thus, after describing Florian's house and mind as places "'inclosed' and 'sealed,'" Pater immediately breaches this enclosure: "But upon this assured place, upon the child's assured soul which resembled it, there came floating in from the larger world without, as at windows left ajar unknowingly, or over the high garden walls, two streams of impressions" (6). Impressions enter the child as trespassers through a relaxation of domestic guard—the window left unknowingly ajar, the garden wall not high enough. The mind here is structured like a vulnerable house, and the boundary-crossing of sensation becomes a trespass onto the private property of the subject: "the realities and passions, the rumours of the greater world without, steal in upon us, each by its own special little passageway through the wall of custom about us" (4).

Pater's essay explores—we might better say luxuriates in—this vision of a subject haunted by home's failed enclosure and of a domesticity haunted by the subject's vulnerability. It insistently rethematizes the risks and pleasures of the domestic subject's vulnerability in the most extreme and eccentric aspects of Florian's aestheticism: his fascination with the transformations of death and decay, the ghostly and the macabre. For while the dead and suffering people who so intrigue Florian and to whom he is most susceptible, mark Pater's decadent interest in the extremes of sensation, in the line between pain and pleasure, these macabre figures also embody and make literal the trespasses the impressionable subject invites. As the essay makes clear, ghostly transgressions bind the sensitive child ever more closely to the home which ought to protect him but cannot. It is hardly accidental, then, that in the story which floats through Florian's window and to which he "could not but listen" (12), the dead themselves are imagined as trespassers who violate home's secure enclosure so thoroughly that, as Ruskin might say, "it ceases to be home":[13]

> For sitting one day in the garden below an open window, he heard people talking, and could not but listen, how . . . a sick woman had seen one of the dead sitting beside her, come to call her hence; and from the broken talk evolved with much clearness the notion that not all those dead people had really departed to the churchyard . . . but led a secret, half-fugitive life in their old homes . . . with no great goodwill towards those who shared the place with them. All night the figure sat beside him in the reveries of his broken sleep, and was not quite gone in the morning—an odd irreconcileable [sic] new member of the household, making the sweet familiar chambers unfriendly and suspect by its uncertain presence. . . . Afterwards he came to think of those poor, home-returning ghosts, which all men have fancied to themselves—the *revenants*—pathetically, as crying, or beating with vain hands at the doors. (12)

The ghosts of this passage mark the domestic sphere's failure; indeed they embody and anticipate that psychic structure Freud will later describe as the *unheimlich*, in which the most homelike and familiar scenes are revealed as intrinsically uncanny. These ghosts are fully at home neither in the cemetery nor in their former houses; they lead a "half-fugitive life in their old homes," or—as *"revenants"* whose return can never be complete—beat "with vain hands at the doors." Equally importantly, in haunting Florian, the dead underline the instability of home, rendering the place of peace itself unhomelike, "unfriendly and suspect." And the anecdote itself mirrors the ghosts' effects: not only does it illustrate young Florian's susceptibility to impressions which come through breaches in the walls of the house but it transforms home itself into the source of trouble—the story floats out from an open window to Florian in the garden. Further, the episode initiates a continuing susceptibility in Florian, as the unsettling image returns in the future to penetrate the most secure gatherings: "Even in the living he sometimes caught its likeness; at any time or place, in a moment, the . . . image with the bound chin, the quaint smile, the straight, stiff feet, shed itself across the air upon the bright carpet, amid the gayest company, or happiest communing with himself" (12).

Elsewhere the dead, as objects of Florian's decadent fascination, emphasize the extreme vulnerability of the perceiving subject by being figured as analogous to it. When Florian, later in life, visits the morgue in Paris and "that fair cemetery at Munich," he is haunted by the "waxen [and] resistless" faces of the dead that then "live[d] with him for many days" (11). These faces double not just the child but, more specifically, his nature as a *tabula rasa*, his inability to resist the imprint of sensations, and they make that vulnerability ominous. Once again the particular susceptibility that dead faces evoke in Florian has macabre effects: the force of their impression on him figuratively raises the dead: "those waxen faces would always live with him . . . making the broadest sunshine sickly" (11). By the end of the essay, such faces have come so thoroughly to haunt the house in which Florian has grown up that home's final impression on his memory appears through its personification as a dead person: "As he passed . . . from room to room, lying so pale, with a look of meekness in their denudation . . . the aspect of the place touched him like the face of one dead" (14). This chain of association extends still further, however, and does so in ways that point to some of the social terms through which domestic space was imagined as both enclosed and vulnerable. For the waxen, resistless faces which so disturbingly double Florian, and which come to provide the face of home itself, evoke cities like the one just beyond his home. These faces become the very sign of the urban to him. He "could trace . . . a pervading preference in himself for a kind of comeliness and dignity, an *urbanity* literally, in modes of life, which he connected with the pale people of towns, and which made him susceptible to a kind of exquisite satisfaction in the trimness and well-considered grace of certain things and persons" (3–4).

"The Child in the House" links the child's openness to sensations with the vulnerability of the domestic sphere; it thus underlines the feminization of childhood that was a commonplace of Victorian culture at the same time that it establishes a more eccentric vision of a specifically aestheticist femininity (Nelson; Felski 91–114). The aesthetic child is further rendered vulnerable—and feminine—by association with a specifically feminized suffering, which Pater will link in turn to the dangerous, sensuous power of metaphor that structures his own prose.[14] Florian's susceptibility to sensations in the essay is a double one: his "fascination by bright colour and choice form" (6) runs alongside a "sensibility to the spectacle of suffering" (6). Indeed the influence of his childhood home is colored by the series of suffering females who live there, from an aged aunt mourning the death of Florian's father in India to a terrified sister and a haunting picture of the doomed Marie Antoinette. These suffering figures, like the dead who haunt him, will personify the susceptibility they evoke in him and feminize it. When the narrator notes "some of the occasions of [Florian's] recognition of the element of pain in things" (7), for instance, he turns to his encounter with the picture of Marie Antoinette. Her face here, like those of the dead and, by association, the child's waxen mind, is "resistless" (7), both suffering and susceptible; and this resistlessness in turn produces in Florian the sympathy which marks him too as susceptible. Thus "the face [Marie Antoinette's] that had been so high had learned to be mute and resistless; but out of its very resistlessness, seemed now to call on men to have pity, and forbear" (7). Similarly Florian owes his sensitivity, the "mercy he conceived always for people in fear," in part to the presence around him of mourning women; "impressible, susceptible persons, indeed, who had had their sorrows, lived about him; and this [i.e., his] sensibility was due in part to the tacit influence of their presence" (7).

The eerie domestic suffering that feminizes Florian is associated with an ominous power of metaphorical transformation, which threatens the subject's identity much as the identity of home risked dissolution earlier.[15] The cry of Florian's aunt, for instance, "seemed to make the aged woman like a child again" (7). This tendency reaches its most bizarre extremity in the story of Florian's dying rabbit, which, already linked by its dumbness to the "mute and resistless" Marie Antoinette, is explicitly personified—made a person—by its pain. "There were the little sorrows of the dumb animals too—of the white angora, with a dark tail like an ermine's, and a face like a flower, who fell into a lingering sickness, and became quite delicately human in its valetudinarianism, and came to have a hundred different expressions of voice" (7–8).

"The Child in the House" associates Florian's vulnerability to others' suffering with just this kind of metaphorical transformation, for it is precisely the "sensible," embodied, highly particular nature of metaphors which appeals to his preference for the visible and helps bind him to those who suffer: "It was the trick even his pity learned, fastening those who suffered in anywise to his affections by a kind of sensible attachments" (10). But such metaphors, though they reinforce the pity that is the best result of his susceptibility, suggest in the end that Florian's "diseased sensibility" (6) actually initiates the decay and self-dissolution it claims merely to make sympathetic. Thus he "would think of Julian, fallen into incurable sickness, as spoiled in the sweet blossom of his skin like pale amber, and his honey-like hair; of Cecil, early dead, as cut off from the lilies. . . . what comforted him a little was the thought of the turning of the child's flesh to violets in the turf above him" (10). While the passage's metaphors begin by aestheticizing a sickness they cannot alter, this same transformation of flesh into flower is in fact, by the end of the passage, the very sign of the death and decay it would make palatable. The metaphors themselves seem to initiate a process of decay that passes out of the realm of the metaphorical as well as out of control; the passage moves from Florian's self-conscious use of a floral figure to the recurrence of this transformation as an apparently nonmetaphorical fact lying beyond his powers and from which he merely takes comfort. And as such metaphors are firmly linked to the subject's impressibility, as more effective summonings of the sensible outer world into the subject, they begin to take on an autonomy that appears increasingly threatening, indeed that promises an ominous self-dissolution.

Pater's essay thus bases its vision of the aesthetic subject, a subject all too open to the sensations of beauty, pain, and the peculiar affinities between them, in the contradictions of a feminine sphere that is tremblingly open to infiltration and dissolution. In Pater's writing the dangerous appeal of this vulnerability pervades everything for the aesthete; it is lodged in every sensation; it inheres in the very fabric of language and it does so because of the aesthetic subject's affinity for the specific, sensible details of the world around him, which draw him into a delightfully self-dissolving identification. As I have suggested, Pater's essay ultimately attempts to dissociate its model of subjectivity from the feminized domesticity that enables it. And it is through its shifting relation to specificity—through its use of a generalizing rhetoric—that "The Child in the

House" begins to modify both its subject and the visibility of that subject's relation to the historical paradigm of domesticity that shapes it.

We have seen the way the essay associates Florian's susceptibility with his inclination toward the specific, with his preference for the vivid concrete metaphorical vehicle over the abstract thought it conveys. "The Child in the House" asserts this preference explicitly when it describes Florian's assessment of philosophies:

> In his intellectual scheme, [he] was led to assign very little to the abstract thought, and much to its sensible vehicle or occasion. . . . that sensible vehicle or occasion became, perhaps only too surely, the necessary concomitant of any perception of things, real enough to be of any weight or reckoning, in his house of thought. There were times when he could think of the necessity he was under of associating all thoughts to touch and sight, as a sympathetic link between himself and actual, feeling, living objects; a protest in favour of real men and women against mere grey, unreal abstractions. (9)

But Pater ultimately undermines the privileging of the specific over the abstract in this essay as he attempts to resolve the dilemma that sensation and specificity pose for the subject. He does so with a strategy familiar from his formulation of subjectivity in the "Conclusion": he redefines as generic types those very elements he once cast as particular. This redefinition works metaphorically to reenclose specificity within the mind and thus to ward off the threatening penetration from without that the specific detail, and the subject's susceptibility to it, entails. In a sense then generalization offers a more powerful fulfillment of the promise made by the domestic sphere, the promise to enclose the subject.

Florian's preference for the sensible over the abstract is treated most fully when the essay discusses religion. Christianity's virtue at first seems to be that it "translate[s] so much of its spiritual verity into things that may be seen, [and] condescends in part to sanction this infirmity, if so it be, of our human existence, wherein the world of sense is too much with us" (9).[16] But the essay goes on to shift Florian's view of religion. Even as he is shown to love the sensible expression of the church for its own sake, the "church lights, holy days, all that belonged to the comely order of the sanctuary" (13), this sensible vehicle becomes, not a cluster of specific details, but "the type of something he desired always to have about him in actual life" (13). Christianity, that is, rather than fleshing out abstract spiritual verity, begins instead to provide an alternative to everyday life. Florian now conceives of religion as an abstracting narrative, "a sacred history indeed, but still more a sacred ideal, a transcendent version or representation, under intenser and more expressive light and shade, of human life," "a constant substitution of the typical for the actual," in which the sensible is aligned with something other than "actual" sensory experience (13). Now "all the acts and accidents of life *borrowed* a sacred colour and significance; the very colours of things became themselves weighty with meanings" (14, my emphasis). Most crucially, in Pater's words such a substitution of the typical for the actual is figured as providing an alternative enclosure, another, more powerful home that recasts the entire question of the sensible and the specific wholly *within* the mind. Thus, through religion, "a place adumbrated itself in his thoughts, wherein those sacred personalities, which are at once the reflex and the pattern of our nobler phases of life, housed themselves" (13).

　　We can see here a contradiction between the essay's many claims for the priority of the sensible, for the mark of the outer world on the subject, and a set of competing claims for that sensation's affiliation instead with the abstract, ideal, or typical, figured as a sheerly metaphorical inner home rather than an all-too-real outer one. This contradiction, this shift, I would argue, lies at the heart of the essay's function as a whole. It suggests the pattern of Walter Pater's engagement with domestic ideology, and offers the model through which modernist impressionism will engage with the structures of gendered subjectivity.

　　"The Child in the House" takes a dilemma that it understands as social—the subject's susceptibility to external impressions, a susceptibility derived from and figured as an anxiety about the penetrability of the middle-class home—and resolves this dilemma by making it generic, so that it not only transcends its context by converting specific social influences into abstract material for the senses but refigures the problem of perception as purely internal, recontained within a closed subject. For instance, we can see how this technique of abstraction might work to modify and ultimately to contain a social threat like the one the city poses to the child. Thus, after describing the city's potentially ominous presence near the house, its "twisting weather-vanes . . . its beds of rolling cloud and smoke," Pater denies that it has any ill effect upon the child, and does so by converting the city entirely into abstract colors or sensations: "The child of whom I am writing did not hate the fog because of the crimson lights . . . and the white which gleamed . . . on turret or pavement" (3). This abstraction effectively reencloses the child and transforms the city from an influence that threatens to permeate him from without to a play of simple colors which he can "see inwardly" (3). Indeed the passage removes the troublesome force of the outer world entirely, arguing that the child in fact *only* sees "inwardly": "For it is false to suppose that a child's sense of beauty is dependent on any choiceness or special fineness in the objects which present themselves to it . . . earlier [in life] . . . we see inwardly; and the child finds for itself, and with unstinted delight, a difference for the sense, in those whites and reds through the smoke on very homely buildings" (3).

More importantly, abstraction is also the central strategy at work in Pater's rhetorical positioning of the essay itself—in his attempt to find a form of cultural authority for the aesthetic subject and for his own writing that both uses and avoids the powerful discourse of domesticity. Just as Pater's essay abstracts the fleshly particularity of detail into the typical or generic, "The Child in the House" transforms the hypersensitive consciousness and sensibility of the aesthete, concerned with such decadent, eccentric pleasures as the sight of dead faces and the exquisite smell of flowers, into the far less controversial mind of a child who offers a paradigm of the problems of all perception and sensation, so that the essay may see in "the story of [Florian's] spirit . . . that process of brainbuilding by which we are, each one of us, what we are" (1). But this authorization of the aesthetic subject works equally through an abstraction away from the feminized domestic sphere on which it relies. For in proposing the aesthetic male child as a model of the perceiving subject, Pater appropriates and shifts contemporary definitions of interiority that base it in a specifically female domestic sphere. The shift in gender, which works here as a shift from the specific to the generic, allows him to subsume and internalize those elements of domesticity that might limit the subject by their specificity. In making the quintessential subject a child shaped explicitly by the forces of home, Pater draws upon conventional associations of domesticity with universal interiority and uses them to authorize his model of subjectivity. But at the same time, by making this child male, he transforms one aspect of the domestic subject that persistently limited claims that it stood for everyone: the domestic subject was conventionally a woman; no matter the universality attributed to her, her gender was seen to make her specific, and her connection to home, though symbolic and symbolically entitling, was always also a literal restriction to a specific place. By making his representative child male, Pater avoids the gendered particularity associated with women and purges him of the specificity associated not only with femininity but with the concrete, and concretely limited, social space of the home.

We can see this relation to and adaptation of conventional notions about the domestic sphere spelled out in the essay's title. This title, in addition to encapsulating the essay's concern with the house, also alludes to contemporary domestic ideology directly through its reference to Coventry Patmore's "Angel in the House"—a poem praising the ideal of domestic femininity, if paradoxically according it little in the way of interiority. Interesting indicators of the relationship between Pater's essay and the domestic mythology enshrined in Patmore's poem register in the differences between its title and Pater's, as well as in the shift in Pater's own title before publication. Pater's essay was originally to be called "The House and the Child"; his editors changed it to "The Child in the House," although it is unclear whether they intended the echo of Patmore's enormously popular poem (Levey 156, 160). The change underlines the degree to which Pater's child, while drawing upon a powerful domestic ideology, replaces the woman as the reigning spirit of the home. It emphasizes as well the degree to which Pater's shift makes its subject generic. For Patmore's angel, while technically ungendered in the poem's title, is entirely and essentially feminine; she is angelic because she is female, and to call her an angel simply describes that femininity metaphorically. Pater's child, on the other hand, is not defined as inherently or specifically gendered; we are meant to accept the male Florian as a representative example of a universal category, "child," which transcends gender. His masculinity, that is, is not supposed to mark him as specific; it does not interrupt his ability to provide a general model.[17]

This shift in title anticipates the various enclosing gestures which frame the essay as a form of philosophical meditation. Appearing throughout the essay as part of its invocation of the generic, these frames provide a form of literary containment linked to the essay's use of the male child as model subject. The revised title, with its "in" replacing the former "and," places the child clearly within the house and thus becomes the first in a series of containing frames which, the essay claims, make Florian's story intelligible. With these frames, the narrator argues both for the privileged context of the "half-spiritualised house," in which Florian "could watch the better, over again, the gradual expansion of the soul which had come to be there" (2), and for the illuminating context of the dreaming mind which "bring[s] its object to mind with a great clearness, yet . . . raised a little above itself" (1). Such frames enclose the essay's subject, balancing the threatening claim to interpenetrability of inside and outside that the dream's substance suggests, reinstating a border between them by arguing for the priority of one over the other. But the frames also work—paradoxically, given the title—to enclose the whole setting of home within the mind, the mind of the adult Florian who meditates upon his home after hearing the story of a man he encounters on the road.

It is precisely this containment of domesticity that posing a male child as the generic subject ensures, for male children, unlike female ones, grow up to leave home, transcending its physical limitations, able to recall its charms and fears from a philosophical distance. The essay's appropriation of the domestic model of subjectivity guarantees that just as Pater's essay cannot be restricted to the popular genre of domestic tale, the male aesthete cannot be limited by the specific realm of the home; instead he has incorporated into himself its authority, its claim to be symbolically universal. He is, in a sense, authorized by his metaphorical definition through the home; but we are always, despite Pater's insistence, meant to read through this sensible vehicle to the abstract idea of generic subjectivity underneath. The essay's elaborate frame of memory is thus a necessary mechanism for the strategically generic aesthetic subject it posits and for the domestic essay Pater has produced. Memory provides the connection that retrieves domestic authority for the aesthetic subject and securely encloses its feminized associations—its history and its permeability—within the mind of a subject who is free to move on.

2 The New Woman and the Modern Girl: Egerton, Grand, and James

The Victorian ideal of domestic enclosure that shaped Pater's aestheticism faced serious challenges in the late nineteenth century. Critics debating about young women's education, mobility, and entry into the professions argued vigorously over whether the seclusion of home might not do as much harm as good to female character. Innovations in the novel raised similar questions about the power of marriage and domesticity to resolve female character development—criticizing the constraints of marriage and the family, and envisioning alternate narratives for women. A wide range of literary and cultural commentaries thus questioned the ability of home to anchor spiritual authority, social critique, and subjective interiority. As critics have recently discussed, such critiques provide a crucial transition between Victorian and early-twentieth-century cultural and literary formations by recasting premises about women's—and the novel's—proper plots (Ardis; Boone, *Tradition*; De-Koven; DuPlessis).

The central figure in the reevaluation of domesticity in the 1880s and 1890s was the modern young woman. Named the "New Woman" by Sarah Grand in an 1894 article entitled "The New Aspect of the Woman Question" and linked by her newness to the period's modernity, this young woman disturbed a range of conventions of domestic femininity, most centrally middle-class woman's limitation to the home.[1] She might walk abroad, read what she chose, refuse to marry; she might advocate professional training for women or premarital chastity for men. She took as her sphere the slum, the university, and the political podium, and she offered an increasingly compelling—if also fiercely contested—model of female identity that exceeded the plots of courtship and conclusive marriage for middle-class women. The New Women who appeared throughout magazine debates and novels as well as in drawing rooms and lecture halls thus made the perceptions of the modern female subject the source of a critique of domesticity and marriage. Through her critical stance, her expanded knowledge and activity, this figure recast the ideal Victorian home as the site of those very cultural terms it was supposed to exclude; she recast home as corrupt rather than pure, as worldly, conventional, and commercial rather than transcendent and spiritual.

The newly public woman who emerged in this period is a crucial figure to explore if we are to trace the way a self-consciously modern twentieth-century fiction emerged out of and was indebted to the structures of nineteenth-century culture. I will be arguing here that this figure can help us understand both the accounts of subjectivity offered by modernist impressionism and their complex gendering. For modern woman centered many of the well-known debates on the subject in the 1890s that helped generate modernism's characteristic narrative experiments. Reading her presence at the center of these discussions about interiority and social health, about domesticity and the New Woman's psychology, will allow us to see the way impressionism's attention to subjectivity grows out of a concern with a specifically modern feminine subject.

Indeed the New Woman of the 1890s in particular was defined through turn-of-the-century debates about a crisis of subjectivity. In such discussions, the nation's health seemed threatened by a subject who failed to maintain a proper balance between the risks of solipsistic enclosure and radical dispersal, and the solution commentators imagined required fortifying the subject. In this context, when modern woman was imagined as either social threat or savior, she was defined through her psychology—by the nature of her mind. Critics might argue that women signaled social decline because they were either too self-enclosed or too public; advocates argued in contrast that women could in fact save the country because they were ideal subjects: healthily open, but not indiscriminately so. This attention to the defining power of woman's subjectivity was so pervasive that it linked New Woman writers with otherwise divergent views of female sexuality and the nature of marriage—advocates of chastity, for instance, and advocates for freeing female desire. Such writers worked within (and reshaped) a common cultural grid of ideas about female subjectivity which often cut across those differences.[2]

Reading the power ascribed to modern women's subjectivity further allows us to register the complex relationship between Victorian domestic ideology and the emerging public, mobile woman who will be important to modernism. For it is important to acknowledge the way this figure, like modernism, signals something more ambiguous, and more interesting, than a simple break with Victorian culture and domestic ideology. Instead, the subjectivity of the modern woman both refuses and refigures domestic ideology. In particular, discussions of the rebellious New Woman joined with related debates about a young girl's exposure to potentially corrupting worldly knowledge in order to propose the modern young woman as a powerful extension and revision of the domestic subject. Rejecting the insularity of an enclosed home, this subject responded to impressions ranging from the most intimate confidences to the most sordid social realities. And yet this model female subject importantly adapted domesticity's social function as much as she rejected it. For writers claimed that her openness to the world might in fact strengthen the individual and manage the problematic relation between subject and social world. Indeed texts attempted to render her permeability compatible with new forms of unworldliness, and with an inviolate privacy.

In this way discourses on the New Woman and the modern girl imagine a privileged figure who is both subjectively open and closed. They begin, that is, to render subjective openness compatible with personal depths, and to use the combination to create a claim to modern cultural authority. They thus render the contradiction between interiority and permeability both central to the subject and culturally productive. This subject strategically both open and individuated allows us to see the relation between the modern women of the 1890s and the domestic ideology they both revised and continued.

This figure's central position also allows us—as recent critics of New Woman fiction have suggested—to rewrite a history of the novel and of culture at the turn of the century. For if the New Woman enters the field in part as a way of reworking nineteenth-century versions of subjectivity, reshaping the apparent crisis of the domestic subject's openness into the source of its power, such a revision of subjectivity is crucial to literary experiment in the period and to modernist redefinitions of literature's authority. In particular, we need to note the way late-nineteenth-century fiction's vision of the powerful, even exemplary subjectivity lodged specifically in a young woman or girl—and lodged in a young woman or girl exposed to dire social situations the better to redeem them—centers the period's famous turn to foregrounded narrative innovations. Such innovations both record and shape the doubleness of this subject, her openness and enclosure. Writers will come to suggest not just that narrative experiment is necessary to accommodate this compelling, enigmatic figure but that such experiment may be the exemplary discourse for appropriating—and transcending—her cultural authority.

This chapter thus explores the way the claims for proto-modernist literary experiment draw upon the contradictions of female subjectivity at the end of the nineteenth century. In order to discuss this dynamic, I explore debates over female interiority and knowledge in the early 1890s, drawing together magazine debates with a series of stories and novels, both popular and highbrow. I begin by reading discussions of both decadence and the decline of the domestic sphere together with two popular and controversial New Woman fictions of the early 1890s that helped shape ensuing impressionist understandings of subjectivity, narrative, and gender: George Egerton's *Keynotes* and Sarah Grand's *The Heavenly Twins.* I then turn to Henry James's transitional writings of the late 1890s, and in particular to *What Maisie Knew* and *The Awkward Age.* I consider the way his developing narrative experiment in these novels is tied to a vision of the subjectivity and moral authority of young girls. Part of James's long-standing interest in feminine subjectivity, such experiments join in the period's debates about a powerfully exemplary female subject. In them we see James drawing from this discursive field the defining terms for his canonically celebrated constructions of narrative and cultural authority, as he develops, alongside Grand and Egerton, a vision of experimental authority that will shape the terms of modernism.

George Egerton was the best-known New Woman writer to define modern woman as a powerful enigma, and her vision of woman's mysterious doubleness offers a useful model of the contradictions of feminine subjectivity that writers of the 1890s would play out. Egerton became famous with the 1893 publication of her collection of short stories, *Keynotes*, a book that both author and critics saw as distinctly, controversially modern because it depicted female characters as figures of mystery, possessed of depths that escaped masculine knowledge as well as the conventions of domestic life. Looking back in a 1932 essay "A Keynote to *Keynotes,*" Egerton described these depths as the "one small plot left" for the woman writer, "the *terra incognita* of herself, as she knew herself to be," "a closed door" she might "unlock . . . with a key of my own fashioning" (58). The stories in *Keynotes* define their female characters through a mysterious interiority that makes them enigmas to the male characters they meet. The protagonist of "An Empty Frame," for instance, tells her puzzled husband that "I have a bit of a complex nature; you couldn't understand me if you tried to, and better not try!" (130). This enigma produces a universal divide between the sexes, for as a character from the story "A Cross Line" puts it: "The wisest of them [men] can only say we are enigmas; each one of them sets about solving the riddle of the *ewig weibliche,*—and well it is that the workings of our hearts are closed to them. . . . [Men] have all overlooked the eternal wildness, the untamed primitive savage temperament that lurks in the mildest, best woman. Deep in through ages of convention this primeval trait burns,—an untamable quantity that may be concealed but is never eradicated by culture, the keynote of woman's witchcraft and woman's strength" (29–30). Using contemporary discourses of primitivism to praise women rather than disparage them, Egerton casts female subjectivity and sexuality as an antisocial wildness that challenges convention because it is buried deep within the psyche.[3]

This view of woman's inaccessible mystery anchors the stories' criticism of marriage as well as their narrative experiments. By removing female character to a realm of presocial interiority, *Keynotes* suggests that female subjectivity cannot be encompassed by conventional categories like adultery, innocence, or propriety. And in evoking these psychic depths, the stories in the collection—which catalogue a series of marriages from inert to abusive—reposition conventional marriage as artificially constraining at best. They suggest that woman's inner nature would send her on another path, could she bring herself to follow its demands and could society tolerate the results. The critique of marriage that results from this notion of female interiority also shapes the innovations of narrative in *Keynotes.* As critics have noted, the stories proceed less by familiar sequences of external events, by the stages or barriers of courtship, for instance, than by a focus on moments of psychic revelation, reversal, or decision (Bjorhovde 129–132; Boumelha 66–67; Harris). In *Keynotes* such patterns, which claim to disclose the rhythms of woman's internal self, seem to reveal a truer plot for female character, and cast such a narrative—like female subjectivity—as disrupting convention in general and conventional marriage in particular.

This definition of woman as enigma thus renders feminine interiority as a challenge to domesticity rather than as its finest result. Here Egerton paradoxically shares with her critics a view of the power of female interiority to threaten social stability. Her interest in female subjectivity highlights the extent to which contemporary social commentary—especially the discussion of modern degeneration—shares Egerton's fascination with the subject and her concern with the disruptiveness of interiority. Indeed commentators on the New Woman and in particular the new fiction of psychology and sexuality associated with her found this interiority to be among the most disturbing qualities of what they perceived as a new, and potentially degenerative, social movement.

When critics considered the danger posed by the modern woman, they were inclined to discuss her as an example of a new or newly problematic subjectivity. Indeed in reviewers' hands the dilemma of modern femininity becomes the problem of psychology itself. We might note the power of this connection between woman and the psyche in an anonymous essay from 1889, "The Apple and the Ego of Woman." Ann Ardis has recently commented on this essay as a key example of late-Victorian alarm at the New Woman. But what must strike us here, aside from the apocalyptic upheaval the essay sees following upon the New Woman's rise in the world, is its insistent but unexplained association of modern woman with psychology, or "Ego." If, as the essay tells us, "countless papers on woman have now poured out for several years from the periodical press, besides numerous works throwing quite an electric light on her psychology . . . we are all very well informed as to the Ego of woman" (374), nonetheless the essay itself wishes to reemphasize the connection. Indeed the essay's peculiarity is how thoroughly woman herself is subsumed into the category of "Ego" she introduces.[4] For while the essay at first refers occasionally to "the Ego of Woman" (375, 377), it soon speaks almost exclusively of "Ego" alone: "The Ego now prefers a day without vacancies" (376); "the position of the Ego has always been greatly modified by race instincts" (378); "Especially hidden is the Ego's destroying power" (382). The danger of woman here *is* the danger of psychology.

This association of the New Woman with a socially dangerous psyche is shared by her other critics. Psychologizing the New Woman writer as well as her readers and the characters in her fiction, commentators defined modern woman as a pathological subject. What is particularly interesting, however, is the extent to which such comments focused on the dangers of feminine enclosure. Of course this critique is not universal. Predictably enough, some critics accuse the New Woman of violating the codes of domestic femininity by being too public. The prominent antifeminist Elizabeth Lynn Linton, for instance, uses her essay "The Wild Women as Social Insurgents" to attack modern women for an immodest, unsexing social display, for their participation in that "vagrant and self-advertising" "spirit of the day" which must publish or exhibit, and exhibit for money (600). Similarly, Hugh Stutfield's "The Psychology of Feminism" objects to modern woman's insistence on "baring . . . her soul" in fiction (105), and James Ashcroft Noble, in his essay "The Fiction of Sexuality," compares the disproportionate focus on sexuality in recent fiction with "the host who holds a reception and cleans his teeth in the drawing room before his assembled guests" (495).

However critics equally often—and more surprisingly—turn their attention and their censure to the overly private subject associated with scandalous New Women and their fiction. Noble's all-too-public reader is doubled by the equally decadent reader who hides his unhealthy reading as "a secret, only to be confided to intimates" (494). And when Stutfield objects to woman's baring her soul, "dissecting it, analysing and probing into the innermost crannies of her nature" ("Psychology" 105), he is disapproving of introspection, the turn inward, as well. It is thus not simply the inappropriate exposure of interiors that marks the fiction of the modern woman as a disruptive sign of social decay, but the assertion of a subject so emphatically internal to begin with.

We must link such objections to interiority and New Woman fiction with the rhetoric of degeneration that became popular in English cultural criticism in the mid-1890s. This account of degeneration followed upon the 1895 translation of Max Nordau's 1892 book *Degeneration*, a text that diagnosed European cultural and physiological decline.[5] Particularly in the essays of Hugh Stutfield and Janet Hogarth, modern women were cast as degenerates whose disease was both social and subjective. And while both writers saw cultural degeneracy extending beyond New Women, "'yellow' lady novelists" (Stutfield, "Tommyrotics" 833), and "modern women's books of the introspective type" (Stutfield, "Psychology" 104)—most threateningly to male homosexuals—for both writers modern woman and her fictions make up the most problematically widespread signs of English decline.

Both writers see decadence in female interiority, in modern woman's apparent self-absorption and enclosure. Stutfield, for instance, defines the problem with explicit echoes of Egerton. Modern writers, he says, are "oppressed with a dismal sense that everything is an enigma" ("Tommyrotics" 835); this enigma is incarnated in a woman unknowable to man, "forever examining her mental self in the looking-glass" and glorying in her "'complicatedness'" ("Psychology" 105). Men, he suggests, would be "better mated with an open-hearted natural woman, who wore her heart upon her sleeve, than with an animated riddle or an enigma in flounces and furbelows" ("Psychology" 106). Hogarth—noting that English degeneration appears in the nation's female writers rather than, as in France, in male ones—describes modern women's writings as a pernicious form of "impressionism" focused on the "[culture] of the emotions; or . . . 'living one's own life'" (589).

In criticizing feminine interiority, both Stutfield and Hogarth draw upon a category they take from Nordau, "morbid ego-mania" (Stutfield, "Psychology" 109). The connection should make us note the extent to which Nordau's own analysis of degeneration criticizes overly enclosed subjectivity and imagines social health to derive from a subject whose borders are properly managed. Indeed the subcategory of egomania, like degeneration more generally, attributes a social problem to a disease of the subject's nervous and perceptual boundaries; it does so to anchor scientifically Nordau's claim that the social health of civilization requires that the individual subordinate himself to the community and the race. To this end Nordau pathologizes pleasures that he thinks gratify the individual in defiance of normal standards and at the expense of the race— for instance the preference of poets like Baudelaire for "carrion, maladies, criminals, and prostitutes" (275). In contrast, healthy pleasures are turned outward because they further the greater good of the species. "With feelings of pleasure are united, in healthy, fully-developed human beings equipped with the social instinct (altruism), only those ideas the content whereof is conducive to the existence and prosperity of the individual being, society, or species" (328).

For Nordau egomania is a disease of the individual's development and nervous system in which interiority, taken to extremes, leaves the subject insufficiently open to the external world. Paradoxically the egomaniac, for Nordau, has failed to reach "the highest achievement of living matter"—"the formation of an 'I'"—because he has not learned that the "highest degree of development of the 'I' consists in embodying in itself the 'not-I' . . . in conquering egoism, and in establishing close relations with other beings, things and phenomena" (252). Thus the normative individual triumphs through a forgetting of self; he "perceives little and rarely his internal excitations, but always and clearly his external impressions" (253). There are neurological causes for egomania: the egomaniac's "sensory nerves may be obtuse. . . . [Or] the brain is not sufficiently excitable, and does not perceive properly the impressions which are transmitted to it from the external world" (254). But in either case, the egomaniac has become all interiority, as it were. He, or she, has no saving access—or insufficient access—to the external world. In Hogarth's adaptation, egomaniacs "exhibit a love of self never met with in a sane person in anything like the same degree, and at the same time are often completely impervious to various forms of external excitation" (587).

The normative subject on whom these writers rely is an open subject, or rather, it is a subject in whom the relation of internal to external stimuli is proper, or regulated. Thus if the diseased female psyche Stutfield and Hogarth construct from Nordau's account of decadence fails to admit or register "external excitation," then the cure requires a turn to the outside world. And indeed both writers advocated some sort of external object as a way for the morbid woman to cease attending to her own sensations. The cure, Stutfield suggests, is to "take women out of themselves" ("Psychology" 115). For Hogarth, the solution comes as a revision of domestic ideology that nevertheless reinforces the power of home. If she sees the disease's origin in woman's departure from the family, the cure lies in a return to the home, but to a home explicitly cast as the least inward of spheres. In the family, Hogarth suggests, woman has "something [outside herself] upon which to expend her emotions" (591); if this does not happen, "completer training," greater maturity, and "the philosophic mind" (592) will have to provide her with new external objects to save her and her culture. Like Nordau, then, Stutfield and Hogarth propose a healthy female subject as one with a regulated openness to the world, and they see in that subject's openness the mechanism and safeguard of social health.

But while critics described Egerton's stories as examples of the New Woman's absolute interiority, their debates may instead let us see the way her work echoes theirs, for her stories are in fact concerned to imagine a balance between female interiority and an acute sensitivity to the external world. In fact woman's enigmatic power in *Keynotes* derives precisely from the mysterious doubling of enclosure and openness. If Egerton's female characters are admired and powerful in these stories in part because their truest selves are inaccessible to others, their power also comes from an exceptional sensitivity to others' hidden concerns. This is strikingly the case for the protagonist of "A Cross Line," whose pregnancy allows her to intuit that her maid once bore an illegitimate child and thus to forge an emotional communion between them. This same power of joining responsiveness to reserve belongs to the mysterious woman at the center of "The Spell of the White Elf." As the female narrator notes, "We sat and talked. . . . I don't remember what she said; I only know that she was making clear to me most of the things that had puzzled me for a long time. . . . How she knew just the subjects that worked in me I knew not; some subtle intuitive sympathy, I suppose, enabled her to find it out" (85). Indeed this character's power to move beyond herself is so strong that another woman's child inherits her features.

The protagonist of "A Cross Line" comments on this powerful mixture of response and solipsism at length. "'Women have told me that I came into their lives just when they needed me; men had no need to tell me, I felt it. People have needed me more than I them. . . . I have touched sore places they showed me, and healed them,—but they never got at me'" (32). The passage underlines a tension in Egerton's enigmatic women: fully interiorized, their interiority nonetheless yields a power defined as the ability to fulfill the desires of others. It is this doubleness envisioned within female subjectivity that accounts for the notorious orientalist scene in which this same story's protagonist fantasizes about dancing before an audience of responsive men.

> She fancies she is on the stage of an ancient theatre, out in the open air, with hundreds of faces upturned toward her. . . . She bounds forward and dances, bends her lissome waist, and curves her slender arms, and gives to the soul of each man what he craves, be it good or evil. And she can feel now . . . the grand, intoxicating power of swaying all these human souls to wonder and applause. . . . She can feel the answering shiver of emotion that quivers up to her from the dense audience, spellbound by the motion of her glancing feet. . . . [One] bound, and she stands with outstretched arms and passion-filled eyes . . . asking a supreme note to finish her dream of motion; and the men rise to a man and answer her, and cheer. (27–28)

This fantasy plays out a familiar contradiction in modern cultural imaginings of female sexuality that becomes particularly marked at the turn of the century: it is at once wholly interior—the secret desire buried in a woman's mind—and defined through a response to others—the fulfillment of male desire. The contradiction has raised questions about the sexual politics of Egerton's story for critics who focus on either the interiority of the scene or its theatrical publicity, its reliance on an audience. Does Egerton imagine an internal female sexuality and psyche here, or does she offer such a notion of femininity as literally staged in response to others (Chrisman 55; Pykett 173; Ardis 100)?

But isolating these two alternatives does not allow us to read either Egerton's characteristic definition of feminine enigma or its troublingly ambiguous sexual politics, since both are based on a vision of feminine contradiction. This contradiction between a subject interiorized and impervious to the world and one wholly responsive to it does not dismantle feminine subjectivity, but rather defines its unique power for Egerton. Egerton's mysterious woman resists domestic convention with the force of interiority, and finds lodged at the heart of her interior a response to others that seems never to threaten her own boundaries; she refigures subjective openness so that it is compatible with interiority, so that it may not imply a loss of self.

Women's contradictory subjectivity in turn generates the narrative innovations of Egerton's stories, as it places new demands on her fiction's narrators and on narrative stance more generally. The presentation of female subjectivity is central here, for that subjectivity possesses the empowering inner truth resistant to conventional stories. And yet the subject to be captured seems both disorientingly attuned to everything outside her and remotely unfathomable. How might narrators speak of, or indeed transmit, either of these two conditions? Egerton's experiments in narrative method seem to work toward the translation of women's responsiveness when she uses a form of impressionism to echo the movements of subjectivity (Harris). Following a character from charged moment to charged moment without conventional narrative transitions, the stories produce the effect of a female mind that lives through emotional intensities and encounters, one occupied with "producing pictures and finding associations between the most unlikely objects" ("A Cross Line" 9–10).

But narrative authority is also severely challenged by the insistence in *Keynotes* that women's power derives as well from their inaccessible interiority. As Penny Boumelha has noted, these enigmatic women create a dilemma for a traditionally omniscient narrative voice; their mysterious interiority would be compromised if fully open to and transmitted by a narrator. To preserve women's status as possessors of mysteries, Egerton must imagine a narrative voice whose knowledge and power are uniquely unsettled: narrators must convey the authority of female characters without ever entirely shifting that authority to themselves and thus diminishing it. As a result her enigmatic women tend to describe their own power through extended speeches in these stories, controlling revelation and readerly knowledge with their own voices and dislodging, however slightly, the terms on which the stories' narrators acquire the authority of female characters and their knowledge (Boumelha 91–92).

George Egerton's stories thus produce an unavoidable—and central—dilemma for narrative authority with their belief in women's powerful inaccessibility to conventional plot, a dilemma crucial to the modernist innovations fueled by the figure of female consciousness. If privileged and enlightening consciousness inheres in a character and that privilege is defined precisely through inaccessibility and contradiction, how might narrators gain or even approach the authority of character without destroying the very terms that produce it? It is a problem and a dynamic that haunts fictional experiment at the turn of the century, one furthered by the perpetual inquiry into just what it is that gives specifically female subjectivity access to privileging truth to begin with. What does woman know, how does she know it, and what social force might that knowledge possess?

The concern with modern woman's psychology articulated in Egerton's fiction was not restricted to accounts of the highly rebellious New Woman. A variety of social and fictional debates about young women in the 1890s took up the question of female openness and interiority. Like the New Woman, the figure of the innocent young girl newly abroad in the world anchored discussions of cultural health and the stability of the social order. Just as diagnoses of English degeneration saw the shape of the modern woman's mind as a refraction, cause, or cure of social problems—so too did debates about the failure of marriage and the corrosive effects of commodification turn to the promise and perils of the young girl's open mind. Indeed her subjectivity became central as writers attempted to refigure sources of cultural authority when the domestic sphere itself seemed invaded by the market values it claimed to oppose.

A particularly charged instance of this concern was the debate over the changed nature of modern girls living at home and poised on the verge of marriage. Several magazines published collections of essays on the topic, among them a long exchange entitled "The Revolt of the Daughters," which began in the journal *Nineteenth Century* in 1894, and a collection by writers such as Walter Besant, Sarah Grand, and Thomas Hardy entitled "The Tree of Knowledge," which appeared in the *New Review* in 1894.[6] Such exchanges considered the cultural dilemmas that arose as young women began to move more freely outside the home— walking without a chaperone, reading literature and attending plays that discussed current social problems. Exposed to the public world even as they lived within the shelter of the domestic sphere, these newly mobile girls raised questions about the power and appropriateness of the enclosed home, and about the ideal of total feminine innocence it assumed. The debate about young women's enclosure from or contact with the world rendered questions about female subjectivity as questions about female knowledge. Just what might a young woman know—or need to know— about the troubling world outside the home?

The debate about girls' knowledge of the public world drew upon growing suspicions about the stability of domestic enclosure itself. Critics wondered whether the domestic realm might not invite social corruption precisely because of its much-vaunted insularity; they asked whether home's enclosure might not endanger the purity of young girls by keeping them ignorant of the world around them. This critique of domesticity drew upon contemporary discussions of venereal disease, a social problem that seemed to threaten the sanctity of home as men infected unsuspecting wives and children, blurring the line between home and a corrupt public world.[7] Public discussion in the early 1890s often traced this problem to a lack of female knowledge. Were not respectable girls made vulnerable because "the state of ignorance in marriageable women . . . [was idealized as] innocence," and encouraged? (Grand, "Modern Girl" 706). Might greater knowledge of the world's corruptions, and in particular of their prospective husbands' pasts, allow young women to choose pure men, redeeming domesticity and the English race?

Discussion of the perils faced by modern girls thus suggested the cultural importance of female knowledge and of a female mind healthily open to the outside world. And they often turned to such an impressionable figure as a way of revitalizing the values of domesticity, critiquing the home to better save it.[8] We can see the connection between these terms elaborated at length by Sarah Grand in her essay "The Modern Girl" (1894) and in her best-selling novel *The Heavenly Twins* (1893). The link also shapes the debate of "The Tree of Knowledge," in which writers ranging from Besant and Grand to Hardy and Elizabeth Lynn Linton discuss possible solutions to the contemporary fear that the impurities of the public world had infiltrated marriage and the home. Their debate, however, is less a critique of domestic unworldliness as an ideal than an attempt to find ways of restoring it in fact. Grand notes in "The Modern Girl" that "if girls could be kept in perfect seclusion . . . and married . . . to men worthy of them, then there could be little question that the preservation of what we call their innocence would be as practically right as it is poetically beautiful. But the condition of a girl's life at the present time makes the old ideal almost impossible and quite unsafe" (710). The contributors to "The Tree of Knowledge," with few exceptions, agreed that their goal was to restore the endangered purity of the domestic sphere, to remove marriage from the corrupting conditions of commercial exchange, and to reimagine a virtuous world where "a girl should [and could] marry for love, and for love only" (Hall Caine in Besant et al. 679).[9]

These critics objected that marriage had become a part of, rather than an alternative to, the commodified world outside the home, that it had become a "marriage market" (Caine in Besant et al. 679). The source of this corruption was the social convention that dictated that marriageable girls should know nothing about social evils of the world such as prostitution and disease. Young girls' lack of knowledge—their enclosure—had thus become a symptom of the commodification of the domestic sphere itself. Grand argues this point at length in "The Modern Girl." Society keeps girls in ignorance for "vulgar commercial purposes" (711); "brought up . . . exclusively for the marriage market . . . [they are] exhibited like fatted fowls whose value depends upon the color and condition of their flesh" (712). If society commodifies the sacred institution of marriage, it can do so because even the foundation of home—a mother's pure and protective love—has been warped. Among "society mothers[,] position and how to secure it is their first consideration, the position which is conferred by mere money and rank . . . there is nothing that brutalizes a woman like the struggle for rank" (712).

In seeking solutions, the contributors to "The Tree of Knowledge" turned to female knowledge as an answer; indeed the debate was cast in advance as a referendum on female knowledge, as responses to the question: should girls receive instruction in the "physical conditions of marriage and conjugal life" (Madame Adam in Besant et al. 675), "the social condition of the world" and the "past history of [their] lover[s]" (Besant in Besant et al. 676) in order to solve the debasement of the marriage bond? While a few hesitated to go so far as to recommend that young girls learn the physical facts of life or the sexual histories of their lovers—citing the demoralizing influence of "certain books" (Besant in Besant et al. 677) or the prurience of "the despised woman-novel itself" (Israel Zangwill in Besant et al. 690) as evidence of a world gone wrong—most agreed that female knowledge could solve the spread of the home's corrupting commodification. They argued that a young woman "ought to be wise to know where her love is deserved" (Caine in Besant et al. 679), and that "knowledge aids self-preservation—the preservation of the race" (Björnsterne Björnson in Besant et al. 678).

In debating whether young women should know about social corruption or their husbands' purity, the writers of this series thus propose an ambitious—and, for the period, characteristic—link between the questions of female knowledge, social corruption, and the status of the domestic sphere. Their discussion imagines that both the authority of home as a sacred and unworldly space and the fate of the social disease threatening it can be controlled through the knowledge taken in by respectable young girls. The debate, that is, maps the question of the authority and health of home and the social world onto a question about the boundaries of female subjectivity, about the openness or enclosure of a modern girl's mind. But unlike the connection imagined by Pater, the link here is not one of simple analogy. Here the female subject's enclosure leads to home's corrupted openness, its unsettling resemblance to the fallen world. In contrast it is the young woman's openness which saves. Writers hoped that by taking into herself a knowledge of corruption, she might turn it to domestic, indeed national, purification, producing a world in which modesty and knowledge may coexist. The very openness of a girl's purity here conquers social evils and testifies to the saving transformations of the female subject.

Sarah Grand's *The Heavenly Twins* elaborates more fully than any other text the cultural logic of this account of how female subjects may save modern society. It also reveals how these questions about female knowledge and openness may come to shape the terms of narrative at the turn of the century. For while Grand's text, unlike Egerton's, does not focus on figures of enigmatic subjectivity or offer narrative methods that we might consider highly experimental, nonetheless this popular novel shapes its heroine according to contemporary ideals of impressionability and interiority that will influence modernism, and it reveals a complex relation between masculine narrative authority and female subjectivity that similarly endures.

The novel explicitly illustrates the debates played out in "The Tree of Knowledge" and Grand's own essay, "The Modern Girl." It argues openly for women's knowledge of their prospective husbands' pasts, criticizing the damning constraints of woman's domestic enclosure; it explores the corruption of the home and imagines its potential resurrection by a woman exposed to the hard facts of a fallen world. The novel arranges its argument through a contrast between two of its protagonists: between the innocent domestic lamb, Edith—who dies of syphilitic madness—and its heroine, Evadne, who embraces knowledge, refuses a tainted husband, and may point the way toward a renewed world and a renewed domestic sphere. In contrasting these characters and their fates, Grand's novel aligns its consideration of the social problems tainting the domestic plot with questions about the proper shape of female subjectivity—like Egerton, refiguring the relationship of female interiority to the outside world.

The book's most explicit critique of domestic ideology works through the plot of Edith Beale, a veritable angel in the house raised in ignorance of the world as the path of true womanliness. Edith is above all enclosed in this novel. Her home is inward-looking: "the walls were thick, the windows gothic . . . with unexpected alcoves and angles and deep embrasures" (154). Her character too is one of virtuous inwardness. "Her simple unaffected manners were the plaingarment which concealed the fine quality and cultivation of her mind," just as "the ornamentation [of her dress] was out of sight, the lining of her gowns being often more costly than the materials of which they were made" (158). However in the text such inwardness is a sign that the world's truths are walled out—only to return in the disruptions of dreams. If Edith's life is "one long beatific vision" (156), this spirituality signals less a virtuous transcendence of the world than a denial of it: "she was unconsciously prepared to resent in her gentle way, and to banish at once, if possible, any disturbing thought that might break in upon [this vision]" (156).[10]

For *The Heavenly Twins* such inwardness fails because it refuses all contact with the outside world, indeed refuses to recognize the connections between public and private spheres. The plot of the novel insists that such contact is necessary to maintain both virtuous domesticity and virtuous womanhood—the sanctity of the home and of woman's mind. Thus when Edith and her mother ignore a young woman and her baby lying by the side of the road and decline to "take the poor dusty disgraced tramp into their carriage," they insist that the public space of the street and the private space of carriage and home can neither touch nor resemble each other (160).[11] The novel is devoted to disproving this maxim. Not only does it criticize Edith's uncharitable actions and show the destitute girl restored to health in domestic safety but its plot hinges on the resemblance between Edith and this fallen woman—who is an earlier victim of Edith's own diseased fiancé. When Edith refuses to hear the woman's story, she seals her own fate, guaranteeing that she will marry the man and wind up as his next victim. Domestic enclosure and its psychology thus cause their own undoing in *The Heavenly Twins*; by splitting the world between public and private, they ensure that there will ultimately be no difference between the fallen woman and the angelic daughter of the house. Domestic virtue thus remains the novel's central value— the marker of what can be lost; however the novel will suggest that the only way to preserve the domestic sphere is to open that sphere in limited fashion to the world.

In thus linking domestic enclosure with social corruption *The Heavenly Twins* underlines the connections between the dangers of the too-enclosed home and the risks of the too-enclosed subject. For the novel marks the domestic woman's downfall with a vision of interiority both intensified and undone. Syphilitic infection destroys Edith's mind, by destroying its characteristic virtue, placing the most unwomanly thoughts deep within her. Fighting valiantly "for her reason with the fearful malady . . . [Edith at first] presented outwardly only the same dull apathy, giving no sign and speaking no word which could betray the fury of the rage within" (281); soon she is tormented by uncharacteristically sacrilegious thoughts she cannot control, which are lodged deep within her and yet make that interior unrecognizably foreign. By novel's end, the inner sanctum of the domestic angel's bedroom has, like her mind, been transformed into the site of terrifyingly unnatural impulses; the angel in the house madly shrieks of her desire to kill her own child.

In contrast, *The Heavenly Twins* offers as its central heroine an exemplary modern young woman. Through the character of Evadne Frayling it explores the paradigm of the newly open female subject and considers how her impressibility might produce a renewed form of feminine principle and domestic virtue. Indeed Evadne's openness is introduced to us as a model for healthy education: "Ages of education, ages of hereditary preparation had probably gone to the making of such a mind, and rendered its action inevitable. For generations knowledge is acquired, or, rather, instilled by force in families, but, once in a way, there comes a child who demands instruction as a right" (3). Evadne exists to take in information about the outside world, "a word being enough on some subjects to make whole regions of thought intelligible to her" (3). Such impressibility, however, bears little resemblance to vulnerability or to instability. For while she takes in the advice of others, she does so only to become more securely and independently herself, to reach permanent truths. We might note here the way that this figure revises the image of woman offered by a Victorian advocate of domesticity like Sarah Lewis. For while Lewis's woman could judge by the "unalterable principles of reason and religion" (66) because she was secluded from the world, Evadne in contrast can find such principles because she is open to the world, and thus can "put prejudice aside in order to see beneath it, deep down into the sacred heart of things, where the truth is" (3).[12]

In the course of the novel's plot, Evadne's admirable embrace of information—and the individual principles and virtue it produces—indicts the contemporary practice of keeping knowledge from marriageable girls. Thus her openness to knowledge of the public world allows her to avoid Edith's end by a principled insistence on taking in information and judging for herself. Learning of her husband's "wild" past, she refuses to be his wife in more than name (77). The individual rectitude learned through her education continues to allow her to evaluate and reject pernicious influences—from the salacious French novels with which her husband attempts to corrupt her to the seductions of "coarse conversation" (202) and the "objectionable stories" (203) that circulate promiscuously in the debased society he frequents. Indeed the primary effect of Evadne's openness is a capacity for selective closure later; the principles formed in her early education produce an inviolable core that keeps her safe from too much susceptibility in future years.

Grand's novel thus depicts the unique capacity for virtue of the modern young woman. She is both open and closed and these qualities complement each other in her; indeed her permeability to the world provides a means of ensuring the boundaries that make her upright and genuinely unworldly. Thus *The Heavenly Twins* uses modern woman's mind to provide a new definition of virtue. Evadne is exemplary not just because she is an ideal subject for education but because her mind's unique qualities constitute a renewed, modern form of purity or unworldliness. It is this purity which keeps her from being disruptively altered by what she takes in, which limits the harm of innumerable influences, allowing her to read "with intellect clear and senses unaffected by anything" (23). Purity makes Evadne a superior student of medicine, for instance—a superiority linked to her exemplary femininity. She can read medical texts "quite unharmed, because she made no personal application of her knowledge as the coarser mind masculine of the ordinary medical student is apt to do. . . . She possessed, in fact, a mind of exceptional purity as well as of exceptional strength, one to be enlightened by knowledge, not corrupted" (23). The knowledge that some feared would debase young girls is here rendered a tool for a girl's protection of her virtue and the social order, for the structure of her mind has the power to absorb external influences and convert them to a strength for individual morality.

The Heavenly Twins does not reward its exemplary protagonist with a happy ending. Despite the moral power of this figure, the text stops short of imagining that female subjectivity might fully triumph over the many corruptions of the world. In the end Evadne's spirit and health are broken; her first husband's restrictions and the conventions of domestic privacy weaken her by interfering with the openness and individuality that the novel has defined as mental and social health. Having promised to keep her first husband's name out of public view, she cannot enter the public sphere, cannot "publicly join societies, make speeches, or publish books, which people would know [she] had written, on the social subjects" she cares about. As a result, "her mind grew sluggish, her bodily health decreased, and the climate began to tell upon her" (350). Even a second marriage to an enlightened man, Dr. Galbraith, fails to cure her. While he can diagnose her as a victim of contemporary illusions about women's place in the private sphere, and while he believes as she once did that "if we refused to study the bad side of life, no evil would ever be remedied" (560), he cannot prevent her decline into a melancholy, self-enclosed dreaming that echoes Edith's tragic end. At the novel's conclusion, its exemplary modern woman can hope for little more than a tolerable life, for she has been irrevocably crippled by the social dictum that is the text's target: the spectrally voiced phrase, repeated throughout the novel, "HOME IS THE WOMAN'S SPHERE!" (295).

The Heavenly Twins does not use particularly experimental narrative methods. It is conventionally plotted in comparison with a text like Egerton's, and for most of its plot the novel is narrated by a traditional omniscient voice, which possesses the power to reveal characters' thoughts and motivations and to frame them in a broader social, philosophical worldview. However, like Egerton's *Keynotes,* Grand's novel imagines a set of complications for narrative voice to arise from its vision of female subjectivity, and these complications are tied to the novel's significant final swerve into an alternative method of narration. In its final section, the novel switches to first-person narration, to the more restricted voice of Dr. Galbraith, who recounts his meeting with Evadne, his investigation into her problem and its sources, and their eventual marriage. We might read this shift—as Lyn Pykett does (174–75)—as a questioning of narrative certainty, since Galbraith's knowledge in the text is partial.[13] The novel does mark him as in some ways limited, both because he is a character—one unfamiliar with Evadne's past—and because of his occasional lapses from the novel's view of the world. However Galbraith's principles do ultimately let him understand Evadne's psychology and problems in terms congruent with the novel's own. His medical knowledge has enabled him to diagnose her and to understand the relation between her nervous inwardness and her restriction to the private sphere.

I would argue that the shift into the narrative voice of a male character at the end of *The Heavenly Twins* does something quite different: it proposes a close connection between the text's model of ideal feminine subjectivity and its definitions of masculine narrative authority. We might approach this relation through a question that recalls Egerton's text: what access do we have to the modern woman's mind? For while this novel, unlike Egerton's stories, does not obviously limit either a character or a narrator's access to female psychology, the shift to Galbraith's perspective late in the text nevertheless draws attention to this problem of access. When we read his story, the novel forces us to reencounter through him, bit by bit, Evadne's character as an enigma to be deciphered through a set of signs—signs whose potential opacity becomes obvious in Galbraith's progressive hypotheses about their meaning. Though her psychology cannot be a mystery to us, and ultimately will not remain one to Galbraith, the novel's narrative progression here offers the familiar uncovering of woman's mysterious psychology as the structure and fuel of narrative, making the task of a narrator the deciphering of female opacity and equating this plot with—if not substituting it for—the conventions of courtship and marriage.

We might read the relation of narrator to female character here as one in which the narrator gains mastery, comprehending woman's mystery as well as finishing her story. But we might want to consider another relation as well—one of likeness and even substitution. *The Heavenly Twins* opens with Evadne Frayling as its exemplary female subject—taking in information while remaining uncorrupted, forming principles and measuring the world against them, and promising a purified society as a result. It closes with Galbraith taking in information, referring to principle, and speaking for social change. We may say, with reason, that Galbraith has triumphed in taking over the moral and subjective authority Evadne once held. But we may also say that he gains narrative power by echoing the process of learning first established through the novel's portrait of a modern woman, that his authority comes from occupying a space—epistemological as well as moral and critical—defined in the novel through Evadne as its prototypical, idealized female subject. If the novel somewhat disconcertingly proposes a masculine, professionalized narration as the final voice of its feminist critique of domesticity, that voice nevertheless resembles, and receives authority on the basis of, the shape of a young girl's mind.

Henry James is a figure more familiarly linked to the rise of modernist impressionism than is Sarah Grand. However, his work shares her concern with the parameters of female subjectivity, and indeed this concern shapes many of his most important narrative experiments. Like Grand—whose work he read—James was fascinated by the position of girls in a corrupt society, the dilemma of young women entering into scenes of social complexity or compromise.[14] If such concerns located Grand in popular, sentimental literary traditions and led many critics to read her work as didactic and topical (Mangum 85–89, 141–43), the same set of questions ultimately offered the terms through which James placed his writing in the sphere of artistic high culture. For James used his female characters repeatedly as the central figures through whom he developed the ideas about subjectivity, artistic perception, and cultural authority that were to be so influential for literary modernism.

While the subject of the young girl interested James throughout his career, in the late 1890s the question of what and how she knew became the center of his particularly intense scrutiny in two novels: *What Maisie Knew* (1897) and *The Awkward Age* (1899). The predicament of girls in a modern social setting becomes entwined in these texts with questions of narrative and literary authority for James; it does so at a moment when, suffering from his public failure as a playwright, he attempted to redefine the form of cultural authority that he might attribute to fiction. In this period, and in particular through the writing of *What Maisie Knew*—with its view focused closely on the perceptual processes of its female subject—James begins to elaborate the narrative strategies so vital to the method of his late novels, to the definition of technique offered in the prefaces to the New York Edition as a basis for his authorial identity, and to the model of narrative authority he provided ensuing writers of modernist impressionism. The shape and cultural authority of female subjectivity centrally forms those strategies, as James investigates the familiar question of what young girls might know and what form of virtue they might possess when they encounter social corruption within their own homes.

James's experimental writing of the 1890s reworks the concern with the public or private nature of subjectivity that absorbed him in the 1880s, when he wrote a series of novels about the dilemmas of explicitly public women. In *The Bostonians* (1885) and *The Tragic Muse* (1890), for example, James used the figures of the feminist speaker Verena Tarrant and the actress Miriam Rooth to explore questions about the viability in contemporary life of a private sphere or subject, especially a female subject, secured from the commercial demands of the public world. These are characters in whom interiority is rendered problematic because of their public vocation—becoming more prized as its terms are more suspect.[15] In *The Tragic Muse*, for instance, Miriam's gift as an actress is her ability to enter the roles she acts, a quality which lingers off the stage and makes it difficult for others to locate a solid self beneath the actress testing a role. And *The Bostonians* imagines Verena as a figure through whose powerful but absorptive voice others hope to speak and over whose fate—private or public—its protagonists fight. As Lynn Wardley has suggested, James saw the apparent breakdown of the private sphere and genteelly insulated individual in *The Bostonians* as both a crisis and an opportunity for a newly exemplary form of cultural authority. For James, Wardley observes, it is the public woman who signals the possibility of a figure bridging public and private (640). If this figure marks a breakdown between spheres, she nevertheless compensates with an alternate authority: she can circulate publicly without being fully absorbed into the terms of commerce and she thus may serve as an exemplar of civilization in modern democratic culture.

James's novels of the 1890s shift from this focus on women's place in the public world to an interest in the way identities are formed in more intimate, domestic interactions. However this turn inward (as critics have often described it)—to a more restricted social sphere and to a greater focus on the processes of subjective perception—only intensifies the dilemmas about female identity and cultural authority raised earlier (Weinstein; Allen). For the "private" realms of home and subject James envisions are not distinct from the power more conventionally visible in the public realm. Rather, his examination of the home and the female subject located there unravels the very possibility of a clearly delineated interior space. This subject is a permeable entity, radically shaped by impressions as by the demands of other characters, formed and reformed within interactions that are always relations of power.[16]

In these texts of the 1890s, then, James considers whether a young girl's openness may not simultaneously mark a cultural crisis and the opportunity for a new model of cultural authority. James's fictions hardly give themselves over without qualms to the idea of a world lacking the authority of private identity or a private realm. A world fully permeated by power, commerce, or exchange is as dire in these novels as it is nearly unavoidable. Indeed these novels receive their ethical and narrative impulse from the scandal that results when disinterest and innocence dissolve, even as they exploit the seductive melodrama the problem generates (Brooks). We might read James's work of the 1890s as attempting to reimagine sources of authority out of this situation, sources that could function the way the model of domestic interiority and transcendence did, given the disintegration of those very terms. This desire to locate a technique or figure of transcendence and resistance in a world of corrupting power draws him repeatedly to the fate of young girls in such a world. Through them James makes visible the terms in which cultural crisis and compensating authority might be mapped.

Both *What Maisie Knew* and *The Awkward Age* join contemporary journal debates and Grand's *Heavenly Twins* in asking whether some form of privacy is left to girls in a corrupt society. In each text the young protagonist inhabits a debased family in which the domestic sphere has virtually expanded toward a horizon at which it is inseparable from the public realm (Heller; J. H. Miller, *Versions of Pygmalion* 29–62; Walters). In *Maisie* the problem begins, like the novel, with her parents' divorce and multiplies with a consistent logic through their ever-widening circle of lovers, spouses, and household staff. In *The Awkward Age* the problem arises when the manipulative Mrs. Brookenham refuses to separate her family life—and her teenage daughter Nanda—from her own adult social set. Inappropriately immersed in a dissolute, gossiping society, Nanda is thus endangered, simply through "exposure" to her mother

(129). In both cases public and private spheres blur and young girls risk corruption when the family begins to operate by the rules of exchange, in a kind of promiscuous circulation; in both novels this failure of domesticity culminates in the scandalous vision of mothers who reject their daughters for participating in a circulation they cannot escape.[17]

What Maisie Knew marks the publicity of its disintegrating family when it introduces its domestic dilemma in the terms of a court case, in which Maisie is divided and circulated between her parents in exchange for a sum of money owed by one to the other. But the court's public circulation merely underlines the terms of her parents' social set—a society in which "the many friends of the Faranges drew together to differ about them"—and indeed echoes the public nature of her parents themselves, who produce "the sense indeed of a kind of abuse of visibility" and move about ceaselessly, carrying clothes "as a train carries passengers" (14). In this light it makes perfect sense that Maisie should tragically become the "little feathered shuttlecock they could fiercely keep flying between them" (19), part of their cycling attempts to find new partners to supply them with money and approval. The corrupt society of Mrs. Brookenham's drawing room in *The Awkward Age* is similarly, if more politely, based on public exchanges of gossip and on the overlap of social with monetary value. A circle ruled by the logic of "'giving each other away,'" by the terms of "'London life . . . tit for tat'" (13), its members encourage each other to rotate through extramarital affairs in order to provide fodder for conversation. This unseemly gossip, like the adolescent Nanda's immersion in this world, exemplifies the ills of modern culture, the crude "English periodical public washings of dirty linen" characterizing the age (70). The novel's central plot—in which Mrs. Brookenham seeks to capitalize materially on old-fashioned Mr. Longwood's attachment to Nanda—merely complicates the financial matchmaking already implicit in modern society. And for James, this troubling publicity of the family becomes a problem of character. Culpable adults lack any distinct interiority. Either they become sheer material or commercial surfaces—like Maisie's parents, who glitter as shields and shopfronts—or they are themselves merely embodiments of the social order—"produced," like the cartoonish Cashmore in *The Awkward Age*, by the circle that discusses them and given identity only in relation to those they gossip about (113).

The problem of character becomes acute in these novels when it raises questions about how we are to understand, and distinguish, the texts' young protagonists. For the young girls whose imperiled innocence lies at the heart of these novels do not themselves possess easily defined centers by which we may mark their difference from public corruption. Nanda describes her dilemma—that she is potentially unmarriageable because she has been exposed to inappropriate knowledge—in terms of this all-too-open nature. She suggests that she may be a mere transparent conduit, just a figure through whom the world around her becomes visible. She shows, she says, "my situation, my exposure—all the results of them. . . . Doesn't one become a sort of a little drainpipe with everything flowing through? . . . it sticks to [me]" (241). Maisie too notoriously begins as a "ready vessel for bitterness, a deep little porcelain cup in which biting acids could be mixed" (13). As a result, neither heroine offers a reassuring sense of interiority to anchor her innocence. Indeed Maisie acquires what tenuous interiority she has as a form of secrecy, discovering "the idea of an inner self or, in other words, of concealment" as "a new remedy" for "the feeling of danger" (20). Her new capacity for concealment does remove her from her parents' circuits in one sense— keeping secret her knowledge about others, she now "spoiled their fun, but she practically added to her own" (20). However, such hidden thoughts do not remove her from the problems of circulation; they only reinscribe her differently, placing her in the manipulative exchange of keeping others' secrets as her knowledge.

These novels, with their failed domestic circles and their young girls wholly open to the world around them, offer a privileged and intensely charged site for James to work out the implications of a subject entirely permeable from without. As we have seen through Grand's text and through the period's debates on feminine knowledge, the stakes of Maisie and Nanda's openness are particularly high because as young girls their potential for innocence, for opposition to worldly corruption, is so culturally charged; it so centrally represents the possibility of untainted transcendence in the period.[18] Thus James's turn to the figure of the young girl not only intensifies the drama of his texts but shapes the terms in which interiority might be imagined as innocence and openness figured through a drastic analogy with a "drainpipe with everything flowing through."

However such culturally overdetermined protagonists also dictate that both *Maisie* and *The Awkward Age* must imagine a way in which their young heroines may differ—however problematically or temporarily—from the debasing world, in order to generate and satisfy the demands of ethical and narrative suspense. In Nanda and Maisie, then, the open subject is laden with the weight of supplying a resistance to social corruption and an authority that seem structurally denied it. Through revising what that openness means, James will attempt to reimagine the terms of the young girl's cultural privilege, and in doing so he will redefine the authority of the novel as well.

The issue through which James's novels remap the subject's potential authority is a familiar one—the question of a young girl's knowledge. And in neither novel may female authority be construed as the conventional virtues of enclosure or lack of knowledge. To reject this view, *The Awkward Age*, like *The Heavenly Twins*, depicts an unknowing domestic lamb as a foil for its heroine in order to illustrate the complicity between false ideals of purity and the reality of social corruption. In *The Awkward Age* that lamb is Little Aggie, who possesses "no consciousness but that of being fed from the hand with the small sweet biscuit of unobjectionable knowledge" (159). But Aggie's purity is a spectacle; her "admirable training appeared to hold her out to them all as with precautionary finger-tips" (63), and she has been kept ignorant for the most cynical of motives. In fact the openness with which her aunt has aimed to make of her "a particular little rounded and tinted innocence" has the opposite effect: it labels Aggie as a product "deliberately prepared for consumption" (158). Her plot fulfills the novel's description of her as a product; her aunt forms her to sell on the marriage market and dangles her as a possible prize to keep her own lover nearby. When Aggie begins an affair with this lover immediately upon marriage and joins Mrs. Brookenham's scandalmongering circle, this is merely the logical outgrowth of a system in which her version of secluded innocence was only ever a market value designed to move her into circulation faster.

By contrast the novel's heroine Nanda sees and knows nearly everything around her and the novel explores the paradoxical possibility that such knowledge may not corrupt her—that she may be something other and better than her surroundings despite the fact that they enter her, shape her, and show through her. "'Don't I know everything? . . . You know what I know'" (228), she tells Van, the unworthy man whom she loves and who will reject her for her knowledge. Nanda knows so much because she has absorbed the world around her in the characteristic manner of a modern English girl, "'tak[ing] in things at [her] pores'" (228). Thus she explains to the elderly Longdon why she differs from her grandmother Julia: "'if we're both partly the result of other people, *her* other people were so different'" (153). "'There's so much else that's extraordinary [now],'" she observes, "'that if we're in it all so much *we* [young girls] must naturally be [extraordinary]'" (366).

But while *The Awkward Age* is fascinated by the proximity of Nanda's virtue to the cynicism of those around her, it never offers stable terms for distinguishing her as a subject. For the qualities that make her appeal-

ing reappear in other characters as the work of their most extreme cynicism. Thus Nanda, unlike the hypocritical Van, does not try "'to dodge
[the state of modern girls' knowledge] . . . to make believe . . . that it isn't
so'" (229), and she similarly insists with integrity to Mr. Longdon that
he accept her knowledge. But her mother's machinations take the same
guise; she too claims merely to accept the sad state of things, but she does
so in order to manipulate them the better—as when she tells Van "'You
won't do it [i.e., marry Nanda]'" (198), and so he doesn't. Nanda is also
echoed by her mother when Mrs. Brookenham cynically acknowledges
her own departure from Longdon's ideal in order to ensure that he will
give Nanda money. She confesses "'that compared with her [Julia], I'm a
poor creeping thing . . . of course I ache in every limb with the certainty
of my dreadful difference . . . I've helplessly, but finally and completely,
accepted it. Won't *that* help you [bear me]?'" (126).

The doubling underlines the problem Nanda's character poses in the
novel—a problem that fascinated James in novel after novel. How do we
know that she offers an alternative? Is it possible that she too is cynical,
manipulating others into tolerating her modernity for her own best advantage? *The Awkward Age* does not place great weight on this possibility. However, it is nonetheless fascinated by the social predicament of
young girls that makes the possibility imaginable, that threatens to make
them indistinguishable from the world around them. For as James notes
in his 1908 preface to the novel, Nanda's dilemma is created by the characteristically modern English "compromise," by which girls are immersed
in a society, yet still expected to remain paragons of innocence (xxxiv).
James exploited the tensions of this compromise for their full effect.

The narrative method of *The Awkward Age* is designed to highlight
this tension, by setting against each other the undecidability of Nanda's
character and the readerly and narrative desire for her innocence. As he
describes it in the preface, James refused in this novel to "go behind" the
dramatic presentation of conversational scenes, thus refusing to give us
a view of any thoughts that might constitute his protagonist's interior
and differentiate her from those around her (xl). He leaves us instead with
a contrast between Nanda's uncertain motives and the thematic and
structural necessity of her virtue. For the ethical stakes and the narrative suspense of the novel in fact require the possibility of Nanda's innocence, so that the corrupt glitter of her mother's circle may register
through its betrayal of her, and so that their endless circulation might,
with resistance, produce the trajectory of a plot. The closest the novel
comes to offering an image of Nanda's alternative innocence is the picture of virtue constructed from the funneling of vice, embodied in our

view of Nanda reading a scandalous French novel to decide whether it is safe for an already compromised friend.[19]

In turning to *What Maisie Knew* we find a text wholly centered on the problematic vision of female subjectivity implied by this contradiction. Indeed *Maisie* is the text in which James most clearly connected the powerfully enigmatic nature of such a subject with his experiments in narrative method, linking the social predicament of the modern young girl with the formal techniques that would influence modernism. The novel places the mysterious workings of a young girl's mind at its center by the narrative strategy of focusing on her perceptions of the world; in doing so it underlines the tentative difference between her views and those of the corrupt adults around her, and capitalizes on this potential difference as the source of readerly suspense and interpretation. For while we might wish to differentiate Maisie from a figure like Nanda—defining her as a character who signally does *not* know certain things (primarily the sexual and mercenary logic of her parents' repairings)—the novel is less interested in her ignorance than in her knowledge and its nature. The virtue she promises in the text does not hinge on a simple lack of exposure, so much as on what she makes of endless exposure itself. Our interpretation of the novel is thus a constant process of attempting to assess what she understands of the world in order to evaluate her motives and her virtue in acting as she does.

The novel focuses our attention in particular on how Maisie perceives the corrupt exchanges of her expanding circle of parents and stepparents, and how she comes to understand her role within them. While we may see Maisie's misinterpretations and developing understanding in terms of her initial lack of knowledge and her movement toward ending that lack, James also asks us to think of Maisie's innocence as producing an alternative interpretation or knowledge, one that articulates another, better vision of relations between characters.[20] In particular, Maisie's misunderstandings may offer a view of the world freed from the logic of exchange, nowhere more so than in her repeated conversations with her stepparents Sir Claude and Mrs. Beale about the fact that she has "brought them together." When they first meet, Mrs. Beale tells Sir Claude that she will:

"never give up any rights in [Maisie] . . . I shall hold very fast to my interest in her. What seems to have happened is that she has brought you and me together." "She has brought you and me together," said Sir Claude. His cheerful echo prolonged the happy truth, and Maisie broke out almost with enthusiasm: "I've brought you and her together!" Her companions of course laughed anew and Mrs. Beale gave her an affectionate shake.

"You little monster—take care what you do! But that's what she does do,"
she continued to Sir Claude. "She did it to me and Beale." "Well then,"
he said to Maisie, "you must try the trick at *our* place." (54–55)

While her stepparents speak the self-interested language of rights and
interests and frame Maisie's "bringing together" as the pretext for a series of liaisons, Maisie—especially clearly at this early stage—has access
to none of these meanings. Instead she seems to take the phrase in its
most domestically benevolent sense: she sees herself as bringing them
all together familially, recasting exchange as reunion, and imagining that
she truly is "sav[ing]" them by giving them a duty to fulfill (99).

Maisie's alternate reading here pits a logic of compatible union
against the various rules of exclusion governing adult sexual relations.
This reading will be pressured again and again in the novel as events force
her to wonder why "the general reunion should have broken down so in
fact" (128), why, with her governess Mrs. Wix, she may not join her stepparents. "Why after all should we have to choose between you? Why
shouldn't we be four?" (201). But importantly—and familiarly—James
never locates Maisie's reading in a safely autonomous subjective source.
The difficulty of interpreting her (mis)understanding is that she creates
it from the material others provide her—visible here in Maisie's sheer
repetition of others' words. On the one hand, the fact that Maisie merely repeats what other characters say makes her meaning uncertain, makes
it possible that she here, as much earlier in her life, is simply an empty
vessel. But Maisie's repetition also offers a mysterious instance of how a
girl might take in corruption and turn it to something quite different,
without recourse to an autonomous subjectivity.[21] In thus figuring
Maisie's repetition of adult exchanges as an internalization that may
purify the world, the novel emphasizes an ethical ambiguity: just what
does it mean that Maisie is so intimately "mixed up" in the most worldly and corrupt of affairs (128)?

Further, Maisie's understanding is not restricted to poignant misread-
ings of others. Eagerly desiring a knowledge that might make sense of the
adults on whom she depends, she accurately deciphers many of the relations of power in which she is so impossibly enmeshed—from appreciating her function as a vessel to be filled, to gauging the effects of her blank-
ness or apparent knowledge on her unreliable parents. The acuteness of
this knowledge registers in the painful scene in which her father not only
cuts his familial ties entirely but asks her to take the blame: "Then she
understood as well as if he had spoken it that what he wanted, hang it,
was that she should let him off with all the honors—with all the appearance of virtue and sacrifice on his side. It was exactly as if he had broken

out to her: . . . There's only impropriety enough for one of us; so *you* must take it all. *Repudiate* your dear old daddy—in the face, mind you, of his tender supplications" (142). The accumulation of Maisie's worldly understanding that is visible here merely reinforces the question posed by her repetitions: "As she was condemned to know more and more, how could it logically stop before she should know Most?" (208–9).

We might, then, paraphrase James's question: Does appreciating the terms of power around her doom Maisie to know them so fully that she reenacts them? Can she know and remain pure? These questions, of course, become most acute in the novel's conclusion, with Maisie's final decision. Faced with the choice of joining her adulterous stepparents or staying with her governess and renouncing ties to her beloved Sir Claude, Maisie in turn forces him to choose between his lover Mrs. Beale and herself, refusing to accept the quasi-familial threesome she had earlier "brought together." In offering Sir Claude these terms, Maisie, the text suggests, is acting on a conclusive stage of knowledge: "What helped the child was that she knew what she wanted. All her learning and learning had made her at last learn that . . . bewilderment had simply gone or at any rate was going fast" (263). What Maisie wants is Sir Claude and she knows it; but, the novel asks, what kind of knowledge is this? Is Maisie's desire for Sir Claude now a fully sexualized one in the social terms in which the novel has defined that desire, so that to acknowledge it would be to enter the circuits of exchange by insisting that he must leave Mrs. Beale? Or is Maisie still essentially unworldly in her choice, renouncing Sir Claude and the hopelessness of the economy he and Mrs. Beale inhabit—either because she has a better, less commodified version of desire that can accommodate loss or because of a lingering childish ignorance of sexuality itself? The novel's final uncertainty about a female subject immersed in the world and in power is freighted with all the cultural weight of ideals of girlish innocence. Should we doubt their force, a century's worth of commentary on the novel will remind us: critics from James's time to the present have attempted to confirm Maisie's ultimate innocence or bewail its loss, to praise *What Maisie Knew* for its vision of her triumph or revile James for pornography in terms just as charged as the novel's own (J. Hynes).

It is important then that *What Maisie Knew* makes it impossible to decide conclusively just what Maisie knows and thus what this ending might mean. The novel leaves us perpetually wondering, like Mrs. Wix at its close, about the dimensions of her knowledge. In doing so it renders Maisie as a powerful mystery, as it reveals the simultaneous pressures that combine to keep the question of the female subject's innocence constantly in play. The novel's structuring logic both requires the possible existence of an alternate, purer knowledge in Maisie and refuses to confirm its saving presence. The text is sustained affectively by the pathos and irony of Maisie's difference from the mire around her even as it refuses a stable subjective source for that difference. And the very ambiguity of Maisie's subjectivity and her final choice may reinforce the possibility—even the necessity—of a young girl's virtue. For what could keep innocence more thoroughly present to a reader than its constant vulnerability, the risk of its disappearance or violation, and the vision of the modern girl as a subject structurally liable to both? Maisie's potential for innocent knowledge is thus the more valued the more uncertain it is, and the text offers this evanescent but powerful purity as its relentless center, as Maisie becomes an enigma to be endlessly explored but never fully accounted for in her simultaneous openness to others and promise of thorough separation from them.

What Maisie Knew transforms the thematic problem of the nature of female knowledge into a central structural concern for the novel. In doing so it links James's developing narrative experiments of the 1890s—often read as preparation for his experimental late novels—with the shape of female subjectivity so compelling to the period's cultural debates (Isle). For it is the novel's experimental narrative strategy that keeps Maisie's subjectivity before us as an enigma reminiscent of George Egerton's mysterious heroines. The technique of the central consciousness that James intensified so dramatically in *Maisie* is vital to her contradictions; it both responds to and produces the terms in which her ambiguous innocence is constructed. By making Maisie's limited view of the world the focus of our attention, the narrative asks us to figure out what she knows by contrasting what she sees with the sense she makes of it; indeed the novel requires us do so in order to interpret each exchange. In this manner James's text structurally insists on the question of whether the influences around Maisie determine her knowledge—insists on the question of how much permeates her and how untouched she remains. This is the process that offers Maisie as an enigma that must be encountered and can never fully be solved, even as it makes the solution a matter of immense social and narrative weight.

However in the very process of rendering Maisie so ambiguously enigmatic, the text's narrative approach again reinforces her in vital ways as the redemptively unworldly character the novel refuses to confirm thematically. In contrast to the novel's adult characters, whose motives are more predictably accessible to the narrator and the reader—and, as we have seen, in many ways increasingly readable to Maisie as well—

Maisie, as the center of our interpretive efforts, appears ambiguous and undecidable, governed by some logic that is not (yet) fully assimilated into more legible adult terms of exchange. In this sense her uncertainty and the uncertainty she produces in the reader, the "wonder" James will praise in his preface, become sources of authority like the feminine mysteries Egerton insists on (7).[22] And like Grand's Evadne, Maisie builds, on the basis of her exposure to corruption and her risk of absorption in it, a potential form of alternate, purified knowledge.

But James's technique not only investigates Maisie's authority in the novel, it raises questions about the relation of the text's narrative authority to hers. *What Maisie Knew* both identifies narrative authority with the view of a young girl and distances narrative credibility from her. Here the structure of the central consciousness creating Maisie's innocence and our wonder about her must be read as a double view. For while the narrator offers us Maisie's vision of the world around her as our central perspective, we receive this vision from within the narrator's own broader and more worldly view, conveyed in distinctly adult language. In the terms of James's preface: "Maisie's terms accordingly play their part . . . but our own commentary constantly attends and amplifies. . . . Even though it is her interest that mainly makes matters interesting for us, we inevitably note this in figures that are not yet at her command and that are nevertheless required whenever those aspects about her and those parts of her experience that she understands darken off into others that she rather tormentedly misses" (6). Thus if the complications of Maisie's subjectivity generate a privileged wonder in the novel, it is striking how centrally the narrative method insists that we need an eye that sees beyond her in order to produce the Maisie we read. Such narrative doubleness is in fact responsible for constructing Maisie's innocence. Only through a divided view—registering what she sees beside what she doesn't—can the text make visible what Maisie misses and thus mark her difference from the world around her. James chooses the strategy of the central consciousness then, over a total restriction to Maisie's perspective—which he claims in the preface to have rejected as "strangl[ing]" his subject—because it has the power to build redeeming distance between world and character into the text (5).

As he develops this strategy in *Maisie*, James begins to suggest the problematic ways this female subject and worldly narrative voice might reinforce or erase each other—a problem we have seen both Egerton and Grand similarly confront. This narrative issue in turn illuminates the broader social question of how the value attributed to feminine subjectivity might shape or be appropriated by the voice of the professional—

here masculine—writer. Indeed we can begin to understand the necessary proximity, but not identity, between the narrator's view and Maisie's when we consider the troubling terms of the cultural authority a female subject like Maisie may possess. For by offering a symbol of purity and cultural power in the character of a materially disempowered little girl, *What Maisie Knew* stresses the gap between the cultural value Maisie can represent and the power she can wield. This overlap of authority and disempowerment, of unworldliness and discomfort in the world—intrinsic to definitions of female cultural power in the nineteenth century—complicates the ways in which Maisie can provide a model of literary authority for James himself.

It is this complicated relationship to which James returns in his 1908 preface to *Maisie*. The preface, as part of James's career-condensing reissue of his selected works in the New York Edition, attempts to construct an identity for himself as an author and to interrogate the terms of authorship. In that reinterpretation of the novel, he imagines the relationship between his power as an author and Maisie's as a girl transfiguring the debased world around her, both proposing his debt and resemblance to her and imagining a way that his worldly voice as a writer could produce and assume the properties of her more innocent one.[23]

In framing the relationship between them, James's preface, we should note, diminishes some of the novel's more problematic suggestions about Maisie's distance from the world, offering a reading that simplifies as it intensifies her innocence and its power. For while the preface at moments imagines her deriving a "profit" (2, 3) from her situation, the terms of that profit are opposed to the coarseness of the "ugly facts" in which she is submerged (2). The preface makes of Maisie a more emphatically purifying filter. Her immersion in an impure world is clearly transformative here; it allows her not only "successfully to resist . . . the strain of observation and the assault of experience" but to "remain fresh and to have even a freshness to communicate" (7). Here she generates a purity that is marvelous exactly because of the assault. Thus the "active, contributive, close-circling wonder . . . in which the child's identity is guarded and preserved . . . makes her case remarkable exactly by the weight of the tax on it" (10). By this wonder, Maisie turns the grim and unpromising world about her "to fineness, to richness" for herself; the effect of her "imagination" is to "steep" "the small creature . . . in security and ease" (2). The preface's reading underlines the power of Maisie's purity to reinvent a form of domesticity, rewriting the novel's emphasis on the violently false domesticity Maisie suffers—as she is pinched, slapped with hairbrushes, denied dinner, or pushed down stairs—by stressing the alternative bliss imaginatively provided by the subjective transmutation of the world.

More importantly, however, given the New York Edition's interest in authorial method and power, Maisie offers her transformations to James's material and to his narrative technique as well. For in the story James tells of the novel's germination, when he considers an original story of divorce and child custody that seems insufficiently appealing material for a novel, the idea of a child who might imaginatively transform this situation occurs to him not only as the discovery of a more complex premise but also as the all-important narrative method which the prefaces will cast as central to his artistic work. Maisie is to be the novel's "little wonder-working agent" (3) who redeems by her "freshness" (7), by "the rich little spectacle of objects embalmed in her wonder" (7), materials for fiction and "appearances [that would be] in themselves vulgar and empty enough. They become, as she deals with them, the stuff of poetry and tragedy and art" (7–8).

The preface further insists that the magic of the novel—its access to "the stuff of poetry and tragedy and art"—depends on Maisie's particular wonder-working subjectivity as a girl. His "light vessel of consciousness," James notes, couldn't be "a rude little boy" since "the sensibility of the female young is indubitably, for early youth, the greater, and my plan would call, on the part of my protagonist, for 'no end' of sensibility" (4). As a girl, Maisie enables James as the cultural figure who explicitly converts openness to closure, who must be open and at risk for that closure to work its wonders—the thoroughness of her "sensitiv[e]" permeation by sordid surroundings yielding artistic transcendence, or "connexions with the 'universal!'" (8). And while the vision of Maisie's feminine sensitivity in the preface gives James access to a universally authorizing art, her innocence also yields him the complexity and ambiguity so central to his notion of how the subject and the literary text may redeem vulgarity in the very process of registering it. In fact Maisie's creative innocence produces the complexities so fruitful for herself and for the novel, bringing about the plot complications of assorted remarriages and liaisons—"weaving about, with the best faith in the world, the close web of sophistication . . . becoming a centre and pretext for a fresh system of misbehavior" (3). Most importantly, she produces the ambiguities that add mystery and ethical resonance to a scene merely debased without her, illuminating "the close connexion of bliss and bale" (4), "making confusion worse confounded by drawing some stray fragrance of an ideal across the scent of selfishness" (4).

The preface to *What Maisie Knew* reveals James constructing his relationship to this feminized model of social implication and redemption and acknowledging the complexity of the process by which Maisie's cultural authority may be related to his own. For while, as a wonder-working agent, a transformative appreciator of the complexities around her, Maisie has often been taken as a double for James and the novel read as a "portrait of the artist as a young girl," the connection his preface suggests between them is far more charged and problematic than simple identification (Mitchell 168–69; Rowe, *Other Henry James* 134). Like the novel's narrative voice, James in the preface appears at once dependent on Maisie and necessarily more than her. This registers in the essay's alternating presentation of Maisie as a quasi-autonomous, sentimentally personified "little wonder-working agent" (3) to whom James is indebted and at whose power he marvels and an interwoven account of how he developed the story's complexities and its narrative technique in order to create her. When Maisie appears as a figure whose wonders are her own, James casts himself somewhat wryly as profiting from her abilities, rather like the adults in the novel, commenting that his "business" is to "extract from her current reaction whatever it may be worth . . . [to] recognise in it the highest exhibitional virtue" (7).[24]

But James figures his relation to Maisie quite differently in the alternate passages that depict the artistic process of envisioning the novel—a process in which art takes on and takes over the salvational function of the female subject. He imagines this process most fully in a long passage that moves from his first suspicion that the child he considers writing about might have a surprisingly complex response to "ugly facts," through an account of the exultant labor of authorial analysis. Such analysis ends, after the trials of "smothered rapture and . . . obscure victory," with his final discovery of the "red dramatic spark that glowed at the core of my vision," the "precious particle [that] was the *full* ironic truth—the most interesting item to be read into the child's situation" (2). The full truth James describes here is the discovery both of Maisie's salvation and his narrative method: "For the satisfaction of the mind, in other words, the small expanding consciousness would have to be saved, have to become presentable as a register of impressions . . . saved by the experience of certain advantages . . . rather than coarsened" (2–3). Through his story of his artistic process James thus proposes that Maisie will be "saved" and that she will "become presentable as a register of impressions" for the narrative; he suggests that it is the discovery of his narrative method that saves her by turning her into a register of impressions. And he suggests that the artistic need to satisfy the author and reader in fact generates Maisie's cultural power.

In this extended conflict between a power located in Maisie—specifically as a little girl—to possess salvational cultural authority and a power possessed or bestowed by artistic and narrative technique, we can see James struggling to regulate the relationship between what he might owe to the feminized cultural authority he invokes in his subject, and that which he may claim as an author. The conflict partakes of James's broader concern about his literary debt to popular sentimental novels, a concern that might well have grown acute in his rereading of a text that, after all, exploits sentimental conventions of female purity and suffering to great effect, a concern that also inflects his characteristic interest in the preface in moving from the vulgarity of scandalous facts to the complexity of his fiction (Habegger).

This conflict between Maisie's cultural power as a little girl and James's power as her author appears as an intractable tension over the intensity and social specificity of her presence in the preface. For the essay differs from other Jamesian prefaces to novels about young girls—most notably from the preface to *Portrait of a Lady*, where, as one critic has noted, James manages his anxious relationship to feminine cultural authority by reducing his protagonist Isabel from an active character to the most oblique of metaphorical figures, and by casting her as the possessor of an insignificant social problem that must be elaborated into meaning by his technique (Blair 68–69). In contrast, Maisie is by far the most vivid figure in her novel's preface, which reaches its moments of greatest intensity in describing her effects precisely as the culturally familiar figure of the imperiled girl. Rather than being transformed, as Isabel Archer is, into the abstraction of a "figure . . . [that has been] placed" or a "'piece' left in deposit" in the high drama of James's authorial process (qtd. in Blair 67), Maisie is powerfully present in the familiar figure of the piteous yet pure child, praised for her "freshness" as a "little wonder-working agent" (3), as "our small mortal" (4), and evoked in the poignant image of her wondering "to the end, to the death—the death of her childhood" (7). The intensity with which Maisie appears in all the concreteness of her social location in the essay may account for its balance of focus, in which James's own artistic transmutations tend to pale by contrast—and it is through this balance that the preface acknowledges most clearly the promise and difficulty Maisie poses as a culturally enabling figure with whom James must grapple. For we should note the familiarity of what happens to Maisie when she reappears as a sheer product of James's artistic technique and power: these are the moments when she becomes less specified than exemplary. As a result of James's victorious analysis, saved by his narrative method, she is rendered a neutral "register of impressions" (2). And at the essay's end, she becomes, in her appreciative openness to the world around her, a generalized figure for James in his struggle against a "muddled" (9) world, a figure for the reader to whom he appeals, indeed the exemplary instance of the ideal subject more generally. "For nobody to whom life at large is easily interesting do the finer, the shyer, the more anxious small vibrations, fine and shy and anxious with the passion that precedes knowledge, succeed in being negligible" (10).[25]

The tension that James's preface highlights and acknowledges between Maisie's specific incarnation as a female character from sentimental literature and her presence as the exemplary, abstracted figure of his artistic method is a familiar one from Pater. Pater too clarified a pattern by which abstraction promised to lift the burden of a specifying feminine culture and enable a more securely empowered approach to the dilemmas of subjectivity and the cultural claims of authorship. James's cultural work, however, is to take this double burden—of both the subject and its implication in feminine social contexts—and shift its distinctive weight to the function of a foregrounded narrative technique, which becomes the site through which writers may most thoroughly explore and most professionally manage it. Like Grand and Egerton, he offers narrative innovation as the means of shaping and exploiting a powerful female subject that is simultaneously permeable and enclosed. In doing so he assigns to his narrative experiments a cultural power based on the saving resistance of the female subjects they so often describe. When James anatomizes this encounter with female authority, he makes broadly visible—and visible as well in Egerton and Grand—the tension and the advantage involved in abstracting that authority from domestic space and plot to female subject, and from the female subject to one imagined as essentially general.

The thematic and narrative experiments of Egerton, Grand, and James form part of a transition from the structures and emphases of Victorian fiction to those of modernist impressionism, which will use narrative to investigate—and reshape—the subject's perceptions. As it analyzes subjects immersed in the world and formed by social conventions, this new fiction will nevertheless reveal a deep cultural desire to find within permeability itself a way of unlocking the subject from social context as a means of triumph or resistance. And through its distinguishing narrative strategies it will imagine a way for authors similarly to place their texts in the privileging space of the questioning and the experimental. James's work, like Egerton's and Grand's, anticipates the social terms through which modernism will claim both to register the world and to offer un-worldliness. His work, like theirs, points out how far this movement based itself in a female subject already formed by Victorian cultural and novelistic traditions. The presence of a feminine subject at the heart of these traditions will move modernist authors to abstract impressionism's subject and to see experimental narrative technique as a vital means to that abstraction. The shaping force of feminine subjectivity thus appears as impressionist writers construct both authority and social critique in the movement between embodied, gendered subjects and their shadowy universal doubles.

3 "One of Us": Conrad, Scouting, and Masculinity

The texts I have discussed thus far enter explicitly into cultural debates over feminine mobility and subjectivity, and over feminine space. To turn to stories about men and boys, to read debates about masculine agency at the turn of the century as I wish to do now, might seem to resituate modernism in a quite different, familiarly masculine terrain. Indeed critics writing about the period have often described the profusion of adventure tales at this historical moment precisely as a reaction against the feminine: a reaction against the domestic concerns of the Victorian novel and the new public roles women took on in the 1880s and 1890s. Read in this light, early twentieth-century accounts of masculine heroism and its dilemmas share little with those careful anatomies of domestic and emotional susceptibility sketched by Egerton or Grand, James or Pater. The imperial setting of many of these narratives in particular emphasizes this apparent reaction against the domestic and feminine; critics have argued that such settings establish a distinct Western male agency by a contrast with a feminized, colonial landscape and its exoticized inhabitants (Gilbert and Gubar, *Sexchanges* 3–46; McClintock 232–57; Showalter, *Sexual Anarchy* 76–104).

But narratives defining feminine subjectivity and those producing masculinity hardly divide this clearly. In this chapter I read key turn-of-the-century accounts of masculine agency and narration in order to con-

sider their connection to contemporary ideas about feminine subjectivity. I turn to such texts, that is, less to describe the oppositions imagined
there between feminine and masculine subjects—although I do address
such oppositions—than to chart the dependence and doubling between
them. And the resemblances are important ones. For accounts of masculine subjectivity envision cultural dilemmas similar to those framed
by the New Woman. In particular, when discussions of masculinity summon or criticize ideals of heroism, of imperial manliness, and of national health, they invoke familiar questions about subjectivity and interiority. Stories about men and boys ask about the subject's balance of
openness to the world and enclosure from it; they ask whether subjects
need to have interiors in order to be heroes, or to be plausible narrators.

I argue here that heroic masculine identity at the turn of the century is reimagined in terms resembling the identity of modern women—
as a form of impressionist subjectivity.[1] In doing so I draw upon, but also
refigure, current critical accounts of imperial masculinity and its relation
to modernism. For I want to suggest that in the early twentieth century,
the idealized masculine subject is imagined not as substantial and self-
enclosed—a contrast to ostensible feminine weakness—but as impressionable. His authority, his ability to anchor coherent community depends less on his stable difference from cultural others than on the power
to identify with and absorb them. Such identification doesn't unravel
masculine identity so much as confirm it, constructing a mobile subject
whose interiority comes from the constant, fluid incorporation of impressions, the absorption of other stances. And read through such a model,
modernism's very uncertainties, its experimental and high-cultural ambiguities, may be seen to participate in and exploit broad contemporary
visions of masculine character rather than refute them. Thus I trace the
dynamic of impressionist masculinity in texts of both high and popular
culture: in Joseph Conrad's *Lord Jim* and in the handbook of the period's
most popular youth movement, Baden-Powell's Boy Scouts. For just as
the popular concern with molding male character and strengthening British empire takes up familiar impressionist questions about the parameters of subjectivity, so too do Conrad's accounts of the impressionable
subject and his use of new narrative methods participate in broader cultural discussions of masculinity.

Conrad's famous use of impressionism to recast the premises of the
narrative subject formulates a peculiar, characteristically modernist account of the masculine subject: he produces a heroism grounded in *not
knowing*, in both embodying and facing an enigmatic world; he uses uncertainty not to undermine heroism but to refigure it.[2] With this redefi-

nition of heroism, Conrad would seem to claim the thematics of uncertainty solely as the privilege of masculinity. And indeed female characters in Conrad's work have most often been read as wholly "out of it" (Straus).[3] Confined to registers of the overly primitive, overly civilized, or sentimental, they are often read as though separate from the dilemmas of subjectivity, agency, and interpretation confronting male characters and central to Conradian modernism and its claims about literature's authority. My reading here uses the tensions of impressionist masculinity to argue a different point. For the central text I will examine, *Lord Jim*, shows how the model of heroic uncertainty draws impressionist narrative agency irrevocably toward its doubles: feminine uncertainty and feminine narrative authority. As the novel attempts to redefine masculine storytelling through enigma, that is, the text finds in the terms of its narrative authority a resemblance to feminine and colonized subject positions and narrative stories. The disavowed similarities as well as the differences between masculine and feminine subjectivity and narration provide the shifting ground on which Conrad's work will merge uncertainty and authority to imagine modernist fiction's cultural power.

Debates about masculinity intensified in England at the turn of the century, framed by many of the same discourses of degeneration that shaped the idea of the New Woman. Such debates were formed in large part by the social pressures and transformations of a country growing more urban and less industrial, and beginning to face global competition. The rapidly expanding lower middle class of urban clerical workers unsettled established accounts—economic and rhetorical—of British stability. Occupying a new position in the national economy, this class of workers fit uneasily into the language of imperial identity; they seemed unsuited to signify either an idealized British industrial power or the traditional image of English pastoral integrity. This cultural and economic shift raised doubts about masculine national character; it did so all the more when combined with the economic and political pressures of the New Imperialism—which pitted British imperial claims against those of other European powers competing for new colonial territory in Africa and Southeast Asia.[4] As historians and cultural critics have noted, the 1900–1902 Boer War crystallized these concerns with masculinity, class, and the stability of British Empire. Turn-of-the-century commentators wondered whether, like Rome, Britain was beginning to decline, and they traced the causes of that potential failure to the physical and moral deterioration of Englishmen. A range of military reports, government investigations, and popular pamphlets speculated that young English men and boys, reared in unhealthy cities and slums, were unfit for military service and had weakened the empire at its core (S. Hynes, *Edwardian Turn* 22–26; Rosenthal 88–90).[5] Like discussions of the dangerously degenerate subjectivities of modern women, such diagnoses of unfitness cast this broad political problem as a subjective one: as a problem of what they termed "boy nature." Accounts of national and imperial decline located the problem in the questionable agency or firmness of boys and young men. A boy's stability or vulnerability, his balance of autonomy and malleability, it was argued, might determine Britain's imperial fate.

The Boy Scout movement and its handbook, *Scouting for Boys*, have provided critics a central location for reading these discourses on "boy nature" and for exploring the connections between empire, gender, and subjectivity that shaped turn-of-the-century culture and fiction (S. Hynes, *Edwardian Turn* 15–53; Rosenthal 131–60; MacKenzie 228–51; Boscagli 82–91; Jeal; Warren, "Citizens of the Empire" and "Popular Manliness"). Scouting offers a promising field for cultural analysis because it was immensely popular and also because it was in many ways exemplary of how imperial ideals of masculinity were spread through British society. Begun in 1908 by the Boer War hero Lord Baden-Powell, Scouting was the most successful of a number of youth movements which started in the 1880s and gained momentum through the early twentieth century. All these movements were designed to train boys—to render boys, particularly lower-middle-class urban boys, reliable, manly British citizens. But the Boy Scouts are also of particular interest for my discussion of interiority here because while the movement's success derived in part from the prestige of its founder, this success was also often attributed to Scouting's focus on training boys as individuals. In contrast to drilling groups like the Boys' Brigades, which emphasized group behavior through team games and military drills, Scouting trained boys in individual activities and skills. The movement was concerned with forming individual character, and with imagining the mechanisms of subjectivity that shaped it. Scouting thus speculated on how masculine character might be constituted, and how it might serve or undermine the needs of empire.

Like the discourses on modern women and degeneration, the Boy Scout handbook links the question of national health and gendered identity to the parameters of subjectivity; it concerns itself with the proper regulation of the individual's boundaries. Like discussions of degeneration it traces social problems to a diseased relation between subject and world. In particular Scouting diagnoses national weakness as a result of subjects who are either too open to the world or too enclosed from it.

Problem boys are at once self-absorbed, overly enclosed, and yet also too permeable to external influences. On the one hand, they undermine national unity and purpose by their selfishness; untouched by communal ideals and notions of patriotism, they can't be connected to the greater good and thus rendered reliable. As Baden-Powell's *Scouting for Boys* puts it, such boys are bad citizens for "putting self in the first place and ignoring duty or the interests of others" (363), for failing to understand that "'Country first, self second' should be [the scout's] motto" (30).[6] But the Scouting handbook also—and familiarly—imagines unreliable boys as disastrously open to every passing influence: they are far too permeable. Baden-Powell sees bad cultural influences threatening to infiltrate boys' interiors much as he imagines disease does. Just as "microbes, or seeds of disease that are in the air," can enter and sicken boys, so too can cultural diseases enter them (20). To avoid contamination, Scouts must close themselves off, must metaphorically "breathe through the nose . . . [so] they don't suck [dangerous influences] into their insides" (27) as they might the seeds of disease.

Scouting for Boys figures this permeability, unsurprisingly, as a form of feminization. Urban culture, Baden-Powell notes, infects boys by reducing them to passive members of a crowd who are swayed by emotions from without and thus cannot develop as autonomous individuals. Criticizing football spectatorship, he envisions: "thousands of boys and young men, pale, narrow-chested, hunched up, miserable specimens, smoking endless cigarettes . . . all of them learning to be hysterical as they groan or cheer in panic unison with their neighbors. . . . One wonders whether this can be the same nation which had gained for itself the reputation of being a stolid, pipe-sucking manhood, unmoved by panic or excitement, and reliable in the tightest of places" (338).[7] Linking femininity with passive movement, and masculinity as the power to remain unmoved, Baden-Powell would seem to establish a clear division between the gendering of open and closed subjects.

But failed or effeminate boys and men are paradoxical—they possess selves both inappropriately moved and unmoved; thus the masculinity Scouting wishes to inculcate cannot be envisioned simply as the subject's enclosure. Scouting cannot turn to a wholly autonomous individual to ward off passivity. And indeed, Baden-Powell proposes a masculine subject who is imagined no less doubly than the problem he describes. The ideal Boy Scout Baden-Powell imagines is both open to and closed off from the world. We can see this balance at the center of Scouting's methods as well as its ideals. The movement tries to instill such masculine selfhood through a notion of character training that is implicitly paradoxical; it seeks actively to mold boys into firm, immovable citizens. The tension in this project is clear. Relying on the power of good influences in place of bad ones, Scouting requires that a boy be susceptible to training so that he may be shaped by the games, tests, and pantomimes by which Scouting teaches civic and imperial virtue. However the goal of such training is a masculine character defined by its stolidity, by its impermeability to outside influence. For only such an individual, Baden-Powell suggests in anecdote after anecdote, can act under pressure and support the empire.

This tension in the Boy Scout ideal does not undermine the movement's philosophy. Instead Scouting is founded on and enabled by it. The reiterated Scout Motto, for instance—"Be Prepared"—places this doubleness at the center of the Scouting ethos as well as its practices. In section after section, the Boy Scout handbook provides games, sample tests, and exemplary stories. By rehearsing them, by pretending to track animals and thieves or to rescue people from fires, young scouts will have character instilled in them by their susceptibility to the remolding force of habit. And the very solidity of a scout's character will in turn be defined by this preparedness: he possesses an inner "character" because he is so thoroughly trained, because he constantly practices.

Scouting bases its training on the details of everyday life—on a domestic world that it nonetheless promises to masculinize and transform. The handbook offers exercises through which mundane details like the state of a passerby's clothing or the sight of a dropped button might become opportunities for patriotic bravery and crime-solving. A prepared boy can be just as great a hero "in everyday life," Baden-Powell assures his readers, as "the soldier who rushes into the thick of the fight to rescue a comrade amid all the excitement and glamour of the battle" (25). In thus promising to find opportunities for masculinity in a debased world of "cities, mines, and factories" (25) or in the apparently familiar and uninteresting life of small towns, the Boy Scout handbook seeks to make the home country the same alluring terrain for male bravery that was promised at the British Empire's frontiers. Baden-Powell is explicit about this imperial reference for Scouting's more local versions of manliness. He introduces the book by suggesting that Boy Scouts model themselves on both the scouts who served him at the siege of Mafeking and on what he terms "peace scouts": "the frontiersmen of all parts of our Empire . . . [including] the British pioneers, explorers, and missionaries over Asia and all the wild parts of the world . . . real *men* in every sense of the word, and thoroughly up in scout craft" (12).

As the imperial reference for Scouting's methods might suggest,

Baden-Powell's Boy Scouts incorporate a racial component into their notion of character. Character appears in the face and the body, and as the illustrations in *Scouting for Boys* sometimes reveal, the distinction between different characters can be mapped in familiar eugenic and imperial fashion as a distinction between racialized types. Thus Baden-Powell presents an illustration of three heads as a test of a scout's ability to read "character": "The shape of the face gives a good guide to the man's character. . . . Perhaps you can tell the character of these gentlemen?" (77). Implicitly anchoring good character in the stereotypical Anglo-Saxon ideal at center—in opposition to the African caricature at the right and the arguably Semitic one at the left—the Scouting handbook uses a notion of racial identity to ground character within the body.[8] In this sense training and preparation merely confirm the interior character that racializing categories establish as innate. The idea of embodied racial contrast suggests that it is at colonial outposts that distinctions in character are most effectively interiorized and appear most legibly.

But Scouting's notion of identity as both trained in and imperviously innate also yields a rather different importance for the imperial context from which it draws its examples and political import. If scouts practice character-building exercises at the same time that their characters are confirmed as interior, the odd complementarity between these two stages of their training is underlined by the fact that many of their exercises involve imitation. In the context of empire, imitating a colonized other explicitly foregrounds the complex relationship between imitation and a scout's identity. Like the impressionist subject, the Boy Scout takes in or takes on the identity of another; however this provisional identification does not disrupt, but rather confirms, the scout's interior identity.

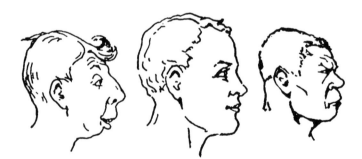

Figure 1. Interpreting character. Illustration from Baden-Powell, *Scouting for Boys* 77.

The handbook foregrounds this version of identification in its intro-
ductory retelling of Rudyard Kipling's "Kim," which Baden-Powell presents as "a good example of what a Boy Scout can do" for his country (14).
For Baden-Powell, Kim offers an admirable example of "strong-mindedness" (15). Tested by the British government intelligence department in
India, Kim refuses to be mesmerized by a government agent, resisting the
agent's attempt—in Baden-Powell's words—to "make Kim's thoughts obey
what was in his [the agent's] own mind. . . . But, do what he would to reach
the boy's brain, he failed," the handbook notes (15). Kim's imperviousness
to external influence—his ability to remain himself under the pressure
of forces that would alter and permeate him—is part of what suits him to
be a government spy, as well as a Boy Scout. But Kim is also suited to
British spying and scouting here because he has been raised with Indian
playmates and speaks their language, because he can identify with and
imitate them. His ability to adopt "native habits and customs" (15) underpins the narrative of pluck and resourcefulness Baden-Powell retells
to inspire his scouts, a story in which Kim repeatedly disguises himself
as Indian in order to uncover secrets for the British. In this account, Kim's
identification with Indians enables him to be a better British spy; his
imitations, that is, do not disrupt a resistant British strong-mindedness
so much as support, and indeed exemplify, strong character as its exercise.[9]

Baden-Powell's Boy Scout movement sketches a version of masculine character and agency I affiliate with impressionism because it imagines a subject for whom external impressions and identifications with
others do not necessarily threaten interiority, but rather may consolidate
it. Such a model envisions an imperial encounter in which British identity may be solidified even in those moments when it seems most dispersed. In placing Joseph Conrad's work within this cultural context and
in relation to this understanding of the subject, I wish to suggest how this
discussion of masculinity is continued in literary impressionism. For
Conrad's texts also reenvision masculine agency and identity in imperial settings. The famous narrating and interpreting subject of Conrad's
fiction—the character who absorbs conflicting accounts and confronts the
ultimately unknowable universe that results—links the structures of
imperial heroism to a subjectivity both endlessly impressionable and yet
repeatedly interiorized. In this connection between empire and the shape
of the subject, Conrad's novels and characters often emphasize the masculine nature of this position. But they also, more provocatively, reveal
the extent to which heroic impressionism is tied to those accounts of
femininity it seeks to distance. The emphasis of impressionist narration
on the subject's confrontation with ambiguity and on his ability to ab-

sorb all other identities thus sets out a masculine subject who not only must encounter feminine subjects and plots but must try to identify with and absorb them. The movement between such identifications and the reassertion of a masculinized, universalized realm of meaning emerges in these texts, shaping both Conrad's famed ambiguities and the cultural work they do.

The contemporary imperial imaginings I have been discussing through Baden-Powell offer Conrad a vision of masculine identity which powerfully joins the subject's dispersal and reconsolidation. The many connections this model forges are important for rereading Conrad's work; indeed they are especially provocative for the way in which they complicate the traditional oppositions on which readings of his work have often rested. In particular, the nuances of Baden-Powell's account may help us reread the relations among imperial ideology, epistemological doubt, and masculine narrative authority in Conrad. This conjunction of issues has long been held to offer central oppositions which make Conrad's texts internally contradictory and which thus enable profound critiques of imperial ideology and coherent subjectivity. While such critiques are surely present in Conrad's work, they do not inhere quite so simply in contradiction. Baden-Powell's "impressionist" masculinity may help suggest why, by showing the ways contradiction may be incorporated into notions of masculine authority, and subjective dispersal may be congruent with imperial heroism.

In reading Conrad's work, I turn to one of his best-known novels, *Lord Jim*, to reconsider this relation between imperial masculinity and impressionist concerns with subjectivity and doubt. The novel has long provided an opportunity for critical debates on empire and modernism. While it has not centered debates about modernism's implication in imperial racism in the way *Heart of Darkness* has, the text's elaborate impressionism and narrative embedding, its doubled and potentially opposed "heroes" (Jim and Marlow), and its apparent generic shift midway through have offered an opportunity for critics to theorize about the effects of the contradiction and ambiguity that form my topic here. Fredric Jameson's influential analysis of *Lord Jim* in *The Political Unconscious* (206–80), for instance, proposes that the novel's historical content is "contained" and displaced by its modernist narrative strategy, and thus sets the two registers of the text apart as the divided implications of proto-modernist style and substance. In an opposed reading that nonetheless repeats this division, Chris Bongie argues that the novel's narrative frame ironizes imperial exoticism as sheer fantasy in the text, recasting it as a self-consciously impossible dream (33–70).[10]

While these two compelling readings draw our attention to potential tensions between imperial and narrative structures, I would like to suggest that narrative uncertainty and imperial heroism bear a different relation to each other, and to the work of modernism. For Conrad's text renders impressionism a way to reconstruct imperial and narrative authority rather than unravel it. And as Baden-Powell's work suggests, the complexities of masculine subjectivity offer the key space through which the novel may bring these categories together. *Lord Jim* insistently addresses the possible relations among masculine agency, interiority, and imperial heroism. It does so at a variety of levels—in an inquiry into its title character, in its presentation of the central narrator Marlow, and through the general problem it poses for a reader attempting to sort through interpretations of both Jim and Marlow, weighing the various, and differently gendered, authorities of different commentators, including that of Jim's part-Malay beloved, Jewel.

The novel frames these issues most overtly as an investigation of Jim's character. At the start of the novel Jim leaps from an apparently sinking ship, the *Patna*, abandoning the eastern pilgrims aboard. In response to this shame he spends the remainder of the text trying to reclaim his honor, with uncertain success. The novel in turn devotes itself to unraveling the implications of his leap, his response, and the notions of heroism, agency, and community involved in interpreting them. Through its shifting redefinitions of his character and dilemma, it will consider how the story of Lord Jim may yield both narrative uncertainty and narrative heroism, ambiguity and a form of cultural agency for the novel.

In inquiring into the motives and implications of Jim's act, the novel seems torn between critique of a Baden-Powell-esque belief that training and social standards can form and rely upon individual interiority, and a wishful attempt to reassert that the subject and the standards of imperial heroism are indeed compatible. The novel opens as an explicit satire of the Boy Scout principle that training can reliably form the subject. For what Jim represents most pressingly in the first half of the novel is the failure of social codes at that precise point at which they might construct individual character and agency—an unreliability which prompts Marlow to meditate on the relation between subjectivity and the truth of such codes.

The novel establishes this interpretation of Jim well before Marlow begins his narration, relating in its first pages a scene that parodies the claim that ideals of manly heroism can be internalized and made to prompt action. On board a "'training ship for officers of the mercantile marine,'" which he joined "when after a course of light holiday literature his vocation for the sea . . . declared itself," Jim illustrates how training may fail (47). He "live[d] in his mind the sea-life of light literature. He saw himself saving people from sinking ships, cutting away masts in a hurricane. . . . He confronted savages on tropical shores, quelled mutinies on the high seas . . . always an example of devotion to duty, and as unflinching as a hero in a book" (47). But while in his fantasies he rehearses the behavior of heroes, aboard ship he fails to act. When a coaster crashes into a schooner, "He stood still. It seemed to him he was whirled round. He was jostled. 'Man the cutter!' Boys rushed past him" (48).

What Fredric Jameson terms Jim's *"bovarysme"* here underlines the failed link between training and the interiority it claims to solidify (211). Jim appears in this scene as merely a hollow container for social codes. Indeed the very presence within him of fantasies of "light literature" reveals the dissolution of masculine interiority: Jim cannot act because he has no truly internal self, nothing that properly belongs inside him; he is merely the site where light literature repeats itself. This permeability and repetition mark the imitative and thus unstable nature of his character, perhaps any character. Rehearsing the exploits of adventure heroes in his mind does not form his character but reveals its absence. Identification with such figures has unraveled rather than molded identity, and the unraveling has made masculine action, and thus imperial heroism, impossible.

The scene thus foreshadows what Jim's more grave and central failure aboard the *Patna* will suggest to Marlow in the novel: the dangerous permeability of the masculine subject—its destabilizing openness to impressions—and the threat such permeability poses to ideals of heroism or standards of conduct. Marlow's investigation of Jim focuses on both these registers at once; it is an inquiry both into the failure of communal codes and into the subject where they should take hold, whose hollowness possesses the secret of this collapse (Winner; Watt 312–19; London, *Appropriated Voice* 29–58). The "horror" Jim represents here is thus the danger that training and character are at odds, a risk which threatens the possibility of stable interiority or identity more generally. In representing such a risk, Jim threatens not only Marlow's notion of a Western seagoing community but his supporting belief that character may be solidified in and read from the faces of European sailors. As Marlow puts it, "'I liked his appearance; I knew his appearance; he came from the right place; he was one of us'" (74). "'I tell you I ought to know the right kind of looks. I would have trusted the deck to that youngster on the strength of a single glance, and gone to sleep with both eyes—and, by Jove! it wouldn't have been safe. There are depths of horror in that thought'" (76). Marlow's desire "'for the impossible—for the laying of what is the most obstinate ghost of man's creation . . . the doubt of the sovereign power enthroned in a fixed standard of conduct'" drives his fascination with whether Jim possesses a hidden interior that might embody and testify to that standard (80).

But *Lord Jim* does not maintain this initial critique of interiority. Indeed the trajectory of the novel works to reestablish an interiority for its title character, despite its assertions that no such stable interior self can exist. In part the very insistence of Marlow's own inquiry helps grant Jim depth by endowing him with a psychology that is the field of investigation. But this psychological depth, at least initially, presents a paradox in the novel. For while Marlow begins his search with the hope that he will find something in Jim that might differentiate him from others—some unique interior—for the most part Jim appears both impossible to individuate, and a refutation of the possibility that there could be anything inside the masculine subject. He comes to stand, that is, for the subjective absence at the center of the community he resembles. *Lord Jim* sustains this skepticism about reliable agency, interiority, and community that Jim represents throughout the first half of the text, and it never entirely parts with it (Wollaeger 78–119). But the novel is nevertheless wishfully drawn to try to reconstitute this ideal of heroism—despite its impossibility—in its second half, in which Jim acts simply, vigorously, and heroically to establish a just imperial community in Patusan, before ultimately failing. The text reasserts the possibility of these ideals by a conceptual shift which recalls Baden-Powell's construction of Boy Scout character: it does so by reconstituting an interiority for Jim that will reanchor—in fact single-handedly re-create—heroic agency.

Midway through the text, the novel reinvents the relationship between Jim and the light literature of the sea: it regrounds this ethos within Jim. In doing so, it individuates him and it gives him an interior. The thematic pivot for this transformation is Jim's obsession with his failure aboard the *Patna*. This insistent concern first appears as a kind of stupidity about the meaning of his failure. Marlow reports somewhat satirically: "'I could see in his glance darted into the night all his inner being carried on, projected headlong into the fanciful realm of recklessly heroic aspirations. He had no leisure to regret what he had lost, he was so wholly concerned for what he had failed to obtain. . . . I whisked him back by saying, "If you had stuck to the ship, you mean!"'" (104–5). But *Lord Jim* gradually recasts this insistence as unique, individual virtue, as an attachment to ideals which distinguishes Jim from others and leads him to a truly heroic fate. Jim, Marlow notes later on, "'had that faculty of beholding at a hint the face of his desire and the shape of his dream, without which the earth would know no lover and no adventurer'" (171). If in the course of the novel Jim comes to appear the only one who still believes in honor and heroism, *Lord Jim* in some sense reimagines these values as properly his, and thus endows him with a form of stable character.

The novel's shifting commentary about Jim continues to reinterpret him in this manner. In particular the scene in which Stein diagnoses Jim as a """"romantic"""" effectively individuates and interiorizes him (199). In what is perhaps the most commented-on moment in the novel, Stein takes Jim's story as an opportunity to speculate on the question of """"how to be"""" (199):[11]

> "'[Man] wants to be a saint, and he wants to be a devil—and every time he shuts his eyes he sees himself as a very fine fellow—so fine as he can never be. . . . In a dream. . . .
>
> [. . .] And because you not always can keep your eyes shut there comes the real trouble [. . .] it is not good for you to find you cannot make your dream come true [. . .] Yes! Very funny this terrible thing is. A man that is born falls into a dream like a man who falls into the sea. If he tries to climb out into the air as inexperienced people endeavour to do, he drowns— *nicht wahr?* . . . No! I tell you! The way is to the destructive element submit yourself, and with the exertions of your hands and feet in the water make the deep, deep sea keep you up. [. . .] To follow the dream, and again to follow the dream—and so—*ewig—usque ad finem.* . . . '" (199–201; unbracketed ellipses in original)

The passage displays a double movement. In it heroic ideals and standards in the guise of dreams move from being opposed to the truth (man "sees himself as a very fine fellow—so fine as he can never be. . . . In a dream") to being the only possible path to truth; the answer to the question of "how to be" is "to follow the dream." But this revaluation of ideas of conduct and heroism from falsehood to a difficult and ennobling truth accompanies a repositioning of this ideology to the interior of character. Here it is worth noting the shift that occurs when Stein recasts Marlow's "standard of conduct" as a "dream." For while the dream here, like that standard, appears as something outside us that we swim in, the word "dream" suggests a source in an individual mind. Jim's refusal to let go of a failed external code—a code whose externality marked its own, and his, failure—is thus reimagined by Stein, and subsequently by the novel, as Jim's determination to follow his own dream, a determination which revitalizes the heroic ideology it interiorizes.

Thus the Patusan section, which follows upon this scene, presents Jim as the heroic source of honor, action, and community. He unhesitatingly leaps from imprisonment and frees the village from a tyrant; he finds a pure, childlike, suffering girl to protect and support; he brings peace, justice, and stability to Patusan's quarreling native inhabitants. His personal devotion to honor gives him heroic agency, and it allows him to embody a fantasy of benevolent Western rule. Such a rule is made possible in *Lord Jim* by the use of an exoticized East as its setting; the residents of Patusan incarnate Jim's literary fantasies ("""It's like something you read of in books" he threw in appreciatively'" [215]). And unlike the oppressive illegibility Jim represented in the novel's first half—where character could neither be fixed nor read from faces—in the world of Patusan, motives and interiors are wholly transparent; villains may be distinguished from faithful servants at a glance.

The fantasy world of Patusan may not last in *Lord Jim*, but the heroic interiorization it yields persists. When the problem of secret doubt returns at novel's end, it does so in the individuated figure of Gentleman Brown.[12] Brown arrives to ruin Patusan by playing cynically on Jim's sense of secret kinship with those who have failed Western standards; the novel here returns to the question of whether Jim and heroism are doomed to fail. But this familiar theme reemerges as a contrast between different individual interiors as much as a reflection on a common problem of human identity. While Brown alludes to his secret resemblance to Jim, we read this "resemblance" at novel's end quite differently than we once read Marlow's earlier speculations on Jim's representative status. We must now register instead a difference between characters only possible in a context in which honor and conduct might be valid standards, potentially embodied in heroic interiors. And if Jim identifies with Brown, that identification testifies less to the waywardness or permeability of his character than it does to its solidity. Indeed Jim's very awareness that he resembles Brown marks him as particularly honorable and responsible.

The narrative of individual heroism Jim enacts takes place in a world primarily occupied by masculine subjects. When femininity emerges in the symbolic landscape of Patusan, a space marked through sexual and maternal imagery (DeKoven 162–75; Mongia, "'Ghosts'" and "Empire"), its presence serves less to feminize Jim than to provide him with the classic imperial contrast that allows him to take up the white man's burden of paternal leadership. But a version of feminine subjectivity does appear in the text, and it may help us frame a question about the relation of the masculine heroism I have been discussing to the categories of feminine subjectivity and narration.[13]

The relation of masculinity to feminine subjectivity and narration is cast in terms that will be familiar from Henry James; it turns out to be one of doubling and uneasy appropriation. Jim's attachment to his sweetheart Jewel is cast in the language of domesticating resemblance. As Marlow describes them, when Jim speaks her name it produces "'a marital, homelike, peaceful effect'" (248). Despite their quite differently gendered behavior—Jim rescuing Jewel, their contemplative strolls with "'his arm about her waist, her head on his shoulder'" (252)—their relationship is described in terms of a mutual absorption that verges on identification. They appear nearly as twins, glimpsed as "'two white forms very close'" in the darkness (252). And their romance becomes picturesque to Marlow in the way it blurs the lines between them. Jewel, for instance, "'had learned a good bit of English from him, and she spoke it most amusingly, with his own clipping, boyish intonation. . . . She lived so completely in his contemplation that she had acquired something of his outward aspect, something that recalled him in her movements, in the way she stretched her arm, turned her head, directed her glances'" (251). The language of Jewel's "boyish[ness]" works less to masculinize her than to render them both identically childlike.

But Jim's absorption into Jewel's world will be more complicated for the text. For Marlow notes that there is visible in the background of Jewel's story "'the melancholy figure of a woman, the shadow of a cruel wisdom buried in a lonely grave, looking on wistfully, helplessly, with sealed lips'" (246). This image of Jewel's mother, with her tragic fate, haunts Jewel and will haunt her understanding of Jim's story. And as Marlow makes clear, when Jim enters into his romance with Jewel, he too becomes absorbed in this memory and this story. "'When I tell you besides that Jim with his own hands had worked at the rustic fence [around her grave], you will perceive directly the difference, the individual side of the story. There is in his espousal of memory and affection belonging to another human being something characteristic of his seriousness'" (246–47). Jim's seriousness and his honor wed him not just to Jewel but to her memories and affections, making them his own. And as Marlow's framing suggests, the effect of this blurred identity is not just to feminize Jim by rendering him like Jewel but to feminize him by inscribing him in Jewel's story—a story about a woman and told by women. The question of the subject's masculinity or femininity in *Lord Jim* relies then on the process of storytelling, and on the process of interpreting a story. It rests in the power to define what Jim's story means. And it is through competing interpretations of Jim, and the question of what it means to interpret him, that the text will elaborate its most compelling

accounts of new masculine subjectivities, and find itself most problematically entwined with feminine ones.

In examining *Lord Jim*'s construction of masculine subjectivity, we
must turn to its narrator Marlow. For while the novel may use this character to call heroic masculinity provisionally into question, the work of
narration in the text as a whole has quite a different effect. *Lord Jim* is
as much concerned with Marlow as it is with its more visible thematic
center, Jim. Marlow's doubts, his complex narration, establish the pac-
ing of the first half of the novel as well as its philosophical inclinations.
And it is these doubts, of course, which have dismantled the possibility
of simple idealistic heroism in Jim. Marlow's investigation of whether a
true Western seagoing community is possible or valuable—his famously ambivalent invocations of the idea that Jim might be "one of us,"
whoever "we" are—is the text's central method for interrogating heroic
masculine subjectivity, and seems to contrast sharply with the latter
portion of the novel, with its more straightforward tale of community
and agency in Patusan. But while both narrator and narrative method in
the novel make the fantasy of unselfconscious heroic integrity impossible, I would argue that they do not oppose ideas of heroic interiority so
much as revise them into the terms of a modernist narrative authority.[14]
The novel, that is, replaces the ideal of Jim's heroism with Marlow's
heroic authority. Such authority works in the text primarily by refiguring the implications of knowledge and epistemological doubt. Uncertainty—the refusal of straightforwardly legible meaning—comes to signal, not
a lack of power or knowledge, but rather a more adequate version of either. This model of narrative authority thus refigures the narrator as the
exemplary masculine figure who can identify with others and yet remain
himself, who gains authority by remaining open to all impressions.

Lord Jim's narrative progression and Marlow as narrator are central
mediators of how such doubt works. The novel is structured as an inquiry
into the fact of Jim's failure aboard the *Patna*; after Marlow begins narrating in chapter 5, it proceeds largely as his investigation. The novel
suggests that such an inquiry will improve upon Jim's official trial; by
its narrative method and Marlow's commentary it suggests that the re-
calcitrance of this more complex investigation—the diffuseness and
ambiguity of knowledge generated through it—is central to improving
upon the trial's verdict, based as that is on a concern with mere "facts"
(63). The difficulty of knowledge in this investigation is directly linked
to the text's famous narrative impressionism—to the way that the text

offers opaque events which only gradually yield the range of possible meanings behind their appearances, and behind our first impressions (Watt 269–304). At the broadest level, the novel proceeds from the fact of Jim's misdeed through Marlow's series of interviews with men who might shed light on the episode. Each interview promises to further unfold the full meaning of Jim and his action; each reveals the failings of any one view and the need to absorb, question, and thus improve upon the limited "knowledge" each figure trusts. The upright Brierly's notion of honor, for instance, is exposed as inadequate when he reveals that he is committed merely to the seafaring community's good """"name"""" (93); the courageous French Lieutenant may acknowledge the complex link between fear and bravery but nevertheless disdainfully fails to offer an opinion on """"what life may be worth when . . . the honour is gone"""" (152). Even Stein's reading of Jim as romantic must be weighed against his aging diminution from hero to collector and cataloguer of butterflies, beetles, or people.

The effect of this multiplication of stories and interpretive sources, as critics have often noted, is to assert the difficulty and deferral of full knowledge.[15] However, in doing so, the novel does not put the possibility of knowledge in question so much as it redefines what knowledge looks like and how it is attained. Locating knowledge beneath the surface of events and within various characters' psychological depths, Conrad's novel recasts it as a form of mystery and ambiguity, and redefines its acquisition as the process of collecting, collating, and questioning different views. The novel thus uses the multiplication of perspectives and its narrator's correspondingly multiple identifications and interrogations to propose a newer, fuller version of knowledge, one that relies upon doubt and ambiguity as its necessary components—precisely the components that will distinguish Marlow's ultimate assessment of Jim, or our own, from the more limited views to which he is exposed. As Allon White has noted, F. R. Leavis's famous comment on Conrad is quite suggestive about this ambiguity (109). Conrad "is intent," Leavis notes, "on making a virtue of out of not knowing what he means" (207). In *Lord Jim* not knowing, if done correctly, itself provides an authoritative position, provides, in fact, a form of knowledge.[16]

Within the novel's narrative progression, Marlow's commentary and his presence as a centering character help convert uncertainty into a new form of masculine heroism. The figure of Marlow begins to collect the multiplication of stories in *Lord Jim* into a potential narrative of his character's internal development, reanchoring the problem of doubt as the stance of an individuated figure whose inability to know with certainty becomes a unique, hard-won interpretive privilege—access to what the novel constructs as a potentially more complex truth, a more difficult truth to face. Marlow is famously explicit about the difficulty of knowledge: offering the repeated *leitmotifs* of Jim glimpsed through a fog, or as a dark shadow against the light (99, 173, passim), and asserting the impossibility of interpreting Jim's meaning. "'I could never make up my mind [he says] about . . . whether his line of conduct amounted to shirking his ghost or to facing him out. . . . as with the complexion of all our actions, the shade of difference was so delicate that it was impossible to say'" (187). This last passage indicates the shift by which the failure to know may become instead a privileged recognition of a truth about the unknowable. Marlow's inability to "make up [his] mind" here properly acknowledges the delicacy of ethical differences that makes them impossible to distinguish. His search for that "'absolute Truth . . . which floats elusive, obscure, half submerged, in the silent still waters of mystery'" (202) thus aligns truth with the obscurity of psychic and philosophical depths. As a result the problem of Jim becomes the problem of the unknowable as a positive essence, constructing what Jameson has described as the text's "existential metaphysic" (259). Thus, meeting with Jim alone, Marlow frames Jim's prolonged argument with himself as "'a subtle and momentous quarrel as to the true essence of life'"; in witnessing it, Marlow claims that he is being "'made to comprehend the Inconceivable'" (111).

Marlow anchors this new interpretive authority—the power to recognize and confront the "Inconceivable"—explicitly in a version of masculinity defined through the maritime community. For it is on the sea that men, in this account, are brought face to face with impenetrable uncertainty.[17] Marlow proposes, for instance, that Jim's contact aboard the lifeboat with a sea and sky that "'merged into one indefinite immensity'" (127) is exemplary. "'There is something peculiar in a small boat upon the wide sea. . . . It is as if the souls of men floating on an abyss and in touch with immensity had been set free for any excess of heroism, absurdity, or abomination. . . . Trust a boat on the high seas to bring out the Irrational that lurks at the bottom of every thought, sentiment, sensation, emotion'" (132).

And as a result he redefines legitimate masculinity itself through the seaman's existential doubt. The novel juxtaposes this professional maritime access to the abyss against the false certainties available to other forms of masculine authority in England. Jim's father is rendered untrustworthy, for instance, when he claims that "'virtue is one all over the world,'" for immediately afterward he informs "'his "Dear James" that he "who once gives way to temptation, in the very instant hazards his total depravity and everlasting ruin. Therefore resolve fixedly never, through any possible motives, to do anything which you believe to be wrong"'" (295). This is framed as domesticated parsonage philosophy, embodied by the "'placid, colourless forms of men and women peopling that quiet corner of the world as free of danger or strife as a tomb, and breathing equably the air of undisturbed rectitude'" (295). And its failure seems most acutely marked when it reduces to a conventional platitude the very "unknowable" that the novel is so concerned to evoke. For as the unnamed narrator notes at the start, "Jim's father possessed such certain knowledge of the Unknowable as made for the righteousness of people in cottages without disturbing the ease of mind of those whom an unerring Providence enables to live in mansions" (46–47).

In contrast, the relationship between Marlow and Jim embodies the privileged form of unknowing available to men at sea. Marlow, indeed the text in general, is fascinated by Jim—driven by an erotically charged desire to look at him, to know his secrets, to cast him as a figure in whom infinite psychological and philosophical mysteries may be revealed.[18] For if the sight of Jim first prompts Marlow to imagine versions of community that are untrustworthy, later glimpses lead him toward a form of intimacy which harbors a more compelling, enigmatic truth. Thus when Marlow first interviews Jim he sees "'these blue, boyish eyes looking straight into mine, this young face, these capable shoulders, the open bronzed forehead with a white line under the roots of clustering fair hair, this appearance appealing at sight to all my sympathies: this frank aspect, the artless smile, the youthful seriousness'" (100). If the description leads him for the moment to the impulsive view that "'He was of the right sort; he was one of us'" (100), further looking at Jim—further "'bizarre and exciting glimpses [of Jim] through the fog'"—yields Marlow a more complex understanding of their relationship, of the notion of "one of us" and what it might imply (127). "'I cannot say I had ever seen him distinctly [Marlow comments] . . . but it seemed to me that the less I understood the more I was bound to him in the name of that doubt which is the inseparable part of our knowledge. I did not know so much more about myself'" (206).

Here looking at Jim produces the fuller, more adequate knowledge that arises from a tie between men, a knowledge inseparable from doubt. It produces, that is, the view of ambiguity that privileges Marlow's narration. But Marlow's final suggestion that he "did not know so much more about [him]self" also suggests that this new knowledge which encompasses doubt is linked to the issues of identification, identity, and masculine agency so central in the novel and in the period. It may seem self-evident that Jim appeals to Marlow because Marlow identifies with Jim, sees in Jim a model of himself—but the nature of that identification, the question of how it frames the problem of subjectivity in the text, needs to be explored further. For the intimacy between the two seems to yield notions of the subject familiarly opposed to one another. Marlow comments at one point that "'It is when we try to grapple with another man's intimate need that we perceive how incomprehensible, wavering, and misty are the beings that share with us the sight of the stars and the warmth of the sun. It is as if loneliness were a hard and absolute condition of existence'" (175). In the spirit of this passage, the intimacy between the two men in *Lord Jim* is ready to dissolve at any moment into the solitude of one. While we may read this passage as describing the inevitable failure of intimacy, we may importantly also read it for an opposed suggestion. Intimacy itself here—cast as the resemblance or identification between two men—seems the precondition for the male subject's realizing his own solitude. Put slightly differently, Marlow's identification with another man here allows him to register his own unyielding, impermeable interiority.

This simultaneous solitude and intimacy—confirming one's isolated interiority by seeing oneself in another—is tied to the seagoing community for Marlow. Indeed the process of maritime training is the method that produces this relation. Marlow rhapsodizes about the results of this training at length, although he doesn't detail its mechanics as precisely as Baden-Powell does:

> "Haven't I turned out youngsters enough in my time, for the service of the Red Rag, to the craft of the sea, to the craft whose whole secret could be expressed in one short sentence, and yet must be driven afresh every day into young heads till it becomes the component part of every waking thought—till it is present in every dream of their young sleep! The sea has been good to me, but when I remember all these boys that passed through my hands, some grown up now and some drowned by this time, but all good stuff for the sea, I don't think I have done badly by it either. Were I to go home to-morrow, I bet that before two days passed over my head some sunburnt young chief mate would overtake me at some dock gateway or other, and a fresh deep voice speaking above my hat would ask: 'Don't you remember me sir? Why! little So-and-so. Such and such a ship. It was my first voyage.' And I would remember a bewildered little shaver, no higher than the back of this chair." (75)

Marlow sums himself up here as a man who has trained a series of interchangeable sailors; indeed what he has trained them in is the craft that will make them both like each other and like him. For he defines the "craft of the sea" virtually as the production of these identical subjects, creating a community in which all subjects resemble each other, and double him—a world in which he can identify with all subjects in order to confirm his own solitary identity. The seaman's community is thus based on likeness—not only through the implied if unstated similarity among Westerners, but through the structural likeness trained into Western sailors.

In identifying with other sailors then, Marlow simultaneously contemplates his own interior; in opening himself to them, he may equally remain enclosed and alone. This paradigm—a familiar one from Baden-Powell's Boy Scouts, both malleable and impervious—shapes what Jim comes to represent in the novel. For if Jim disrupts the seaman's ideal of honor, he enables the relation of identification underpinning it. Reading Jim, Marlow may read himself, indeed he may read any seaman. It is this logic of masculine communal identity that allows Marlow to equate his investigation of Jim's interior—or its absence—with an inquiry into the hearts of all. The seaman's logic allows him to universalize Jim, to make Jim an exemplary figure. Marlow notes his own tendency to universalize when he comments on his "'democratic quality of vision'": "'My weakness consists in not having a discriminating eye for the incidental—for the externals. . . . I have met so many men . . . and in each case all I could see was the human being'" (112). In short, the specialized training of masculine subjects allows Marlow to generalize them. Masculine subjectivity's reconciliation of openness and closure thus shapes the abstracted and universalizing terms which characterize the novel's existential thematics—its images of an everyman facing a hostile universe. This model of the trained masculine subject also yields the shifting reference of the phrase "one of us," as it allows the text to slide from the specificity of any "one" to the apparent neutrality of the universal subject, from a limited community characterized or criticized, to claims for mankind as a whole.

We should note too how powerfully this intersection of the masculine subject's simultaneous identification with others and his persistent, nearly solipsistic enclosure informs Conrad's own aesthetic theory. In fact his account of impressionism's aesthetic power and authority rests upon just such a doubled notion of the subject. If we turn for a moment to his famous preface to "The Nigger of the Narcissus," written a few years before *Lord Jim*, we can find a comparable formulation in his explanation of how the writer should pursue his task: which is "by the power of the written word, to make you hear, to make you feel—it is, before all to make you *see*" (xiv). Conrad's definitions of literary authority sustain themselves on a related paradox.

On the one hand, the artist can create a work that "attempt[s] to find . . . what is enduring and essential . . . the very truth of [this universe's] existence" only by appealing to an interior self (xi). The artist, unlike the thinker or the scientist, "descends within himself" to find truth; this is why "his appeal is less loud, more profound, less distinct, more stirring"; although "sooner forgotten, yet its effect endures forever" (xii). The artist reaches eternal truths by appealing to a similar interiority in the reader: he "appeals to that part of our being which is not dependent on wisdom; to that in us which is a gift and not an acquisition—and therefore more permanently enduring" (xii). Reaching "our capacity for delight and wonder . . . our sense of pity and beauty, and pain; the latent feeling of fellowship . . . [the] conviction of solidarity" (xii), the artist reaches qualities we possess internally, apart from the external pressures of the world, which shape our "prejudices," our "fears," and our "credulity" (xi).

But the preface defines art as something that by definition reaches out, that touches and enters the reader's interior, and does so forcefully (Fogel 41). The imperatives of the preface—that art "should make you hear . . . make you feel . . . make you *see*"—emphasize the disjunction between the violent impositions of a text and the readerly, writerly autonomy that is the mark of the literary authority it invokes. As Michael North has recently pointed out, the preface manages this contradiction with a notion of community that resembles the Western mariner's world I have discussed in *Lord Jim* (37–43). Conrad imagines a community of readers and writers as essentially similar; when he speaks of "*Our* capacity for delight and wonder" he delimits the interiors of artist and reader as identical. In this community, as in the intimate relation between Marlow and Jim, resemblance makes it possible to reconcile persuasion, identification, and the force of impression with a subject who remains securely within his own borders. The logic of the text, that is, construes the reader quite unironically as "one of us."

I have sketched thus far what appears to be a nearly seamless web of masculine subjectivity and community, in which all white men may reflect and stand for each other, aspiring to a version of universality by seeing themselves wherever they look. However Conrad's work interrupts this continuous masculine self-reflection by suggesting an eerie set of resemblances between terms that should not, in this account, be alike—by framing resemblances between colonized women and colonizing men. The novel, that is, will also invite us to question the securely masculine character of the intimate communities Marlow sets out, as well as their universal claims and their assumptions of similarity. Indeed the problem of reading *Lord Jim* as a whole might be taken as the problem of how to evaluate Marlow's narration and its authority, which as we have seen hinges upon the unique privilege of his uncertainty and his knowledge. How far, that is, does Conrad's text also depend on distinguishing between masculine and feminine subjects, and between their respective stories? For the novel suggests that some of Marlow's distinctions are less than fully certain. We can bring this instability into focus by revisiting Marlow's opposition between his own knowledge and the feminized platitudes about the "Unknowable" relayed by Jim's father (46). Indeed, to an unsympathetic reader Marlow's own repeated invocations of the unknowable may well have a similarly platitudinous quality. But we need not read Marlow's claims wholly skeptically to note the resemblance that underpins his opposition. Both the sea and the parsonage claim a knowledge of the unknown; both claim to define character, even virtue, in universalizing terms, as "'one all over the world'" (295).[19]

This proximity between masculine, heroic versions of unknowing and feminine ones is central to questions the novel raises about interpreting Jim's story. How we assess these different sorts of knowledge determines how fully we privilege Marlow's account of Jim in the novel, and how fully we read the text as endorsing those strategies of interiorization and universalization which seem to define the masculine subject there. Marlow's account and his interpretive dominance rely upon the claim that there are vast differences between the world men inhabit and the one occupied by women. Indeed the passage in which he suggests this may be read as one of the clearest examples of Conrad's romanticizing disdain for women: it seems to substantiate the argument that women are "out of it" in *Lord Jim,* and to reinforce Conrad's comment in his author's note that they will not understand the subject of the book, because it is "rather foreign to women's normal sensibilities" (44). Marlow comments that

> "Our common fate fastens upon the women with a peculiar cruelty. . . . One would think that, appointed to rule on earth, it seeks to revenge itself upon the beings that come nearest to rising above the trammels of earthly caution; for it is only women who manage to put at times into their love an element just palpable enough to give one a fright—an extraterrestrial touch. I ask myself with wonder—how the world can look to them— whether it has the shape and substance *we* know, the air *we* breathe! Sometimes I fancy it must be a region of unreasonable sublimities seething with the excitement of their adventurous souls, lighted by the glory of all possible risks and renunciations." (247)

The passage, like Marlow's criticism of Jim's father, is double-edged. In part it relegates women to an exotic, ethereal world far from the one

Marlow says "we" inhabit. The novel's presentation of female characters and their stories in many ways supports this division. Jewel, for instance, is repeatedly described with a miniaturizing language that removes her to a register separate from the masculine world of the sea and its crises. Her incomprehension of Jim's past and motives, and the text's introduction of a new, sentimental narrative about romantic suffering and the shared fate of mother and daughter to account for her, situates women in a different genre and language, removed from the problems and stories framing Marlow and Jim. But the passage also suggests that if women stand apart from men, they double them too. Though they appear to breathe a different air, they nonetheless represent humanity as a whole much as Jim does: women suffer more, but they suffer "our common fate." Their love, like Marlow's affection for Jim, blends fear and attachment. And the "'unreasonable sublimities'" they see suggest that they too apprehend a fundamental abyss of obscurity in the world which until now has been cast solely as the reward of Marlow's intimate knowledge of another man and of the sea.

The terms in which women are simultaneously held apart from men and brought into doubling proximity to them are thus central ones for the text: women both know and cannot know Western men. They stand apart from a man's world because they cannot comprehend it, and yet their incomprehension—the sentimental or gothic narrative that leaves them deserted by the white men they never fully understand—also brings them face to face with a sublime mystery the text has linked with forms of universality, heroism, and ultimately, masculine narrating authority (Mongia, "'Ghosts'"). We can see this in the way that Jewel comes to double Jim, as well as Marlow himself. I have already noted that the novel's romance renders her Jim's childlike twin. But Jewel resembles Jim in more resonant ways; she provokes a crisis of certainty in Marlow which duplicates Jim's effect. When Marlow meets Jewel and tries to dispel her suspicion that Jim will desert Patusan, he encounters a figure of depth and mystery. Jewel here echoes the images of depth and darkness, of enigma and spreading uncertainty that Jim first set in motion for Marlow. Watching "'the big sombre orbits of her eyes, where there seemed to be a faint stir . . . [Marlow felt that he was looking into] the bottom of an immensely deep well. . . . She was more inscrutable in her childish ignorance than the Sphinx. . . . it was impossible to distinguish her features, the darkness of the eyes was unfathomable'" (269–70). This mystery reproduces the sublime disorientation of the sea and brings to Marlow the familiar and profound horror of a life suddenly deprived of its shaping notions: "'There came upon me, as though I had felt myself losing my footing in the midst of water, a sudden dread, the dread of the unknown depths'" (273). Her imperturbable monotone "'troubled my mind profoundly with the passive, irremediable horror of the scene. It had the power to drive me out of my conception of existence. . . . For a moment I had a view of a world that seemed to wear a vast and dismal aspect of disorder'" (274).

The resemblance between Jewel and Jim raises the question of just how straightforwardly Conrad's novel endorses the link between universal depths of consciousness and a Western masculine community that Marlow proposes; it demands that a reader question Marlow's presentation of Jim as both a singular and exemplary figure. But the figure of Jewel is also important because, perhaps more crucially, she resembles Marlow himself; she thus raises questions about his interpretive authority and about the paradigms of impressionist heroism he establishes. Indeed, Jewel appears to Marlow as an inscrutable figure precisely because, like him, she cannot know: she is "ignorant" and uncertain. A continuation of one of Marlow's comments cited earlier underlines the connection: "'She was more inscrutable in her childish ignorance than the Sphinx. . . . She had been carried off to Patusan before her eyes were open. She had grown up there; she had seen nothing, she had known nothing, she had no conception of anything'" (270). This uncertainty may disable Jewel as a competing interpreter of Jim, since she does not know about the *Patna* or about the depths of Western honor and mystery that episode signals (Mongia, "Empire"). But uncertainty also yields her a perceptual privilege to rival Marlow's own: if "'her ignorance made the unknown infinitely vast,'" this signals an accurate perception of a novelistic universe in which the unknown is indeed immense (271). This coexistence of ignorance and knowledge resembles Marlow's but is at the same time distinctly feminized. Emerging from her mother's stories about white men who come from and return to a mysterious Western world, it is equally an instance of feminine exclusion and women's "'sad wisdom'" (271). For we must recall that this feminized interpretation—"""they always leave us"""—is ultimately an accurate one. Its invocation of domestic tragedy registers the fated end of Jim's story and does so through the terms of colonial and gendered politics that are subsumed in Marlow's account (271).

In *Lord Jim* then, masculine storytelling and interpretation are opposed and doubled by the powerful narratives of colonized women, and Marlow's profound doubt about Jim's nature is brought face to face with Jewel's sublime bewilderment. The resemblance troubles Marlow. As critics have noted, he argues against her interpretation of Jim in large part from jealousy. He recognizes that her intimacy displaces his own, and acknowledges that her story—the uncertainty and knowledge produced by her intimacy with Jim—may also displace his. This clash of uncertainties poses the strongest challenge to Marlow's narrative authority in the novel. Not only does her account question Marlow's interpretation but their conflict suggests the personal interests that motivate it, reducing him from narrator to a limited, externally viewed character. It is important to note that this tension in the novel's presentation of Marlow does not wholly undermine his status; we cannot read *Lord Jim* as a text centrally designed to undo the terms of his authority. Rather we must consider the implications of the novel's double stance: What does it mean that *Lord Jim* both centers its narration through Marlow and yet exceeds him; that it depends upon his narrative authority and yet unravels his difference from others; frames an argument about the specifically masculine subject's access to mystery while incorporating a colonized feminine subject as his double?

To consider these questions we must consider the differences between Marlow's and Jewel's stories as a way of asking what is at stake in privileging either account—or in insisting on both. One crucial difference between Marlow's narrative and Jewel's is the degree of social specificity each foregrounds. Marlow frames a story about a universal man facing the abstract darkness within and without; Jewel counters this with a story about part-Malay women perpetually betrayed by Western men on imperial missions. In bringing these stories together as part of a broader assessment of Jim and of the narrative challenges he poses, *Lord Jim* in familiar modernist fashion tries to bring together these two registers of representation. It claims to incorporate both social detail and the universalizing impulses of Marlow's narration, to relate a story that is equally about empire—the actions of specifically imperial subjects—and about the abstract darkness of the soul or the universe.

The novel's attempt to join social detail with abstract darkness thus centers on feminine narration and on the figure of a woman. As the novel concludes with Marlow's final comments on the impossibility of gauging Jim's success, it condenses this difficulty into two different visions of Jim's relation to Jewel, and two different accounts of women's representation in the text. "'It may very well be'" Marlow says, "'that in the short moment of his last proud and unflinching glance, he had beheld the face of that opportunity which, like an Eastern bride, had come veiled to his side. But we can see him, an obscure conqueror of fame, tearing himself out of the arms of a jealous love at the sign, at the call of his exalted egoism. He goes away from a living woman to celebrate his pitiless wedding with a shadowy ideal of conduct'" (351). Is woman merely a figure for imperial ideals and opportunities, or does she stand for what the novel considers a "living presence"? Can women be so fully absorbed into a world of ideals that they exist only as figures for that universalized fate? Or do they represent a materiality or a social specificity that cannot be absorbed into these interior terms without cruelty? *Lord Jim* does not resolve the disparity but instead depends upon it as a crux for evaluating Jim, evaluating masculinity, and evaluating the effects of imperial and impressionist heroism.

Marlow's authority founders on Jewel's story, founders at the moment that he fails to incorporate her interpretation in the way that he has transformed others—rendering it a mystery that may reflect his own universalized interior. But if female subjectivity explicitly raises questions about the power of the impressionist subject to consolidate impressions into an adequate knowledge of mystery, it also prompts us to ask what effect this limit has on Conrad's text, and on *its* claim to authority? How far does the text claim to exceed its narrator's view of femininity, indeed depend on exceeding it?

We should note that this question, which links feminine mystery and narrative power, is one that persists in Conrad's work, lingering there despite his reputation for placing female subjectivity at the margins of his texts when he imagines it at all. Feminine mystery recurs in strikingly similar terms, in fact, at the center of one of his most popular late novels, *Chance* (1913), which not only returns an older Marlow as one of its main narrators but centers much of its attention on the compellingly unfathomable motives of a young girl. The novel—which unsympathetic critics have long read as an unsuccessful reprise of *Lord Jim*'s thematic and narrative strategies—again charts a kind of counterbalance between masculine narrating authority and the power of feminine mystery (Guerard 254–72). Here a domestic melodrama that would hardly be surprising from Henry James (or, looking forward, Ford Madox Ford) is literally transported aboard ship, and its mysteries reported through the limited view of two seamen and their narration. However in *Chance* domestic mystery clearly limits the narrative authority of a figure like Marlow, whose comments on women and mystery lack textual corroboration and are reduced to a cranky and unconvincing misogyny. In thus shrinking Marlow even as it repeats in ever more explicit terms the dilemmas he faces in *Lord Jim*, the novel reiterates the links between narrative authority and femininity.

To return then to *Lord Jim*, we might consider the way this text proposes its own claim to authority both through and against Marlow's. We can approach this relation by noting that the ground of Marlow's limitation defines the terms for the novel's greater success.[20] That is, *Lord Jim* distances itself from Marlow and claims to improve upon him precisely through its own ability to incorporate woman and her stories. In this sense the novel continues to take as its own the project of its narrator. Both endorsing Marlow and exceeding him, the text establishes its credibility through terms that echo his: through its power to be still more open than its narrator, to heroically confront ever-greater uncertainties. While Conrad's impressionism ultimately asserts that it may be impossible for a narrating subject to incorporate all impressions, the novel nonetheless maintains a commitment to this ideal as a definition of literature's power. It thus offers a form of literary heroism like its models of imperial manly heroism. The novel gets its cultural authority, its manliness, by confronting the unknown. If this heroic uncertainty must be held apart from the feminine subject, it nevertheless cannot escape its dependence upon her.

4 Ford, Femininity, and Unreliable Narration

Lord Jim's impressionist narration revealed the paradoxical terms in which modernist masculinity and narrative authority might be imagined. Conrad's narrator shaped a modern heroic authority from his ability to face uncertainty, and from his ability to absorb and retell the stories of others. As we have seen, such a figure sets modernist masculinity in a complicated relation to accounts of femininity. On the one hand masculine narration must disavow femininity; female characters, Marlow will tell us, are inadequate to the task of facing the brutal mysteries of both world and self. On the other hand Conrad's novel defines narrative access to both truth and mystery in terms that complicate this opposition. Impressionist narration comes to resemble feminine narration even in this most male-centered of texts, as impressionist subjects come to resemble women. The challenge for Conrad's text is to absorb and retell women's stories; to manage feminine uncertainty still better than its first-person narrator can.

This definition of modernist masculinity, dependent upon femininity while claiming to exceed it, is both flexible and precarious. Its difficulty and its centrality become even clearer in the work of Ford Madox Ford; there they will anchor one of modernist impressionism's most characteristic narrative figures, the unreliable narrator, and structure the textual labyrinth such a figure yields. Ford's work is particularly resonant for a discussion of impressionism and gender, and not only because he was the most prominent advocate of impressionism's power and modernity. His fiction and essays reveal the extent to which the narrative strategy he desired to place at the center of new forms of modern writing was thoroughly and problematically gendered for him; Ford imagines unreliable narration both as a feminized mode of storytelling and as the modern writer's best defense against this femininity.

The feminization of narrative appears in part through Ford's affinity for the traditionally feminine genre of domestic melodrama. Fond of stories about characters tortured by romantic secrets, about men torn between sympathetic young women and unsympathetic older ones, Ford repeats this narrative pattern in his fiction from *The Good Soldier* through the *Parade's End* tetralogy; indeed he attempted to repeat it in life with his own series of romantic liaisons. Further, such melodrama seems intrinsically linked to impressionism for Ford; its patterns emerge whenever he begins to describe the complexities of character impressionism is designed to reveal. In the second part of his essay "On Impressionism," for instance, Ford describes the way impressionism may improve on a bare fictional statement such as "'Mr. Jones was a gentleman who had a strong aversion to rabbit-pie'" (324). In Ford's unfolding of this sentence, he describes the power of impressionism to locate this simple dislike in an elaborate domestic web: rabbit pie may signal a husband's disaffection from his wife, his passion for another woman, and his wife's hopeless desire for a reconciliation she cannot quite understand.

While this example from Ford's essay on impressionist method seems idiosyncratic amid the essay's deliberate ramblings, the structures of domestic melodrama and with them patterns of gendered subjectivity anchor Ford's understanding of the modern world and the modern subject. In his extended essay "Women and Men," written in 1911–12 and serialized in the *Little Review* in 1918, for instance, his discussion of the relation between men and women becomes an essay on the mysterious inaccessibility of character. Just as gender relations quickly become a question of interior mystery for Ford, so too do the ideas of internal mystery and the narrative means of rendering it lead him inexorably to the unstable relation between the sexes.

In particular, melodrama's revelations of female secrets and infidelities, its fascination with gossip and romantic suffering mark Ford's view of the modern world as a place in which people are not what they appear to be. In this way his work imagines feminine secrecy and interiority, as well as unreliable narration, as the central characteristics of the modern age. But if Ford's fiction describes such a world, it also attempts to imagine adequate masculine responses that might keep modern feminization at bay. Ford's novels idealize versions of masculine character, often by

imagining such figures as the lingering remnants of a simpler premod-
ern culture. And in his fiction, the feminized world and the dream of
masculinity converge upon the double bind of masculine narration. In
Ford's work secrecy, interiority, and storytelling are themselves feminized. A male narrator, particularly an unreliable one, is thus in a peculiar position. He is both feminized and the location of the text's most
wistful fantasies of masculinity; he resembles a woman even as he tries
to distance himself from femininity. The unreliable narrator thus underlines for Ford the way that both masculine knowledge and its absence,
knowing narrators and unknowing ones are defined through femininity
in modernism. In Ford's best-known text, *The Good Soldier*, such narration simultaneously makes an epistemological point about the difficulty of knowing and genders that epistemology. Unreliable narration emphasizes the extent to which modernist storytelling depends on what it
sees as feminized narratives, even as this modernist narrative strategy
attempts to find a distance from femininity.

Ford's fiction thus places feminized subjectivity and storytelling at
the center of its account of the modern world and the modern subject.
This placement is both important and paradoxical. In his work from 1908
to 1909 as an editor of the *English Review*, Ford sought to define what
was modern about the new fiction he was publishing and writing, and
in a now-predictable rhetorical gesture he grounded the artistic value of
this new work in its impersonality and its masculinity. However, a reading of *The Good Soldier* may clarify the logic through which Ford's influential formulation of a modernist aesthetic proposes a complex version of masculine literary authority that is routed through a range of
feminized figures. The novel also clarifies why this central contradiction
in gendering modernism emerges through an examination of interiority,
as it envisions the modern subject as both a cultural problem and a literary solution.

In *The Good Soldier* Ford casts modernity as a social crisis and defines
that crisis in terms of a treacherous interiority. The novel constantly asks
whether characters have interiors hidden from external influence and
from external view. It is these secret depths which produce the range of
disasters that center the text and mark the modern world as a fallen one.
Adultery, the accommodation of adultery, the corruption and dissolution
of a set of social conventions, the dangers of storytelling and its unreliability—all of these perils spring from the problem of hidden interiors in
this novel and from the dangers of relating their secret depths. Adultery
and duplicity—the two central signs here of dangerously hidden interi-

ority—destroy what the narrator John Dowell describes with both nostalgia and cynicism as the fragile, ordered "minuet" (13) of an older, moneyed social world, a world of "good people" (37) who seem constituted by their appearances and by their conformity to an external, communal standard of behavior. Women will provide the quintessentially modern figures who destroy this world for Dowell's story; through them the novel will feminize what it means to have secrets, to know secrets, and to narrate them.

Modern interiority and its feminization thus shape a set of problems that drive Ford's conflicted claims for an impersonal, masculine literary authority. For when the text links interiority with corruption, it also links such interiority with forms of hidden, pernicious knowledge. If female characters hide behind their conventional behavior, they do so because they are disguising a corrupt knowledge. If they equally and paradoxically seem too open, it is because they circulate a knowledge that ought to remain unknown. This association of knowledge with a feminized fall threatens the status of modernist narration, which is defined as the project of uncovering hidden truths, offering special knowledge of the human interior. Like Conrad, Ford turns to uncertainty as a way to refuse the apparent femininity of knowledge, and in doing so he frames a series of gendered dilemmas about knowledge and narration that the use of an unreliable narrator embodies and attempts to resolve.[1] How can a story be told without access to the hidden interiors of others? How can we interpret the stories told by characters whose depths belie their appearances? How can a narrator appear persuasive, indeed appear masculine, if certain knowledge is itself suspect and feminized?

Unreliable narration—the use of a narrator who himself may possess secret interior depths and hide secret knowledge—offers an example of the modern, explicitly feminized narrating subject on whom Ford's story must depend. At the same time such a narrator makes visible the strategies by which modernist narration attempts to manage this feminization and devise new terms for a masculine modern literary authority. Denying knowledge, Ford's narrator offers himself as an impersonal conduit for his story; he frames himself as an everyman universal in his bewilderment, and defines bewilderment as the prerequisite for narrative authority. Proposing a freeing distance between masculine narrators and the feminized stories they tell, unreliable narration thus underlines the productive doubleness of modernism's relation to feminine subjectivity—as the movement asserts an identification with femininity while refusing to be placed by the association.

The Good Soldier is framed as the story of a catastrophic fall. The novel's narrator, John Dowell, opens his tale by announcing that the apparently civilized life he has led with his wife Florence and their friends the Ashburnhams is false—riven by concealed passion, deception, and infidelity. He thus tells his story as the discovery of hidden, guilty depths in character; it is simultaneously an attempt to construct a method of storytelling that would account for those depths. With this opening frame Ford's text introduces its central concerns: adultery, duplicity, mysterious secrets and the problem of how they might be narrated. In this way Ford suggests a reading of modernity as the disastrous, if also compelling, emergence of a world in which appearances are no longer legible—and in particular a world in which character is no longer legible but rather split between opaque surfaces and the murky depths of subjectivity.

Indeed, at the start of *The Good Soldier*, the fact that characters may possess discrete interiors at all is a sign of social corruption and unreliability. It is this implicit unreliability of the interiorized subject and the novel's attempts to manage its gendered associations that I will be concerned with here, and I will begin to trace them through a reading of the text's representation of character. We might begin to clarify the ominous status of interiority in *The Good Soldier* by considering a passage early in the novel in which the narrator attempts to characterize this social world:

> I can't believe that that long tranquil life, which was just stepping a minuet, vanished in four crashing days. . . . Upon my word, yes, our intimacy was like a minuet, simply because on every possible occasion and in every possible circumstance we knew where to go, where to sit, which table we unanimously should choose. . . . No, indeed, it can't be gone. You can't kill a minuet de la cour. . . .
>
> No, by God, it is false! It wasn't a minuet that we stepped; it was a prison—a prison full of screaming hysterics, tied down so that they might not outsound the rolling of our carriage wheels as we went along the shaded avenues of the Taunus Wald. (13-14)

The narrator's movement between two metaphors neatly condenses the central terms in which the novel describes a nostalgic, illusory world of cultural stability as well as its current crisis. Dowell frames here two very different relations between the social order and the subject.[2] Genteel behavior is either a "minuet de la cour," or "a prison full of screaming hysterics, tied down." The opposition hinges on the vision in the second passage of subjects suppressed by, and distinct from, a social order. If the first vision of a social "minuet" represents cultural stability for Dowell, it does so not just as a decorously restrained and patterned dance but as one that supposes a particular relationship of dancer and dance: The *minuet de la cour* is also punningly a *minuet du coeur*; it shapes the subject so thoroughly that no interiors exist apart from social forms; the subject is at every point patterned by the dance of polite conventions. In contrast, the vision of social breakdown, of "a prison full of screaming hysterics," summons the language of subjective depth and interiority—but it does so only to describe disaster. Recasting society as something that forcibly restrains the subject, Dowell imagines a separate self to be restrained. The modern world is thus divided into surfaces and depths, where individuals possess interiors of uncontrollable emotion that can only be touched by social rules in the most violent manner—a world in which the carriage of civilization must tie its passengers up, so that it may progress down suitably quiet avenues.

This pattern of surfaces and depths, of disastrous interiors, will shape the melodramatic tale Dowell will tell, just as it will shape the labyrinth of modernist plot that is *The Good Soldier*. For this double image prefigures the terms in which the novel's narrator frames his tale of disastrous revelation in the first portion of the text. Set in the corrupt but—to Dowell—appealing world of moneyed society at the elegant spa of Nauheim, the novel describes a set of cultural rules that work by presuming that characters' exteriors determine their essences. And when this conventional society is revealed as duplicitous, the revelation comes from the sudden appearance of hidden depths suppressed beneath what must now be recast as a mere surface.

Dowell's definition of the "good people" (37) populating Nauheim, for instance, makes clear the extent to which social convention in this world assumes that exteriority is all-encompassing—that there are no secret interiors. The desires of "good people" no less than their actions are shaped by communal standards. "We took for granted that we all liked beef underdone but not too underdone; that both men preferred a good liqueur brandy; that both women drank a very light Rhine wine . . . — that sort of thing. It was also taken for granted that we were both sufficiently well off to afford anything that we could reasonably want in the way of amusements fitting to our station" (38). The match of desire and convention signals appropriate identity here, an identity which can be accurately interpreted from wholly external signs: "You meet a man or a woman and, from tiny and intimate sounds, from the slightest of movements, you know at once whether you are concerned with good people or with those who won't do" (40). Indeed neither desire nor behavior is interior here; both are productions or embodiments of communal norms.

The "[taking] for granted," that so importantly defines this class of "good people" seals the complete fit of convention and subject. If the "uninterrupted tranquillity" (37) of polite society is characterized by "an extraordinary want of communicativeness," and a "leaving out [of] . . . the personal note," this absence of the personal does not appear as a vital omission but as a neglect of what is considered redundant (37). "Indeed," Dowell adds, "you may take it that what characterized our relationship was an atmosphere of taking everything for granted. The given proposition was that we were all 'good people'" (37). Knowledge is not a problem in this world because everything may be known so thoroughly from the visible; the ethos of "taking everything for granted" reinforces the view that there can be nothing else to know.

The novel's and the narrator's interest in characterization as a means of satire rests upon this account of a society destined to fall. For it is as the perfect embodiments of this ideal identity that Edward and Leonora Ashburnham first make their appearance:

> For I swear to you that they were the model couple. He was as devoted as it was possible to be without appearing fatuous. So well set up with such honest blue eyes, such a touch of stupidity, such a warm goodheartedness! And she—so tall, so splendid in the saddle, so fair! Yes, Leonora was extraordinarily fair and so extraordinarily the real thing that she seemed too good to be true. . . . To be the county family, to look the county family, to be so appropriately and perfectly wealthy; to be so perfect in manner—even to the saving touch of insolence that seems to be necessary. To have all that and to be all that! (15–16)

For the Ashburnhams here, "to look" and "to be," not to mention "to have," are continuous. They fit the social ideal as "the model couple"; indeed they authenticate it by embodying it so fully. This method of characterization as the denial of interiority is emphasized in Dowell's accounts of both characters. Leonora's body, for instance, is continuous with her clothing: "I never thought that Leonora looked her best in evening dress," Dowell comments, because "her shoulders were too classical. She seemed to stand out of her corsage as a white marble bust might out of a black Wedgwood vase. . . . Certain women's lines guide your eyes to their necks, their eyelashes, their lips, their breasts. But Leonora's seemed to conduct your gaze always to her wrist" (36). She appears to Dowell as a statue, as "lines"; she is an artistic artifact, a culturally produced object whose body, like her clothes, may be described as a kind of style, and whose identity may be signaled by her outline.

Edward is similarly shaped by social conventions, and subject to a still more extreme parody. Indeed Dowell's account empties him of all interiority whatsoever:

> His face hitherto had, in the wonderful English fashion, expressed nothing whatever. Nothing. There was in it neither joy nor despair; neither hope nor fear; neither boredom nor satisfaction. . . . I never came across such a perfect expression before and I never shall again. . . . His hair was fair, extraordinarily ordered in a wave, running from the left temple to the right; his face was a light brick-red, perfectly uniform in tint up to the roots of the hair itself; his yellow moustache was as stiff as a toothbrush and I verily believe that he had his black smoking jacket thickened a little over the shoulder-blades so as to give himself the air of the slightest possible stoop. It would be like him to do that; that was the sort of thing he thought about. (29–30)

The description follows a curious progression: from suggesting that the perfection of Edward's glance lies in its inexpressiveness—that is, its ability to hide what may possibly lie inside him ("it expressed nothing . . . neither joy nor despair")—it goes on to redescribe him as though he were simply an assemblage of flat, colored surfaces, a kind of "uniform" of skin and hair. But the passage then reconstitutes an inside for Edward out of his outside, by suggesting that his clothing creates his bodily appearance (the jacket gives him the air of a stoop), until finally this very construction of the interior by the exterior becomes literalized as the only inside Edward in fact has—"that was the sort of thing he thought about."[3]

If *The Good Soldier* figures conventional character as the seamless fit between social rules and personal desires, the novel nonetheless begins with the narrator's announcement that this society has suffered a crisis, that its secrets have been revealed. Recounted retrospectively by Dowell after he has realized both his wife's and Edward Ashburnham's infidelities, the narration of the novel intermingles two different logics in the description of the fallen social world. While Dowell sometimes presents "character" nostalgically, as though he believed in the terms of a once-stable world of congruent outsides and insides, at the same time this presentation of character is intertwined with a postlapsarian vision in which the subject mysteriously escapes convention and reduces it to a mere surface, removing truth to the interior.

Thus while *The Good Soldier* is a story about adultery and deception, the crisis posed to the narrator by Florence's and Edward's many infidelities registers most acutely in the way such infidelities transform his view of character. Where formerly he considered an understanding of appearances adequate, now such appearances have suddenly been transformed into mere surface, rendered unreliable by the suggestion that beneath lurk mysterious depths. So, for instance, Dowell wonders whether "if for nine years I have possessed a goodly apple that is rotten at the core and discover its rottenness only in nine years and six months less four days, isn't it true to say that for nine years I possessed a goodly apple? So it may well be with Edward Ashburnham, with Leonora his wife and with poor dear Florence" (14). This passage has frequently been read for its connection with the novel's thematics of epistemological uncertainty—the double question of whether we can ever really know anyone else and whether all knowledge may not therefore be wholly subjective. But it's worth noting the preliminary step the passage must take to establish this issue, a step perhaps all too obvious because its vision of subjectivity so accords with our own: this passage reenvisions the subject as a hidden interior, and redefines Leonora and Edward and Florence as figures whose real nature can only be known by knowing what lies hidden inside them.

The first half of *The Good Soldier* is unified by this vision of the subject as distinctly interior and therefore treacherously inaccessible; the novel embeds its thematics of bewilderment in the complementary dilemmas of the subject's mysterious depths and its false surfaces. Thus it is to this notion of interiority that we must refer Dowell's parody of other characters as creatures of false surfaces. This new sense of the world as only visible by its surfaces leads Dowell to mourn that he can "know nothing" (14), that "[n]o smoking room will ever be other than peopled with incalculable simulacra amidst smoke wreaths" (14–15). When he satirizes those whom he thought he knew, for instance, it is on the ground that they were in fact merely surfaces. The descriptions of Edward and Leonora we have already examined, for instance, are parodically double-edged. For while they may describe the Ashburnhams as having interiors wholly shaped by convention, these accounts ironically teeter on the brink of suggesting that a conventional interior may be no interior at all. Thus we might note the way the description of Leonora renders her body figuratively as of the same substance as her clothes and then proceeds to convert her into a series of lines that point elsewhere, removing what interiority she may have to a dispatch box: "Leonora's [lines] seemed to conduct your gaze always to her wrist. . . . there was always a gold circlet with a little chain supporting a very small golden key to a dispatch box. Perhaps it was that in which she locked up her heart and her feelings" (36).

The far more evident irony in Dowell's description of Edward draws on this same element of flattening, comparing him to a series of colored surfaces and inanimate objects: "his face was a light brick-red, perfectly uniform . . . his yellow moustache was as stiff as a toothbrush." A few pages later the parody reduces Edward to commercial objects and to fragments that only imitate a whole, disassembling character entirely. "I had forgotten about his eyes. They were blue as the sides of a certain type of box of matches. . . . But the brick pink of his complexion, running perfectly level to the brick pink of his inner eyelids, gave them a curious, sinister expression—like a mosaic of blue porcelain set in pink china" (32–33).

The co-conspiracy of surface and depth reaches its peak when Dowell describes his wife Florence, who throughout the novel is the object of his most outraged criticism. The pejorative charge of a reduction to surface here immediately summons the image of depth as intrinsic falsehood. For Florence appears simultaneously as the most deceptive, secretive character and as the figure most thoroughly, trivially concerned with—and reduced to—surfaces. Her attention to her clothing and to meaningless rituals of behavior turns her into a complete cipher:

> the heels of her shoes were exceedingly high, so that she tripped upon the points of her toes. And when she came to the door of the bathing place, and when it opened to receive her, she would look back at me with a little coquettish smile, so that her cheek appeared to be caressing her shoulder.
>
> I seem to remember that, with that dress [of blue figured silk] she wore an immensely broad Leghorn hat—like the Chapeau de Paille of Rubens, only very white. . . . She knew how to give value to her blue eyes. And round her neck would be some simple pink, coral beads. And her complexion had a perfect clearness, a perfect smoothness. . . .
>
> And what the devil! For whose benefit did she do it? . . . I don't know. Anyhow, it can't have been for me. . . . Ah, she was a riddle; but then, all other women are riddles. (27–28)

The passage flattens Florence out: her dress, her coral beads, her eyes, her skin are all rendered as a series of textured, colored surfaces, her figure made analogous with the "figure[s]" in the silk of her dress, her shallow vanity marked by the way she has orchestrated this continuity, this resemblance, to "give value" to her appearance. But at the same time, the very behavior that supplies a visible surface disconnected from any interior identity (the walk produced by the high heels, the glance expressing no affection for Dowell) actually suggests, by its flatness, the existence of an interior subject that is being deliberately hidden. Thus Florence's glance can be a performance, a mere surface, because it does not express interior emotions, because her interior is a "riddle"; inside, detached from action or appearance, it cannot be known.

Surfaces and depths are complicit in the modern world of *The Good Soldier*—the maintenance of the one guarantees the other. The model will shape both character and plot in the novel. For Dowell suggests that the infidelities and even mistaken fidelities he describes render marriage—the novel's figure for social unity—both a mystery and a sham. Thus we move from the simultaneous surface and depth of a character like Leonora—at once merely a cluster of graceful lines and a mysterious heart locked up in a dispatch box—to the secret disaster of the Ashburnham marriage—maintained as a false front by Leonora's dogged and secretive Catholicism. We move from the false front of Dowell's own marriage back to the question of this narrator's own secret depths.

———

The Good Soldier imagines the fall of an old social order. However it also proposes another—characteristically modernist—kind of stability to put in its place. And we may read this new order through the same terms that revealed the crisis of the old: through the problem of the subject and its interior. For the novel will reestablish interiority itself as a modern source of truth and integrity; indeed we might say that part of its narrative project is to redeem and refigure the interiority which so obsesses the text and its narrator. The very notion of depth that disturbs Dowell's belief in society and in the "character" of "good people" in the first part of the novel paradoxically becomes the ground for knowledge and a sense of "character" in the latter portion of his story. And interiority becomes a stabilizing element in the second half of the novel in precisely that form in which it was most disturbing in the first: as passion. Where passion entered the text as a falsifying infidelity, the novel takes pains to redefine it as the subject's deepest and most honorable truth. Thus, taken in both its senses—as suffering and desire—passion was the element that rendered the civilized rituals of Nauheim society a mere surface: Florence's affairs, Edward's secret passions, Edward and Leonora's anguished private silences. But in the second half of the tale Dowell tells—in which Edward, Leonora, and "the girl" Nancy circle each other destructively at the English estate of Branshaw Teleragh—Dowell recasts passion as an ennobling emotion. Allying passion with interiority, and with a silence that prevents it from reaching the surface of the subject, he reimagines passion as the quality that marks a character as genuinely "splendid"—"those splendid and tumultuous creatures with their magnetism and their passions" (214) he calls Edward and Nancy near the end of his story.[4] And he now claims that his own passion allies him with truth. "I myself," Dowell comments, trying to compare himself with his heroic image of Edward, "in my fainter way, come into the category of the passionate, of the headstrong, and the too-truthful" (227).

We may trace this shift in the text's language of interiority most clearly through its revision of Edward—whose desire becomes something to be taken seriously in the course of the novel—by Leonora, by Dowell, and by the reader—something that raises our estimate of him (Snitow 181).[5] This shift refigures Edward's passion as distinctly interior. In fact it provides him with an interior. For Edward's passion early in the novel does not appear to be a part of a distinct interiority. His affairs result from a sentimentality that signals his incorporation of social conventions rather in the manner of Conrad's Jim, instead of the possession of an interior separate from those conventions. Edward's emotions are here simply the internalization of conventional or literary scripts, of cheap romances and military codes of honor. Dowell observes that "poor dear Edward was a great reader—he would pass hours lost in novels of a sentimental type—novels in which typewriter girls married Marquises and governesses Earls" (32). When Dowell wonders early on what intrinsic appeal women might find in Ashburnham—"Good God," he asks, "what did they all see in him? for I swear [that] was all there was of him, inside and out"—he finds his answer in this internalization of conventional words. "Ah, well, suddenly, as if by a flash of inspiration, I know. For all good soldiers are sentimentalists. . . . Their profession, for one thing, is full of the big words, courage, loyalty, honour, constancy" (31). And when Edward speaks privately with Dowell, rare as such occasions may be, when he speaks of what Dowell describes him as calling "'the graver things,'" his intimate outbursts are themselves a series of ironically inappropriate clichés: "He would say how much the society of a good woman could do towards redeeming you, and he would say that constancy was the finest of the virtues" (31).

But the second part of *The Good Soldier* recasts Edward as a more nearly heroic figure. His silent, indeed unspeakable, love for the innocent Nancy, which focuses the tragic events at Branshaw, gives him depth at the same time that it gives him a passion the novel presents as courageous, honorable, and constant. And it is particularly the silence and restraint of this passion that ennobles him and gives him a true "character." His central dilemma throughout the second half of the text comes from his determination not to speak to his beloved Nancy of his feelings, lest he ruin her faith in the institution of marriage and her belief in him as an ideal man. The transition registers in the text's refiguration of Edward's character, which literalizes this interiority. Ashburnham's "sickening" for love of Nancy—more precisely his sickening because of his silence—creates a genuinely internal self for him inside the conventions. It creates, for instance, a real stooped body within his clothes where once the clothes had created his body from without: "He appeared, indeed, to be very ill; his shoulders began to be bowed" (122). But more crucially this same silent "passion," this "dumb agony," becomes the basis for Dowell's sympathetic portrayal of Edward as a man tormented by the conventions he had formerly seemed to embody, the basis for figuring him as Christ-like, a man whose "dumb agony . . . passes the mind of man to imagine" (26) (Snitow 185; S. Hynes, "Epistemology" 55).

The Good Soldier thus repositions a silent or hidden interiority as the basis of "character" at the very moment that silence, interiority, character are all being destroyed. The second half of the novel—focusing on the events at Branshaw—organizes itself around the breakdown of honorable character. Importantly, what destroys character now is not the silent deception described earlier but its opposite—talk, confession, the revelation rather than the secreting of private knowledge. We can see this alteration in the novel's depiction of Leonora; she breaks down most dramatically, and she therefore illuminates most clearly the way the text revalues interiority. Where earlier Dowell presented Leonora's silence, and particularly her silence about the problems of her marriage, as deceptive, as one instance of the world's tragic split into surfaces and hidden truths, in the latter half of his narration the fact that she had been "drilled—in her tradition, in her upbringing—to keep her mouth shut" and to resist the "temptation of speaking" (162) comes to appear as a more admirable "high reserve"—admirable, we might note, at the moment it is "abandon[ed]" (174).[6]

Her breakdown, which Dowell describes explicitly as the breakdown of her "character," takes the form of talk: "Florence was a contaminating influence. . . . There is no doubt that she caused Leonora's character to deteriorate. If there was a fine point about Leonora it was that she was proud and that she was silent. But that pride and that silence broke when she made that extraordinary outburst" (168). Leonora's deterioration takes the form of a "sudden madness . . . a thirst for self-explanation" (193); "[s]he craved madly for communication with some other human soul" (185). And it is this deterioration ("[s]he relaxed; she broke; she drifted" [184]) and this desire to tell the story of her marriage that brings on "the smash" of all their lives at Branshaw.

The disastrous, character-destroying nature of the events at Branshaw seems to lie in the horror of there having been so much talk: "What had happened was just Hell. Leonora had spoken to Nancy; Nancy had spoken to Edward; Edward had spoken to Leonora—and they had talked and talked. And talked. You have to imagine my beautiful Nancy . . . a silent, a no doubt agonized figure, like a spectre, suddenly offering herself to him—to save his reason! And you have to imagine his frantic refusal—and talk. And talk! My God!" (182) Talking at Branshaw, as the novel describes it, violates the properly enclosed interiority that is now "character." The narrative presents talk as a literal "outburst" in which what is inside the self is forced to the surface, with destructive results for everyone. When Edward announces to Nancy that she must go to stay with her father, for instance, "the girl put her hand over her heart and cried out: 'Oh, my sweet Saviour, help me!' That was the queer way she thought within her mind, and the words forced themselves to her lips. Edward said nothing" (190). This same torturous breach of interiority entailed by speech renders it a weapon, prompting one character to use it against another, despite the self-destruction that must follow. Leonora talks to Edward with just this intent: "'I said a great deal more to him than I wanted to, just because he was so silent.'" And Dowell notes that "[s]he talked, in fact, in the endeavour to sting him into speech" (192).

Talk destroys passion as well as character at the end of this novel. If Edward's love for Nancy must be a silent one, lest in speech he destroy her faith in him and her innocent love for him, then appropriately all of this talk ends by destroying her love, as well as what one might recognize as an interior, her mind. For while Edward remains silent about his passion for Nancy, Leonora does not. Deliberately deciding that Nancy "should not continue to love Edward" (216), she destroys the girl's love for him by telling her of his affairs. "At hearing of the miseries her aunt had suffered . . . the girl made her resolves" (216); she then appears at Edward's bed to announce "'I can never love you now I know the kind of man you are. I will belong to you to save your life. But I can never love you'" (217). By the end of the novel, Nancy ends up empty, "a picture without meaning" (228), vacantly repeating an empty religious creed: "*Credo in unum Deum omnipotentem*" (210).

Talk in *The Good Soldier* is dangerous because it is contagious. Florence contaminates Leonora in part because she is "an unstoppable talker. You could not stop her; nothing would stop her" (168). Florence's volubility makes her contagious and is also the corruption she spreads—she makes Leonora talk against her will. Thus the nightmare of Branshaw is the constantly circulating, boundary-breaking contagion of talk there which guarantees that the sheer nightmare will continue, which makes it impossible to control. Ford's repetition emphasizes this circling: "Leonora had spoken to Nancy; Nancy had spoken to Edward; Edward had spoken to Leonora—and they had talked and talked. And talked" (192).

And just as Leonora's ordeal is to have her character break down until she is overcome by the contagion of talk, the ultimate trial for the silently suffering Edward Ashburnham is to hear all of this talk and yet be unable to halt its circulation: "Those two women pursued that poor devil. . . . Night after night he would hear them talking; talking; maddened, sweating, seeking oblivion in drink, he would lie there and hear the voices going on and on. And day after day Leonora would come to him and would announce the results of their deliberations" (214–15). Until finally he too must talk—to Dowell. "'I am so desperately in love with Nancy Rufford that I am dying of it,'" he confesses. "Poor devil [Dowell comments]—he hadn't meant to speak of it. But I guess he just had to speak to somebody and I appeared to be like a woman or a solicitor. He talked all night" (224).

As I have been tracing the representation of character in *The Good Soldier* and the sense of social crisis its shifting forms provoke, it will have become clear that the problems of interiority, secrecy, and the shape of the subject that I have been examining are consistently gendered for Ford. Despite Dowell's early criticism of Edward Ashburnham as a sentimental philanderer, it is the female characters in the novel in whom he locates the greatest threat to both social and individual stability.[7] Indeed the consistent problem of femininity in the text is all the more evident because its threat is a contradictory one—lying initially in women's secrecy, their hidden interiority, and later in their talk, their disruption of a stability now vested in the individual. Indeed we might read the novel's late reappraisal of interiority as an attempt to remasculinize it—an attempt to link subjective depths with Edward Ashburnham and to associate both with a feudal ideal in which the subject's interiority strengthens a social order. In contrast, female subjectivity will be affiliated with the rootless, superficial modernity of money in the text. Further, in the course of the novel, femininity's depths and surfaces will come to taint both knowledge and its circulation, both hidden secrets and the act of relating them. This affiliation, above all, will anchor and trouble the narrator's and the novel's attempts to establish forms of masculine narrative authority.

We can see this valuation in the narrator's divided accounts of masculine and feminine adultery. Edward's affairs, false as they are, do not truly disrupt existing social patterns. Instead they grow out of a noble, if archaic, system of social ideals. For Ashburnham believes in a feudal code of honor and the failure of his marriage can be attributed more to flaws in his wife's definition of social responsibility than to his own philandering. Edward acts upon "the feudal theory of an over-lord doing his best by his dependents, the dependents meanwhile doing their best for the over-lord—[and] this theory was entirely foreign to Leonora's nature" (136); in contrast, "his wife was a sheer individualist" (136). Edward's attempt to embody feudal ideals, to "[do] his best by his dependents," leads to his estrangement from Leonora, and indeed to his subsequent attempts to deceive her. Their differences and his deceptions center less on his romantic affairs than on the financial ones that follow from this feudal ideal. Their mutual distrust, for instance, does not begin with his infidelities but before them, with his sense of the "generosities proper to his station" (59) and with Leonora's objection that such "generosities were almost fantastic. He subscribed much to[o] much to things connected with his mess, he pensioned off his father's servants, old or new, much too generously" (132).

Even Edward's most damaging duplicities—the lies that most dramatically render his marriage the hollow formality that Dowell takes as the sign of social crisis—concern differences over money rather than infidelity itself. It is the expense of his affairs—the price of the courtesan La Dolciquita, the blackmail—that, on top of his excessive generosity to tenants, drives Leonora to despair of ever repairing their marriage. Thus when Leonora is discovered slapping the woman Edward loves, Maisie Maidan, her slap responds less to the revelation of his love (which is no news to Leonora) than to the threat of a new financial crisis:

> [I]n boxing Mrs Maidan's ears, Leonora was just striking the face of an intolerable universe. For that afternoon she had had a frightfully painful scene with Edward.... Edward's [financial] affairs were in such a frightful state and he lied so about them that she claimed the privilege of having his secrets at her disposal.... [and she had just] discovered that Edward Ashburnham was paying a blackmailer of whom she had never heard something like three hundred pounds a year.... It was a devil of a blow; it was like death; for she imagined that by that time she had really got to the bottom of her husband's liabilities. (55)

Edward's romances, in contrast, appear as relatively open and undisturbing to Leonora. Indeed the first of his involvements with other women, the publicly scandalous Kilsyte case, Dowell notes, "came almost as a relief to the strained situation that then existed between them. It gave Leonora an opportunity of backing him up in a whole-hearted and absolutely loyal manner" (139). And Edward's further romantic entanglements with La Dolciquita, Mrs. Basil, and Maisie Maidan—until Florence—similarly seem to trouble Leonora primarily by their financial implications.

The social world that Dowell describes remains unthreatened by Edward's affairs as well as his expenses; it contains a set of narrative conventions that frame his actions as picturesque and thus safe. Dowell speculates half-parodically that Edward would have been better off if left to follow these impulses: "Because, of course," he comments, "the only thing to have done for Edward would have been to let him sink down until he became a tramp of gentlemanly address, having, maybe, chance love affairs upon the highways" (60). "Or [perhaps] he would have married a barmaid who would have made him such frightful scenes in public places and would so have torn out his moustache . . . that he would have been faithful to her for the rest of his days. That was what he wanted to redeem him" (61). If Edward's infidelities will lead him into decline, the declines are comic ones, mildly humiliating him while ultimately redeeming him— hardly the crisis of truth and secrecy the novel begins by imagining.

The conflict between Edward and Leonora, centering as it does on money more than infidelity, thus appears in the novel as a debate over the nature of expenses and the role of money. In this account Edward's standards are nostalgically contrasted to Leonora's calculations of cost and exchange. If the novel frames Edward's feudal ideals as indulgent fantasies, many of the specific expenses they prompt—the "remitt[ance of] his tenants' rents," the "redeeming [of] drunkards," the redemption of prostitutes and children—nevertheless demand admiration in the text (59).[8] In contrast Leonora's view of Edward's honor as reducible to his wealth, and her resulting concern to preserve the money rather than the ethos, creates the lie of their marriage. For when Leonora considers money to be the essence of Edward's social position, she makes that position a false display, a mere surface, replacing the ostensibly organic logic of ancestry, place, and obligation with the arbitrary equations of wealth. Thus she is capable of selling the Ashburnham family heirlooms—"two Vandykes [as well as] a little silver"—to repay Edward's gambling debts, thinking that "[t]hey were just frills to the Ashburnham vanity" (154). When "Edward cried for two days over the disappearance of his ancestors . . . she wished she had not done it; but it did not teach her anything" (154). And when, as compensation, she offers him dressing cases—"all that pigskin" (154), as Dowell puts it—she provides the symbol of their marriage as a mere social surface. For Edward, on the contrary, money is far more organically connected to those social ideals that wed interior desire with outward action: money enables him to be a good feudal landlord and take care of his tenants and women in distress; he does not consider it to be the substance of that identity. Money for him is simply the element that will allow his desire (for La Dolciquita, for instance) to be transformed into action.[9]

Dowell thus uses Edward Ashburnham to remasculinize interiority, and to associate this form of character with the values of an eclipsed community. He consistently casts feminine character as a sign of a fall from this community and this sense of value. Just as Leonora misunderstands traditional honor and agency, reducing them to the inadequate modern surfaces of money, Florence comes to embody the most destructive aspects of a world broken into false surfaces and unknowable depths. This division provides the figure for a whole series of instances of Florence's deceptiveness. The "little coquettish smile" that masks the riddle of her motivation—"for whose benefit did she do it? . . . it can't have been for me" (27–28)—offers a parallel to the locked bedroom door behind which she retires each night at ten o'clock, the door that keeps her "out of [Dowell's] sight most of the time" (84). Even Florence's "heart" paradoxically reproduces this paradigm of deception: it is that invisible, troubling interior in Florence (or the interior, at least, that she claims troubles her) that makes her marriage one sort of false front, since it remains unconsummated. Marriage is a false front in other ways as well for Florence: she plans it as a source of money to buy her way back into an English landed aristocracy her family has long since left.

But Florence does not have a "heart" in the medical sense—this is the substance of her lie to Dowell. Her deception thus comes paradoxically to be lodged in the absence at her interior. And the reformulation brings us back to the novel's pattern of associating women with both the problem of interiority and the dangers of talk, of publicity, that make such interiority finally impossible. For while Dowell in part casts Florence's deception as a matter of her hidden thoughts and the adultery that takes place behind her closed door, he also denies that she has a "passion" like Edward's, a passion that the novel ultimately associates with a redeemed interiority. Contrary to Florence's claim to Leonora—in which she excuses her infidelity "on the score of an overmastering passion" (81–82)—Dowell insists that she "need not have done what she did. . . . [since] she had not the hot passions of these Europeans" (68). Florence's passions, he asserts, are instead mere public shows with nothing behind them, "theatrical displays" (112). "She wanted," Dowell comments, "to come rushing to me, to declaim a carefully arranged, frightfully emotional, outpouring as to her passion. That was to show that she was like one of the great erotic women of whom history tells us . . . she was always play acting" (112). Florence's passion—indeed her very identity—is the false production of "play acting"; the illusion of her interior is created by a kind of publicity, a theatricality that takes effect only by being visible to others. As a result, for Dowell, she has no interior at all: "I suppose that my inner soul . . . had realized long before that Florence was a personality of paper—that she represented a real human being with a heart, with feelings, with sympathies and with emotions only as a bank-note represents a certain quantity of gold. . . . I thought suddenly that she wasn't real: she was just a mass of talk out of guidebooks, of drawings out of fashion plates" (114).

Just as Dowell relocates Florence's moral bankruptcy from her hidden interiority to her utter lack of an interior, so too, in the latter part of the novel—in which inaccessible interiority becomes a virtue, a sign of character—he attributes the destruction of interiority and passion to feminine behavior. Where Edward comes to represent silent passion and integrity—the gap between social surface and interior emotion that is the mark of honor—Nancy and Leonora come to stand for the destruction of interiority through its publication in talk. The ideal of community itself is degraded through its feminization; feminine communities are the fallen recapitulations of a lost world. Thus, for instance, when Leonora's stories make Nancy resolve to stop loving Edward, Dowell describes her resolution as a characteristic female refusal of passion—its sacrifice to a pernicious collective standard: "[A]t hearing of the miseries her aunt had suffered . . . with the swift solidarity that attaches woman to woman, the girl made her resolves" (216). "I am pretty certain," Dowell writes,

> that [Nancy Rufford] had loved Edward Ashburnham very deeply and tenderly.
> It is nothing to the point that she let him have it good and strong as soon as she discovered that he had been unfaithful to Leonora and that his public services had cost more than Leonora thought they ought to have cost. Nancy would be bound to let him have it good and strong then. She would owe that to feminine public opinion. (219)

This feminine public realm reprises an earlier society, while draining it of any redeeming value. Thus Dowell sees women as possessing insufficient genuine communal feeling at the same time that they sacrifice the values of the private realm—passion and character—to a false version of community, one characterized by specifically feminine "interests" and "solidarity." Although women, he argues "have little or no feeling of responsibility towards a county or a country or a career—although they may be entirely lacking in any kind of communal solidarity—they have an immense and automatically working instinct that attaches them to the interest of womanhood" (219). This same logic that associates women with empty social forms finally equates them with the worst qualities of the fallen world. By the end of the novel, then, Dowell renders Leonora the mock heroine of a sadly modern novel: "The heroine—the perfectly normal, virtuous and slightly deceitful heroine—has become the happy wife of a perfectly normal, virtuous and slightly deceitful husband" (225–26). For the normal is now understood as a thoroughly modern, degraded public realm composed entirely of the external—lacking even hidden passion—and completely devoid of value. "Her husband is quite an economical person of so normal a figure that he can get quite a large proportion of his clothes ready-made" (228).

The Good Soldier's account of female subjectivity as both troubling interiority and troubling talk will cause problems for the text, and for its definitions of narrative authority. This is particularly the case because of the way interiority and talk join in the form of feminine knowledge. The element that distinguishes women most consistently in Dowell's story is their close connection to knowledge, which unites their contradictory affiliations first with interiority and then with its destruction. Knowledge, that is, links what women hide within themselves in the first part of the novel with what they make public in the second half. In each instance women's knowledge threatens stability—whether it be the stability of a society or the stability of individual character. And the association of feminine knowledge and danger will ultimately define narration in a way that poses a problem for modernist narration—its contents as well as its expertise.

In locating knowledge as the source of women's danger, Dowell relies upon the connection between sexuality and knowledge first suggested by his invocation of the apple as a metaphor for the corruption of society ("if for nine years I have possessed a goodly apple that is rotten at the core" [14]). This association of knowledge and sexual knowledge invoked by the Edenic apple in itself suggests that women's knowledge is responsible for the fall from a paradisial society. But the novel reasserts this identification between women as the source of fallen sexuality and women as possessors of knowledge by its literal connection between adultery as a kind of sexual knowledge and knowledge more generally. Florence's secret adultery, for instance, is described euphemistically as her "knowledge." When Dowell wonders how she had time for her trysts, he says, "I don't, you understand, blame Florence. But how can she have known what she knew? How could she have time to know it? To know it so fully" (15). This same secret knowledge passes between women when they talk.[10] Dowell describes Florence's discussions with Leonora as their "tremendously long conversations full of worldly wisdom" (15). And Leonora's conversations with Nancy at Branshaw similarly pass on to

Nancy "knowledge" about Edward. Here Nancy simultaneously acquires general information (she learns what Edward is like), knowledge with a specifically sexual content (she learns about his affairs), and knowledge that is itself a form of sexuality (this information allows her to recognize her own feelings as passion for him):

> Leonora . . . appeared in [Nancy's] doorway, and told her that Edward was dying of love for her. She knew then with her conscious mind what she had known within herself for months—that Edward was dying . . . of love for her.
> . . . And it seemed to her to be in tune with the mood, with the hour, and with the woman in front of her to say that she knew Edward was dying of love for her, and that she was dying of love for Edward. For that fact had suddenly slipped into place and become real for her. (204–5)

Women's knowledge is always dangerous in the text—a danger that inheres equally in its being hidden from view and in its being passed publicly among them. Such knowledge is especially troubling because it lies at the foundation of society, and therefore may unravel society, and because, by its nature, it cannot be separated from sexuality—a separation on which civilized social order and social division here rest. When Dowell, for instance, first tries to reconcile Leonora's apparent embodiment of social ideals with her story of a failed attempt at adultery, his confusion prompts him to speculate about the unfortunate entanglement of women's knowledge, women's sexuality, and social stability:

> I don't know; I don't know; was that last remark of hers the remark of a harlot, or is it what every decent woman, county family or not county family, thinks at the bottom of her heart? Or thinks all the time for the matter of that? Who knows?
> Yet if one doesn't know that at this hour and day, at this pitch of civilization to which we have attained, after all the preachings of all the moralists, and all the teachings of all the mothers to all the daughters *in saecula saeculorum* . . . but perhaps that is what all mothers teach all daughters, not with lips but with the eyes, or with heart whispering to heart. And if one doesn't know as much as that about the first thing in the world, what does one know and why is one here? (16–17)

There is no distinction here between women's secret knowledge and knowledge that passes among them publicly; indeed a woman's secret knowledge is precisely that knowledge which is passed down to her. The threat posed by this knowledge, a threat posed equally by its secrecy, its inaccessibility from without (hidden "at the bottom of [a woman's] heart"), and by its publicity ("what all mothers teach all daughters") comes from the way it is identical to the spread of sexual knowledge.

Thus while Dowell's "civilization" relies upon "the teachings of all the mothers to all the daughters *in saecula saeculorum*" to maintain clear distinctions between a "decent woman" and a "harlot," those very teachings and their secrecy make it impossible to hold such a distinction and to maintain a social order.

The feminization of both knowledge and its circulation in *The Good Soldier* raises a broad problem for narrators and narration and draws us closer to understanding the way Ford imagined unreliable narration might work as a central strategy in the gendering of modernist fiction. The problem inheres in the premise that a traditional narrator should know what he is talking about. For if knowledge is both feminized and corrupt in this text, then the stance of a narrator who tells and implicitly should "know" his story is problematic. No longer a distant observer of the fall, a modern narrator becomes complicit with it. And no matter how emphatically Ford's novel places corrupt women at the source of an imagined modern social downfall, the text also makes such femininity the very basis for narrating a story. The formulation thus troubles the very idea of masculine narration, the idea of a modern narrative authority that might distance the feminine failings of a modern world. In the very act of narrating, the narrator must be feminized.

It is in light of this dilemma that we must read the novel's narrator Dowell and consider his rhetorical and storytelling strategies. In particular we should attend to his persistent disclaimers of knowledge. For his repeated assertion—"I don't know; I don't know. . . . Who knows? . . . if one doesn't know as much as that . . . what does one know and why is one here?" (16–17)—must prompt us to link his presentation of his own bewilderment to the depiction of a troubling female knowledge I have just been tracing. The proximity of these two sorts of "questionable" knowledge in *The Good Soldier* must cause us to return with a somewhat more cynical eye to the problem of narrative uncertainty in the text.[11]

Dowell claims that he "doesn't know" repeatedly in the novel, but the comment occurs most frequently in the opening chapter, in which he comments on the story he is about to tell and provides a context in which it may be interpreted.[12] This opening frames his story as being about a specific impossibility: that of knowing the character of "good people." "My wife and I knew Captain and Mrs Ashburnham as well as it was possible to know anybody, and yet, in another sense, we knew nothing at all about them . . . a state of things only possible with English people of whom, till today . . . I knew nothing" (11). But Dowell gradual-

ly expands his claim until it suggests the impossibility of knowing anything. He moves from the cry "I know nothing—nothing in the world—
of the hearts of men" (14), to a bewilderment about distinctions between
women ("And, if one doesn't know as much as that about the first thing
in the world, what does one know and why is one here?" [17]), until he
finally ends his first chapter with the most absolute of claims: "I don't
know. And there is nothing to guide us. . . . It is all a darkness" (18).

This assertion that he knows nothing is central to Dowell's description of himself as a character, as well as to his narrative stance. He presents himself—as a character within the story—as the consistent dupe
of his wife, and as only dimly aware, if aware at all, of what is really hap-
pening around him. For instance in the central scene in which the Dow-
ells and the Ashburnhams go to look at the Protest in M——, Dowell
offers himself as nearly blind to the implications of Florence's finger laid
upon Edward Ashburnham's wrist as she lectures them on the virtues of
the Protestant Reformation. The closest he comes to knowledge is a vague
awareness: "I was aware of something treacherous, something frightful,
something evil in the day. I can't define it and can't find a simile for it"
(46). And he presents himself as all too easily deflected by a false interpretation—false knowledge—when Leonora offers it: "'Don't you know,'
she said, in her clear hard voice, 'don't you know that I'm an Irish Cath-
olic?'" (48).

Dowell's ambiguous positioning as a narrator underlines his interest in framing himself as an innocently unaware figure within his own
story. Indeed the strategy of foregrounding his lack of knowledge makes
sense of one of the central uncertainties of narrative voice in the text.
For we should note how the ambivalence of Dowell's narrative stance in
the scene above reinforces our sense of him as unknowing—by blurring
the line between the ignorance of Dowell-as-character and his ignorance
as narrator. The narrative voice in this scene shifts its temporal place.
At one moment it comes from the later, narrating Dowell, who comments
that he "was aware of something treacherous, something frightful, something evil in the day," and makes it clear that as narrator, writing in the
present, he considers this past awareness significant because he now
knows the reality to which it actually corresponds. But in the next sentence the narrative voice has moved to the present tense: "I can't define
it and can't find a simile for it," and we can no longer say with certainty
whether it is the past or the present Dowell who does not know and cannot define. This same shift consistently structures the narrative's use of
irony, as Ann Barr Snitow has pointed out (169–70). It is often difficult

to decide whether the irony of the narrative voice—which must know more than someone in order to be ironic—belongs to the Dowell who acts, or belongs to a later, narrating Dowell commenting on his earlier lack of knowledge. The effect of this perpetual shifting is to repeatedly make Dowell's knowledge unclear as both a character and a narrator.

This uncertainty is reinforced by the narrative's method of progression, which stages gradual revelations by withholding the narrator's knowledge of central events. For instance, while the bulk of the story is told after Edward's death, after all the novel's events save Nancy's decline into madness and Leonora's marriage to Rodney Bayham, Dowell's narration reveals information only gradually, returning to scenes and revealing more, and more clearly, each time.[13] Thus when he first describes Florence's death, he depicts her lying on her bed with "a little vial that rightly should have contained nitrate of amyl, in her right hand" (96). Only after he records the scene in which Leonora tells him that Florence's death was a suicide does Dowell retell the scene in such a way as to make this suicide explicit: "She drank the little phial of prussic acid and there she lay" (113). And he does this even though, writing much later, he knows at both moments of his narration the method of Florence's death. The curious result of this gradual revelation is to place Dowell's knowledge as a narrator, as well as a character, in doubt.

Critical discussion of Dowell's ambiguous knowledge—as I will discuss further in a moment—has tended to take this uncertainty as a sign either of the character's unique pathology (an idiosyncratic neurosis prevents Dowell from knowing) or of his representative, universal status (Dowell knows so little because no one can know anything in the modern world). However the feminization of knowledge and narration in *The Good Soldier*, and its troubling implications, demand that we reframe this traditional question. So too does the fact that Dowell himself has suggested this ignorance most emphatically. We must ask instead what the lack of knowledge does for narration. Why might Dowell claim not to know? What advantages might there be in not possessing knowledge? Or, conversely, what dangers might there be in knowing?

We must, that is, link Dowell's repeated claim not to know with his depiction of the dangerous knowledge held by women, and with the risk that his inclusion in the circle of talk and of knowledge may indeed make him "like a woman or a solicitor" (24). If knowledge feminizes in *The Good Soldier*, then we may see Dowell's claims as a distancing strategy entwined with unreliable narration; they divorce him from a feminized and sexualized knowledge, and from the social disruptions it causes. The oppositions here are not knowledge versus ignorance but knowledge versus innocence. Thus Ford establishes the terms of a masculinized, authoritative narration on the ground of bewilderment and uncertainty.

And masculine narration in this text not only claims uncertainty, it claims a form of impersonality or generality. For it is crucial to note the absolute and universal terms of Dowell's denial of knowledge. He does not merely claim not to know, but rather to know nothing at all, "It is all a darkness," he says (18). And he works as well to generalize the implications of this lack, by deliberately casting himself as an exemplary Everyman, moving from "I" to "us" just as he moves from "I" to "one": "I don't know. And there is nothing to guide us . . . are we meant to act on impulse alone?" (18); "I don't know. I don't know. . . . Who knows? . . . if one doesn't know as much as that about the first thing in the world, what does one know and why is one here?" (16–17). The claim to instantiate a universal or generic innocence—in a gesture familiar from the work of Pater or Conrad or James—further distances the stance of narrative certainty from that of women who tell tales—with their specifically female, and culpable, knowledge. Dowell cannot be feminized, that is, if he is Everyman.

We must read *The Good Soldier*, then, as an exploration of the effectiveness and the limits of bewilderment and unreliability as a masculinizing narrative strategy. For the strategy does have limits in the text—and the novel is as concerned to trace and manage them as it is to imagine the advantages of masculine uncertainty. Despite his denials, Dowell risks feminization not just in knowing but in narrating—in the act of circulating knowledge precisely as female characters do. In fact Dowell's story resembles the one Leonora tells at Branshaw with such disastrous effects; it is a story about adultery, which reveals to a potentially innocent reader that the social and moral order of the modern world is not what it appears to be. It is in order to separate himself from this tainted association that Dowell attempts to found his narration on a lack of knowledge rather than on its presence, and ultimately organizes his narrative to defer any acknowledgment of his knowledge, his complicity. He maintains for as long as possible the impression that he is an unknowing, and therefore innocent, observer of events.[14] This is the logic that governs the novel's delayed final presentation of Edward Ashburnham's suicide. For though Dowell introduces the fact of this suicide early in his last installment of writing, he does not narrate this death until the final paragraphs of the book, and he does so apparently as a sort of afterthought: "It suddenly occurs to me that I have forgotten to say how Edward met his death" (228).[15] What this episode reveals most clearly is Dowell's knowledge. Aware that Edward intends to cut his throat, Dowell becomes openly complicit, openly a participant, in the collapsing world he claims only to describe from a bewildered distance. His action in the scene— carrying a telegram from Nancy to Leonora—inscribes him visibly in the very circulation of feminized talk and feminized knowledge that he holds responsible for the breakdown of character.

> A stable-boy brought [Edward] a telegram and went away. He opened it negligently, regarded it without emotion, and, in complete silence, hand- ed it to me.... I read: "Safe Brindisi. Having rattling good time. Nan- cy."... Then he put two fingers into the waistcoat pocket of his grey, frieze suit; they came out with a little neat pen-knife.... "You might just take that wire to Leonora." And he looked at me with a direct, chal- lenging, brow-beating glare. I guess he could see in my eyes that I didn't intend to hinder him. Why should I hinder him?... I trotted off with the telegram to Leonora. She was quite pleased with it. (229)

This final scene closes down the narrative of *The Good Soldier.* The terms Dowell has set out for it—his own innocent detachment—suggest that with such a scene, the story must inevitably end. Paradoxically, in the novel's terms, narration is only possible and a narrator only has author- ity as long as he can claim not to know what he is saying.

Thus far my discussion of *The Good Soldier* has stayed within the frame of the novel's fictive world. I have asked questions about the rela- tion of interiority, femininity, and knowledge as the novel constructs them as problems for its characters. But narrative knowledge, indeed the problem of secret interiors and narrative reliability more generally, must be addressed as a broader question shaping the text and shaping Ford's ideas about modern fiction and its authority. Not only must we ask what the refusal of knowledge does for a character's narrating authority, for the construction of a figure of masculine authority within the text, but we must also consider how problems of gender and narration structure the text itself, and thus structure modernism's aesthetic and political claims. Ford's use of a potentially secretive, unreliable narrator shapes the way his text defines modernism, and the way it negotiates the gendered di- lemma informing such a definition.

The question of whether *The Good Soldier*'s narrator is indeed un- reliable, and if so how and to what effect, has shaped the history of the text's reception. Discussions of Dowell's role and his reliability have been contentious, repetitive, and inconclusive.[16] The central issue debated, of course, has been whether or not Dowell should be trusted by the reader, but this question itself inevitably takes up other questions and values which play a part in making reliability or its lack sympathetic to a reader. In judging Dowell's accuracy, critics have passed judgment on passion, on social conventions, and on definitions of character. For instance, in 1951 Mark Schorer influentially condemned Dowell in an essay widely circulated as the introduction to the Vintage edition of the novel; this reading attributes Dowell's unreliability to his lack of the unconventional passion Schorer finds ennobling. In contrast readers such as Samuel Hynes ("Epistemology") and Paul Armstrong (*Challenge* 189–224) find Dowell's very lack of knowledge sympathetic because they take the narrator as an exemplar of a universal predicament—in Hynes's terms: "the difficulties which man's nature and the world's put in the way of his will to know" (53). Critics like Arthur Mizener have read Dowell as a fairly reliable source of knowledge, a character who shares Ford's sympathies and whose limitations are offset by his attempt to balance the legitimate values of both civility and emotion (255–77). The debate cannot be satisfactorily concluded—in part because observations on either side of the debate are accurate and in part because, as Snitow points out, "to take a final view of [Dowell] obscures the effect Ford has labored to produce," in which the standards of judgment shift constantly (165).[17]

While the question of narrative unreliability is unavoidable in this text, I would argue that its importance lies elsewhere. We must look, that is, at the figuration and effect of potentially unreliable narration and consider the way Ford's decision to employ a narrator whose motives are imagined as lying hidden within him, a narrator whose accuracy cannot be wholly known, contributes to a historically specific formulation of modernist authorship and authority. For it is striking that in using such a narrative strategy, *The Good Soldier* itself takes up the ambivalent stance toward knowledge, storytelling, and gender we have seen presented within the novel. Simply put, in making Dowell potentially unreliable, Ford has distanced himself from his narrator, by producing the effect of a gap between Dowell's storytelling and his own authorial stance. If the novel is read in light of the feminization of subjectivity, of narrative, and of knowledge shaping the text and indeed impressionism more generally, we may note that this authorial distance works to separate Ford from the femininity inevitably shadowing Dowell's narration. Dowell's unreliability, that is, has a double effect on *The Good Soldier:* On the one hand it is the mark of his feminization; to the extent that Dowell masks a secret knowledge and complicity he is feminized as both a knower and storyteller, and he becomes a quintessentially modern, fallen narrator in the novel's terms. He seems as rootless and deceitful as any of the female characters he describes, part of the social decay he records. But on the other hand, the same unreliability that feminizes Dowell ensures and makes visible the distance between the narrator's voice and the author's; it saves the novel-writing Ford from the feminization that plagues the storytelling Dowell.

Such risks of narrative clearly haunted Ford during much of his career and shaped his attempts to define a distinctly modern, indeed a masculinized, literary movement. Writing frequently and self-consciously about the goals and methods of modern literature, Ford felt himself to be in a troubling proximity to a preceding generation of writers—a generation whose authorial stance he personified in the paradigm of the Victorian "great figure" in his essay "The Passing of the Great Figure."[18] Such great figures (Carlyle, Arnold, Browning, Ruskin among them) seemed in many ways admirable to Ford; they stood opposed to the narrow specialization of contemporary writers of social commentary. But he also presents them as haunting his childhood in *Memories and Impressions:* "To me life was simply not worth living because of the existence of Carlyle, of Mr. Ruskin, of Mr. Holman Hunt. . . . These people were perpetually held up to me as standing upon unattainable heights, and at the same time I was perpetually being told that if I could not attain these heights I might just as well not cumber the earth" (qtd. in Levenson, *Genealogy* 56). It is a haunting that seems not to have ceased, driving Ford repeatedly to distinguish his own, modern literature from that of his Victorian predecessors.

Ford characteristically finds these Victorian "great figures" most objectionable in what he sees as their penchant for moralizing and for prophecy, for entering into their writing and voicing personal opinions. This combination of propaganda and the personal—the desire "to get . . . something off the chest"—stands opposed to the impersonality of modern art that impressionism may provide ("On Impressionism, II" 334). The distinction is weighted with familiar gendered associations for Ford, as it was for many early twentieth-century writers attempting to disclaim a nineteenth-century literary tradition. In this context it is particularly significant that when Ford turns to write his essay "English Literature of Today—I," the writer he chooses to embody the dangers of this Victorian great figure is George Eliot.[19] Eliot in this essay becomes the target of Ford's scornful criticism, and the terms of this criticism are now gendered feminine; Ford thus links his anxiety about great figures with the language of feminized knowledge and narration set out in *The Good Soldier.*

Ford frames this essay, not as a contrast between an old generation of writers and a new, but between "the writer of the commercial book and the writer of a book which shall be a work of art" (55). With the distinction between art and the market in place, he begins to sketch the reasons for Eliot's failure: "George Eliot was in fact, a great figure. She was great enough to impose herself on her day. . . . She desired that is to say, to be an influence; she cared in her heart very little whether or no she would be considered an artist" (56). Eliot's failure as an artist is due to her desire for influence; this desire leads her to place herself in her art by moralizing, leads her to insert "her endless comments upon Victorian philosophy" into her writing (57). By contrast, Ford considers that Trollope, though less great, may be considered more truly an artist because he obeys the precepts of art; he is "content to observe and to record" (56). Trollope thus attends to the business of the writer as Ford will define it in the second part of this essay on modern writing: "to register a truth of life as he sees it," and thus provides a proper model for "English literature of to-day" (102).

Ford thus defines Art as that text which is not overly close to the writer's self, as writing which—although it is based in an author's view of the world—nevertheless stands at a distance because it does not suffer from the intrusions of writerly personality or opinion. "It is for this reason," he writes in "On the Function of the Arts in the Republic," "that the work of a really fine renderer of the life of his day is of such great value to the Republic. For whatever his private views may be, we have no means of knowing them. He himself will never appear, he will never buttonhole us, he will never moralize" (33).

By placing this intrusion of the subject, this overly close relation between writer and work, under the sign of "George Eliot," Ford has predictably feminized the figure of the writer who enters too closely into her work, and feminized it too in terms of the knowledge she claims and the knowledge she transmits to us. This feminine writer has "private views" about the world she depicts, and she communicates them to us by moralizing. The artist who avoids this pitfall does so by "rendering" impersonally; far from possessing knowledge, he merely records what he innocently sees around him. Ford's distancing of himself from his narrator John Dowell thus echoes, paradoxically, Dowell's own distancing strategy. Each tells a story which he claims is something other than "his" story; each claims this distance by focusing attention on the unreliability of those feminized others who are given the burden of knowledge. But if the opposition Ford proposes—between feminine figures who possess secrets as well as relate them and the heroic modernist masters of impersonality who observe at a distance, moving freely apart from their texts—sounds too familiar, we need to recall the formulations of writing and knowing that anchor and unravel the divide. Ford's opposition attempts to distance masculine narration in the face of a definition of narrative that renders such distance impossible. The feminized, interiorized, knowing subject *is* the narrating subject for Ford. And he defines modern narration, just as he defines the paradigmatically modern subject, as implicitly feminine. The tale narrated in *The Good Soldier* is a tale feminized by his own account—a story of mysterious hidden motives, of secret interiors, of sexual knowledge and a social fall. To narrate modern fiction, to be a modern subject, is to be feminine; the gesture of masculinizing distance—as we may see with the novel's narrator—can never move the subject far enough.

5 Pilgrimage: *A Woman's Place*

In turning from the work of Conrad and Ford to that of Dorothy Richardson, I turn from versions of modernist impressionism in which the shaping influence of feminine subjectivity is often evaded or denied to a feminist modernism that explicitly grounds narrative in the powers of modern women. Indeed Richardson's work has been important to recent feminist writing about modernism for precisely this reason. Critics often turn to her texts to imagine an alternative female-authored and feminist modernism, one that may offer more progressive accounts of feminine subjectivity and literary experiment in the period and thus provide an alternative to the masculine canon (E. Friedman, "'Utterly Other Discourse'"; Hanscombe, "Dorothy Richardson versus the Novle"). Richardson's work is in many ways ideal for such critical revisions; she herself saw her writing as an alternative to contemporary masculine fiction, and she offers definitions of modernist literary experiment and authority that ground them without ambivalence in the modern feminine subject.

Richardson's work is similarly important to my account of modernism here, although for different reasons. Her explicit redefinition of impressionist experiment through feminine subjectivity extends the trajectory of fiction I have been exploring, by linking the narratives of modern women to the problems of interiority and narrative form. However I will be suggesting here that Richardson also allows us to reread the oppositions structuring our ideas about modernism—and to reread some of the tropes by which feminist criticism of modernism has framed the feminine subject. In particular Richardson's complex figuration of modern woman as simultaneously foreign to her culture and as its ultimate embodiment—a figure never fully at home, yet at home everywhere—may complicate the way the category of marginality works. Without wishing to ignore the powerful ways that the institutional canonization of modernism has relegated Richardson's work to the movement's margins, I read her experiments as in fact central to modernism rather than as opposed to it, and her feminine subject as a figure as authoritative as she is marginal. For as I have been suggesting, a coherent set of ideas about femininity centers modernist impressionism in its many incarnations; when Richardson imagines feminine subjects as characteristic modern subjects, she theorizes a relation that is far from eccentric. Further, Richardson will importantly elaborate the idea of femininity's productive doubleness that we have begun to trace in the period—the notion of woman as both socially formed and autonomous, historically specific and universal, outsider and ultimate source of cultural authority. Richardson's feminist modernism thus lets us read femininity and modernism less as divided categories than as categories that share central historical and formal tensions and generate related definitions of cultural authority.

Richardson's questions clearly stand at the center of impressionist literary experiment, and at the center of the discussions of subjectivity, gender, narrative distance, and abstraction that I have framed thus far. Her writing proposes woman as the exemplary modern subject—the figure through whom long-standing debates over subjectivity are played out and through whom the ideological contradictions of the enlightenment subject become acute, even as they receive imagined aesthetic resolutions. *Pilgrimage*, Richardson's extended impressionist narrative of such a subject, centers on the question of whether the female subject is open to and shaped by the details of the world around her, perpetually malleable, or whether she collects such impressions into an interior and stable self. In meditating upon feminine subjectivity, Richardson addresses the persistent problem of whether subjects are socially detailed, formed by local and historically specific contexts, or whether they stand apart from such details, inhabiting instead a realm of abstracted and permanent truth.

In *Pilgrimage* the exemplary subject is not simply a woman but an explicitly modern woman. And this modern woman is defined for Richardson by her social mobility. No longer confined within the single context of the home, the female subject centering *Pilgrimage* works and lives independently in the city, and the novel envisions her as moving among a series of public spaces. In turning to the mobile feminine subject to establish the modern novel's authority, Richardson not only adapts on-

going cultural claims about intrinsic female difference, she simultaneously offers a reading of middle-class women's new social position at the turn
of the century. This newly mobile, newly public female figure sets the
terms in which Richardson frames characteristic impressionist questions
about the subject and about narrative. For as this figure circulates through
different social spaces in *Pilgrimage,* she raises the question of how fully she is formed by her immersion in any particular place. Furthermore,
female mobility will equally shape the way the novel reimagines familiar modernist questions about narrative distance. If the modern woman
moves from one context to another and is shaped by each in turn, can
she acquire any distance from these historically specific settings and from
her construction by them? And if the modernist novel inhabits the view
of such a radically shifting and contextually formed character, can the
novel itself be imagined as standing apart from the characters, social settings, and cultural discourses it articulates?

For Richardson, the female subject who circulates between contexts
and spaces can anchor the innovations of modernism because she does
not merely raise the problem of historical immersion versus subjective
distance, of the subject's specificity versus its universality; she also offers the privileged terms that might resolve the tension and confer literary authority on the modern novel. Richardson's female subject—in her
very circulation—promises a subjectivity with a new relation to social
spaces, simultaneously within and abstracted out of historical contexts.
In doing so, she gives Richardson a vehicle for imagining literary texts
anchored in modern female subjectivity as themselves reconciling an
immersion in social contexts with distance from them. Here modern
woman's mobility offers a form of that privileging ambiguity we have seen
in modernist claims for cultural agency stretching back to Pater's child-
aesthete. The ambiguous female subject, both public and private, socially formed and yet free, local and yet universal, grounds claims for modernist literature as similarly mobile and enigmatic, similarly double.
Richardson thus clarifies the way the feminine subject offers a basis for
modernist abstraction as much as she may resist it.

In this gesture, Richardson's texts let us consider the connections
between femininity and modernism's famous appeal to great literature's
international status. As I have begun to suggest, mobility is central to
this account of both feminine subject and text; through this term we may
link Richardson's argument about explicitly feminized narrative with
modernist claims to make an art that, like women, is tied to its place and
yet may transcend any location. Committed to reconciling place and
displacement in the figure of the feminized text, Richardson's work thus

brings into sharper focus a strand of cultural argument threaded throughout impressionism, and throughout this study. It shows how the modern female subject may provide access to ideologies of international or universal modernism; but her work also makes clear the way modernism renders such internationalism compatible with ideals of national identity. Like Ford, Pater, and many of the other writers I have read, Richardson connects the possibility of an interior self to the dream of a stable English identity. In defining what makes a subject English, Richardson simultaneously attempts to imagine what might make the English subject universal. In doing so she asks an analogous question: what might allow a modernist text to be both nationally placed and internationally mobile? This question, so crucial to definitions of modernist literary authority, devolves in Richardson onto a female subject who alone promises the ground for a literary experiment that can join the national and the international. If the feminine subject allows Richardson to imagine a modern novel that can summon place and rise above it, this subject will also allow English feminine identity to become the precondition for a fully European experimental art.

Richardson defined the goal of her lifelong fictional project—the multivolume stream-of-consciousness novel *Pilgrimage*—as the revision of the modern novel: the rewriting of the feminine subject in the name of a greater realism. This change of modern fiction's object and its methods and this redefinition of subjectivity emerge through the novel's famously expansive narrative experiment, which details the impressions, thoughts, and responses of its female protagonist, Miriam Henderson, as she moves from setting to setting, job to job, and year to year. The impressive scope of Richardson's goal is matched by the scope of the novel she produced: The first volume of *Pilgrimage* appeared in 1915; the thirteenth, published posthumously, was still in progress at the time of Richardson's death in 1957, leaving its protagonist's fate unresolved—quite possibly deliberately. For Richardson, this extended and more accurate rewriting of subjectivity required attending to what conventional novels overlooked, attending to everything "preceding and accompanying and surviving the drama of human relationships; the reality from which people move away as soon as they closely approach and expect each other to be all in all" (4:525).[1] As she put it in the 1938 foreword to the collected edition of the first twelve volumes, when she first attempted to write a conventional novel about a young woman she instead became "aware . . . of the gradual falling away of the preoccupations that for a while had dictated the briskly moving script, and of the substitution . . . of a stranger in the form of contemplated reality having for the first time in her experience its own say and apparently justifying those who acclaim writing as the surest means of discovering the truth about one's own thoughts and beliefs" (1:10).

As critics have long noted and as Richardson often stressed, this narrative experiment in giving an ignored "reality" "its own say" grew from Richardson's belief in the difference of feminine subjectivity.[2] It is the unique nature of female subjectivity for her which may generate the new form of fiction, which demands narrative revision, demands a "feminine equivalent of the current masculine realism" to rework explicitly masculine conventions of novel-writing (1:9). Thus when *Pilgrimage*'s protagonist criticizes conventional novels and their methods, she categorizes them as masculine. "'The torment of *all* novels is what is left out,'" Miriam says to Hypo Wilson, the text's stand-in for H. G. Wells. "'The moment you are aware of it, there is torment in them. Bang, bang, bang, on they go, these men's books, like an L. C. C. tram, yet unable to make you forget them, the authors, for a moment'" (4:239). For *Pilgrimage*—which narrates what Miriam sees, thinks, and feels—the female subject offers the privileged ground for an anti-conventional modernist narrative and a new reading of subjectivity. Richardson's desire to see what is "left out" of conventional novels—what "preced[es]" or "surviv[es]" the drama of human relationships"—links the idea of an untold feminine narrative to the question of whether and how the subject exceeds relationship. She thus explicitly makes feminine difference central to modernist debates about how far the subject is formed by its relationship to the external world, how fully it is constructed by perceptions and interactions, or whether it may instead stand autonomously beyond them.

The female subject provokes such questions because Richardson imagines her as uniquely outside the categories of rational, developmental, or argumentative analysis. This opposition of woman and reason renders her a productively confounding enigma in Richardson's view, and locates her power in a merging of incompatible models of subjectivity.[3] As Richardson proposes in a 1924 *Vanity Fair* article, "Women and the Future,"

> the essential characteristic of women is egoism. . . . For the womanly-woman lives, all her life, in the deep current of eternity, an individual, self-centered. Because she is one with life, past, present, and future are together in her, unbroken. Because she thinks flowingly, with her feelings, she is relatively indifferent to the fashions of men, to the momentary arts, religions, philosophies, and sciences. . . . Only a complete self,

carrying all its goods in its own hands, can go out, perfectly, to others, move freely in any direction. Only a complete self can afford to man the amusing spectacle of the chameleon woman. (412–13)

The woman of this passage may sound familiar from a range of modernist and proto-modernist texts we have already examined. Not only does she oppose instrumental reason with enigmatic mystery but this enigmatic nature is imagined as her ability to reconcile two opposed models of subjectivity. Woman is an egoist, self-absorbed and self-contained, but this very self-completion allows her to reach out to others. An ever-changing chameleon, she is nevertheless unchanging and indifferent to fashion; a spectacle for men, she is yet autonomous, with all her goods in her own hands.

Pilgrimage will take the familiar woman of this passage—egoistically whole yet responsive to others—as a ground for its claims about modern woman's immense cultural importance. Within the novel, Miriam Henderson argues that such a woman exemplifies the power of the individual to resist the constraints of evolutionary determinism. Freed from social forms because she occupies a sphere of "being" rather than "becoming" (4:362), her "'emancipat[ion]'" allows her to create art, "'the art of making atmospheres'" (3:257).[4] The novel itself casts Miriam as just such a figure joining apparently incompatible models of subjectivity, for she is both shaped in response to the details of her world and stands apart from them. If in the course of the text Miriam is narratively formed and reformed by the world around her as a "chameleon woman," a permeable, ever-changing subject whose discontinuities mock our desire for her essence—a "myriad-I-am," as Heath (128) and Radford (*Dorothy Richardson* 61) have noted—the novel nonetheless also imagines her as a "complete self" continuing beneath the surface of the world, standing apart and resisting its coercive force.[5] And the text envisions Miriam's cultural potential in precisely the ability to mediate between these two modes of subjectivity; it will stake its own power, its modernity and its access to what it claims as a deeper truth, on the narrative ability to encompass this female subject.

This doubleness of feminine subjectivity in *Pilgrimage* is linked to the tension between two aspects of Miriam's experience: her immersion in a flux of socially anchored, historically particularized events and impressions, and her repeated turn to an alternate register of epiphany—a register she associates with the "real" and which she claims as the expanding core of her continuing identity. The relation between these two modes of being forms the central problematic for the novel's claim to power, for its reimagination of character, and for its innovative narrative

construction. Because these registers arise through *Pilgrimage's* characteristic narrative technique—the text's presentation wholly through
Miriam's views of the shifting scene around her—it is worth pausing for
a moment to consider a passage and the implications of its method.

The following passage from the opening volume, *Pointed Roofs*, concludes an account of Miriam's visit to a confectioner's with her students
while she is teaching in Germany. Surveying the scene with a pleased
sense of being abroad, freed from home, Miriam observes the German
women around her:

> Orders for *Schokolade* were heard from all over the room. There were
> only women there—wonderful German women in twos and threes—la-
> dies out shopping, Miriam supposed. She managed intermittently to
> watch three or four of them and wondered what kind of conversation
> made them so emphatic—whether it was because they held themselves
> so well and "spoke out" that everything they said seemed so important.
> She had never seen women with so much decision in their bearing. She
> found herself drawing herself up.
>
> She heard German laughter about the room. The sounds excited her and
> she watched eagerly for laughing faces. . . . They were different. . . . The
> laughter sounded differently and the laughing faces were different. The
> eyes were expressionless as they laughed—or evil . . . they had that same
> knowing way of laughing as though everything were settled—but they did
> not pretend to be refined as Englishwomen did . . . they had the same hor-
> ridness . . . but they were . . . jolly. . . . They could shout if they liked.
>
> Three cups of thick-looking chocolate, each supporting a little hillock
> of solid cream arrived at her table. Clara ordered cakes.
>
> At the first sip, taken with lips that slid helplessly on the surprisingly
> thick rim of her cup, Miriam renounced all the beverages she had ever
> known as unworthy.
>
> She chose a familiar looking *éclair*—Clara and Emma ate cakes that
> seemed to be alternate slices of cream and very spongy coffee-coloured
> cake and then followed Emma's lead with an open tartlet on which plump
> green gooseberries stood in a thick brown syrup. (1:88–89)[6]

The passage offers Miriam's observations and responses: her view of
the German women, her admiration, emulation, and then her excited
horror of them, and her refocusing upon the sensations of cup and cocoa
and the colors and textures of pastry. Through this sequence the passage
registers several of Miriam's most important, recurrent concerns in *Pointed Roofs:* her linked fascination with and repulsion at patterns of female
behavior and her desire to emulate and rebel against them; an interest in
national categories as a way of imagining her relation to these possible
identities (perhaps German womanhood provides options English womanhood doesn't; perhaps she might grow up to be a German woman); and

a related concern with middle-class refinement and its alternatives—whether "jolly" or vulgar. Finally the text raises the problem of the connection between these issues and the juxtaposed sensations of eating or looking at food and the materiality of the food itself. These sensations seem to contrast social questions about femininity with the material substance of cake and cocoa, proposing a register of sheer elemental being which resonates throughout the novel in Miriam's concern with the miracle that things exist at all (Powys 34). "What is much more astonishing than things behaving after their manner," she comments much later, "is that there should be anything anywhere to behave. Why does this pass unnoticed?" (4:455). The divide is uncertain here, however; for sensation also reincorporates the scene's preceding social questions about agency, desire, and propriety in Miriam's helplessly sliding lips and the uncertain refinement, the discordant sensory appeal of "plump green gooseberries" in "thick brown syrup."

The passage may clarify the way the novel's protagonist shifts from an immersion in her surroundings to a potential distance from them, and between a world of concrete social details to one of timeless and essential qualities. Here as throughout the novel, *Pilgrimage* offers us a character formed through her impressions, through the particular scene she sees and her responses to it. Not that Miriam is a blank slate—she is already marked by presumptions that shape her view and derive from earlier contexts (particularly from her girlhood in a genteel, intellectually advanced household and school). But the text constantly reconstructs her in reaction to her surroundings. Further, because *Pilgrimage* offers the continuing narrative of Miriam's life as a ceaseless flow of such impressions and responses, unshaped by an overview, it renders Miriam a constantly particularized and unsettled subject, endlessly reformed by the accumulating details of each successive social milieu. The opening volume, for instance, registers her reaction to the family's sudden loss of upper-middle-class security and status and to the German school where she then must teach. This school in turn frames her in a charged atmosphere whose rules and erotic attachments embody clashing, class-inflected views of female propriety and aestheticized purity. *Pilgrimage's* subsequent volumes will present Miriam through no less specified environments, from a provincially genteel North London suburban school to a wealthy household, from a professional dentist's office through London's radical intellectual and political circles, and the religious community of a Quaker farm.

But the tension visible within the passage I have been discussing—between Miriam's culturally marked responses to German women and her sensory encounter with material objects, however unstably the latter realm is distinguished—points to an impulse in *Pilgrimage* at odds with its commitment to the shifting determinations of social specificity. The text clarifies in Miriam and its own structure a desire for a plane of being that transcends cultural place, and it thus provides the female subject with an enabling distance from the social world. In *Pointed Roofs*, for example, German high culture and especially German music point beyond national specificity to something more: they are local traditions alien to English culture and yet offer Miriam access to something both internal and transcendent. When she hears German students play, the music can summon a mysterious vision of a mill-wheel from her English childhood: "she saw, slowly circling [. . .] a weed-grown mill-wheel. . . . She recognized it instantly. She had seen it somewhere as a child—in Devonshire—and never thought of it since—and there it was. [. . .] Her heart filled. [. . .] She pulled herself together, and for a while saw only a vague radiance in the room and the dim forms grouped about" (1:44). This same music, in another ecstatic moment, lifts her above the details of her life entirely. "Miriam, her fatigue forgotten, slid to a featureless freedom. It seemed to her that the light with which the room was filled grew brighter and clearer. She felt that she was looking at nothing and yet was aware of the whole room like a picture in a dream. [. . .] It came from everywhere. It carried her out of the house, out of the world" (1:43).

The novel thus associates Miriam's epiphanies with an abstract world in which she acquires distance from the specific social terms of her life. This sort of epiphanic access to "featureless freedom" recurs increasingly often in *Pilgrimage*. As Miriam immerses herself in the city, returns from office work to the attic room where she writes, or later recalls her childhood in a garden or encounters Quaker silence, she enters a space distinct from the detailed world. As she walks in London, the specificities of the city give way to abstraction through the shape and substance of paving stones. Miriam muses on the "flags of pavement flowing—smooth clean grey squares and oblongs, faintly polished, shaping and drawing away—sliding into each other. . . . I am part of the dense smooth clean paving stone . . . sunlit; gleaming under the dark winter rain; shining under warm sunlit rain, sending up a fresh stony smell . . . always there . . . dark and light [. . .] Life streamed up from the close dense stone. With every footstep she felt she could fly" (1:416). In the course of *Pilgrimage* Miriam becomes increasingly attuned to this register of sheer unmarked "life" and the placeless freedom of flight; she associates it with an internal voyage (S. Rose; Gevirtz 118; Radford, *Dorothy Richardson*). At a Quaker meeting near the novel's end, for instance, she aligns their commitment to silence with the epiphanic abstraction she increasingly finds within herself: "she felt herself once more at work, in company, upon an all important enterprise [. . .] the labour of journeying, down through the layers of her surface being, a familiar process. Down and down through a series of circles each wider than the last [. . .] nearer to the living centre" (4:498).

Thus the register of epiphany links abstraction and subjective distance with the image of a subject who powerfully possesses an interior— one who is not wholly formed by her contexts. Such moments will reshape the novel's reading of character, by offering an alternate account of the nature and source of Miriam's subjectivity. These privileged moments suggest to Miriam that she possesses a core identity beneath the surface of her daily life; they cast doubt on the status of the subject constructed by a flux of detail. In such moments social interactions and categories seem to constrict rather than produce her. Waking to one such moment early on, she "felt that her short sleep [. . .] had carried her down and down into the heart of tranquillity where she still lay awake, and drinking as if at a source. [. . .] 'It's me,' she said, and smiled. [. . .] She wanted to have the whole world in and be reconciled. But she knew that if any one came, she would contract and the expression of her face would change [. . .] She knew that if she even moved she would be changed" (1:149–50).

We should note that these epiphanic moments do not consolidate a conventionally unified subject; they do not, that is, create Miriam as an autonomous and unique individual. Instead they propose a subjectivity whose identity emerges from its contact with broader universal forces. Miriam describes one such moment, for instance, as filling her with an "impersonal joy" at emotions "that seemed at once the inmost essence of her being and yet not herself; but [rather] something that through her, and in unaccustomed words, was addressing the self she knew" (4:281).[7] But these moments nonetheless importantly supply *Pilgrimage* with a register in which the subject may be distinguished from a socially detailed world and given a kind of coherence. For the subject's permeation by abstract qualities reveals them here as something already internal. Miriam speculates at one point that "all the things of the mind that had come her way had come unsought; yet finding her prepared; so that they seemed not only her rightful property, but also in some way, herself" (3:236).

In Miriam's arguments as in Richardson's, this doubleness of the subject will be marked as a feminine characteristic. The ability to reconcile permeability with forms of interiority, to find the abstract self in the socially specified one provides the feminine subject with an enabling distance from false social forms. It also allows feminist impressionism in Richardson to become at moments compatible with a rhetoric of the individual, as women oppose the pressures of social and species determinism both as social critics and as free, untrammeled selves. (Recall Richardson's comment in "Woman and the Future" that "the womanly-woman lives, all her life, in the deep current of eternity, an individual, self-centered.")

The recurrence of epiphanic moments by the novel's late chapters also promises a potential narrative continuity for the feminine subject, one that complicates the character endlessly remade by the flux of detailed impressions. Miriam can thus unite her present self with its distant past when, instead of seeing in the mirror "her image entangled with a thousand undetachable associations, she saw only her solitary self, there had come that all-transfiguring moment during which in the depth of her being she had parted company with that [other] self, masquerading under various guises, with whom she had gone about ever since leaving home, and joined company with the self she had known long ago" (4:407). We can see this continuity as *Pilgrimage* evokes a growing artistic vocation for its protagonist and places this vocation against the social world it threatens to reduce to "wreckage" (4:299). Even the novel's final shift toward reconstructing the possibility of human relationship extends this abstracted narrative by repositioning others within the transcendent zone, so that Miriam may communicate with "the unlocated being of these people [. . .] and not at all with the sight and sound of their busy momentary selves" (4:141).[8]

The novel's fascination with feminine subjectivity, with the question of whether it has an internal essence to be recovered or is instead wholly contextual, thus links a debate about how the modern female subject occupies place with a familiar debate in modernist fiction about the power of abstraction. As critics have noted, *Pilgrimage* sustains a well-developed critique of abstraction in Miriam's arguments against masculine philosophical and narrative generalization (Felber 103; Radford, *Dorothy Richardson* 17–19). I would argue, however, that *Pilgrimage* is centrally committed to joining abstracting models of the subject with localizing ones—and joining them precisely in modern female subjectivity. For in reading the novel we must register Miriam's frequent assertions of the power of the local. She posits a greater truth in stories which offer "the little real everyday things that give you an idea of anything" (1:265); she attempts to make Hypo "aware of the reality that fell, all the time, in the surrounding silence, outside his shapes and classifications" (3:360); and by novel's end she has ready to hand a "useful indictment of the limitations of [masculine] abstract reasoning" and the way they raise "a demand for feminine thinking" (4:378). But we need also note that Miriam herself is not averse to generalization, which she describes at one point as potentially the deep, informing "shape of truth." After a lecture, countering the complaint that "'large speculations are most-fatiguing,'" she claims that "'when you see truth in them they are refreshing. They are all there is. All I live for now, is the arrival in my mind, of fresh generalization. [. . .] What does it matter what they cost? A shape of truth makes you at the moment want to die, full of gratitude and happiness'" (3:235). And her speculations throughout the novel draw her repeatedly to the question of what general patterns of behavior motivate the specific details we can observe. (Thus, for instance, she theorizes to Hypo and Alma about how the desire for authority lies behind a range of particular class-based speech patterns [4:163–63].) *Pilgrimage*, then, cannot be read as a straightforward critique of abstraction, for it is persistently drawn to balancing local and generalizing accounts, to grounding character in specific places while claiming the privileged view possible from the abstract depths of the self.

But before we go on to explore further how this doubled view of character and plot are tied to the position of modern woman in Richardson's text, we should pause first to note how fully the narrative method of *Pilgrimage* helps construct this dilemma of generality or specificity. For the text's experiment with stream-of-consciousness perspective incorporates the subject's specificity or abstraction as a problem made both crucial and undecidable by narrative distance. As critics have noted, the novel's presentation of all events through Miriam's view renders the relation between the narrator's and protagonist's voice uncertain and thus constantly foregrounds it (Radford, *Dorothy Richardson* 68–70).[9] But unlike James's use of a central consciousness in *What Maisie Knew*, for instance, which required a clearly distanced narrator to register its character's limited if privileged view, *Pilgrimage* plays on the ambiguous distance, if any, between what the narrative endorses and what its protagonist asserts. The problem does not derive simply from the novel's autobiographical basis, the patterning of Miriam's jobs, friends, and lovers on Richardson's own life. Nor does it derive simply from the overlap between Richardson's essays and Miriam's views—their similar commentaries on feminine aesthetics, for instance, which have often led critics to read Dorothy Richardson and Miriam Henderson as one. The ambiguity also arises from the novel's use of point-of-view narration. For the text's narrative restriction to Miriam's responses installs distance as an active problem: we can consistently assume neither proximity nor disjunction between novel and character, even as we must constantly consider their relation.

At times *Pilgrimage* signals ironic detachment clearly. Early on the text uses Miriam's overemphases to indicate her immaturity or snobbery. Thus when early in *Pointed Roofs* Miriam worries about whether she knows enough to teach her students, she adopts a tone of self-reassurance and an attitude toward cultural authority which the text marks as an aspect of her character it does not share. The novel distances its view from Miriam's own by juxtaposing her assertions with her earlier uncertainty, and by using an ironizing internal repetition: "But she had no provincialisms, no Londonisms [Miriam thinks to herself]—she could be the purest Oxford English. There was something at any rate to give her German girls. . . . . She could say: 'There are no rules of English pronunciation, but what is usual at the University of Oxford is decisive for cultured people'—'decisive for cultured people.' She must remember that for the class" (1:48).[10] This clarity is unusual, however; *Pilgrimage* offers few such signs. We cannot know whether Miriam's contradictory opinions, for instance, invite us to read the text or the character as contradictory. Nor can we know whether such contradictions even mark a character's inconsistency as an individual symptom or sign of social placement, given the text's apparently straightforward commitment to the contradictory nature of the real. For here we might note Miriam's comment, rereading Emerson, on the "increased power of the contrasted adjectives" (4:533), or her own frequent pairings of incompatible adjectives to describe the world (Blake 162).

One important effect of this ambiguous narrative distance is to intensify the question of Miriam's specificity or generality as a character. For a narrative voice separated from Miriam's point of view frames her as a character with specific borders, limited views, a character shaped by social place among other factors. Narrative distance, for instance, encourages us to read Miriam's praise of Oxford English as the class-bound belief of a genteel English girl anxious about her loss of cultural status. In this reading she fully inhabits that world of social detail and category in which the novel's flux immerses her; her central thoughts appear as responses to rather than as distance from such forces. In contrast, the narrator's lack of clearly signaled distance from Miriam's later views—on women's freedom from masculine convention, on the superiority of London to the suburbs, on the limits of radical intellectual circles—may suggest that Miriam voices an opinion the text considers broader, more general; it suggests that her responses are not wholly circumscribed by her social location and join with the views of a narrator otherwise distinct from her.

The structural uncertainty about the generality of Miriam's character which I have been tracing so far underlines the novel's characteristically modernist concern with the ways subjectivity may escape, exceed, or remain immersed in particular contexts. And as I have begun to suggest, for Richardson feminine subjectivity, most crucially the subjectivity of modern women, provides the central ground for this question and for its cultural as well as its narrative implications. *Pilgrimage* will claim that modern women change the way we think about the subject precisely because they inhabit place differently. And in its presentation of potential models by which they might do so, the novel attempts to imagine modern female mobility—and in particular the movement of modern Englishwomen—as reconciling the claims of abstraction and interior identity with those of impressionist permeability.

In doing so, the novel—recalling the texts of the New Woman in the 1890s—transforms nineteenth-century claims about the power of women as domestic subjects into assertions about their power, as modern ones, precisely to leave home. We should note the way *Pilgrimage* at moments associates the ability to stand above cultural constraints with an older model of feminine domesticity. For instance, partly altering her early association of traditional homebound women with false social convention, Miriam (as we have seen) comes in the course of the text to praise domestic women for their potential social autonomy. She sees in their genius for creating "atmospheres" a lack of subjugation, an independence from masculine logic. Thus, although the novel often juxtaposes its freed modern woman with a conventional, complicit one whose charms reinforce masculine power, it draws as well on the image of domestic insularity to imagine a model for the modern woman's cultural autonomy. We might see the connection as Miriam uses the rhetoric of domesticity to shape her very repudiation of it. When she says she's "'been flying, almost desperately, from domesticity, all m'life,'" Hypo redefines domesticity as her "isolation" (4:225) and she agrees. "'Women,'" she says, "'carry all the domesticity they need about with them. That is why they can get along alone so much better than men'" (4:226). Richardson thus connects her account of the modern woman who rejects home and hearth with one of the central strands of domestic ideology—its claim that women and the home establish an interiorized subjectivity.

But *Pilgrimage* is concerned to shift the claims of this by now old-fashioned figure to modern women, and the novel far more centrally associates women's power to surmount social convention with the modern figure of the middle-class woman who works in and travels through the city—imagining ways that she may, in effect, "carry all the domesticity [she] need[s] about with [her]." It is on this figure that I wish to focus. It is this woman—so important to the narrative's reworking of the traditional marriage plot—who embodies the mobility suggested in Miriam's last comment about flying alone. Her circulation among a range of urban settings and social circles gives the text a way of rearticulating the relationship between occupying social place and remaining free of it, reconciling an immersion in social detail with critical distance.

In this focus on the centrality of newly mobile women, *Pilgrimage* both responds to and constructs a new cultural meaning for a shift in women's working patterns: namely, the wide-scale movement of women into office work in the late nineteenth and early twentieth centuries. This shift, which gained momentum from the 1890s, when *Pilgrimage* is first set, brought large numbers of middle-class women into the rapidly expanding field of clerical work, and brought them visibly into a public sphere, much more so than did earlier, more conventionally "domestic" professions like teaching or governess work.[11] Richardson herself lived a version of this transition, moving from a conventional middle-class household to work as a teacher and governess to work in a London dental office. Her novelistic account of this alteration proposes the female office worker, traveling through the public spaces of the city, as the central modern subject. In doing so, she redefines this figure's mobility—her movement between spaces—as grounding woman's claim to a culturally privileged view, by arguing that this movement gives her a powerful and characteristically feminine mode of inhabiting place as a result. Miriam's circulation through London—from work in a dental office to rooms in boardinghouses or garret apartments to intellectual and political meetings—increasingly shapes her access to freedom in the text, both in the power accorded to this movement and by the way it refigures the female subject's relation to social contexts.

In this way *Pilgrimage* importantly feminizes one of the central figures of modernity: the *flâneur* (Hidalgo). This figure had long been associated with the masculine privilege of roaming the streets, watching but unseen. In contrast women were cast as visible and vulnerable spectacles—as prostitutes and as the objects of the *flâneur*'s gaze.[12] The distinction, as critics of Richardson note, haunts *Pilgrimage*—particularly in those brief moments when Miriam encounters or is taken for a prostitute (Radford, *Dorothy Richardson* 53–58).[13] But it makes Richardson's claim for the affinities between *flânerie* and modern femininity—indeed the essential femininity of *flânerie* in the text—the more striking. For the novel claims for women precisely the movement and the subjectivity claimed for the *flâneur*. Both circulate through the city and in doing so both enact the doubleness which characterizes the subject of modernity. Absorbed into the crowd as they merge into the city's anonymity, both nonetheless also claim an autonomous private identity as they assert a fundamental distance from what they see. Like the *flâneur*, that is, Richardson's modern woman immerses herself in the disconnected sensory impressions provided by urban modernity; and like the *flâneur* she reconsolidates the notion of an autonomous private self as that figure who can move from impression to impression and yet remain untouched. Indeed *Pilgrimage* does not claim that women may be *flâneuses* so much as it claims that the *flâneur*—the quintessential modern subject—is fundamentally feminine.

We can trace the urban dynamic of *flânerie* through *Pilgrimage*. As critics have noted, the novel links Miriam's epiphanic moments with both city streets and the solitary room in which she writes (Radford, *Dorothy Richardson* 52–53). London generates epiphany because its unmappable multiplicity removes Miriam from the constraint of dwelling in a single place: "now her untouched self here, free, unseen, and strong, the strong world of London all round her, strong free untouched people, in a dark lit wilderness, happy and miserable in their own way, going about the streets looking at nothing, thinking about no special person or thing, as long as they were there, being in London" (2:76). The city thus allows her to "pass into that strange familiar state, where all clamourings seemed unreal" (3:106). The text renders this urban freedom compatible, even continuous, with a new social space of privacy—the working woman's rented apartment. For Miriam's solitary room and desk likewise alter her relation to the other places she inhabits: "the paper-scattered lamplit circle was established as the centre of life. [. . .] Held up by this secret place, drawing her energy from it, any sort of life would do that left this room and its little table free and untouched" (3:134). In *Pilgrimage* the impersonally public street and the private room both free the female subject by enabling mobility and an altered relation to the other spaces she inhabits; they offer a similar distance from constraint, from that absolute definition by convention which the novel links to relationship and stasis. Indeed *Pilgrimage* figures solitary rooms as producing the abstracting imagery of epiphany in a sort of merging with the city: "London could come freely in day and night through the unscreened happy little panes; light and darkness and darkness and light. London, just outside all the time, coming in with the light, coming in with the darkness, always present in the depths of the air in the room" (2:16).

In these privileged locations we can see the novel's commitment to linking modern women's financial and physical independence with their privileged critical view. And we may see the way women's status as itinerants gives them a form of authority that will anchor the text's own aesthetic project. This authority derives from the mobility that makes such women quintessential Londoners. For both the private room and London's streets provide Miriam with a critical relation to the social, by defining subjective freedom and epiphany as suspended between spaces. Miriam, for instance, muses on a lecture hall inhabited "by people who gave no thought to the wonder of moving from one space to another and up and down stairs. Yet this wonder was more to them than all the things on which their thoughts were fixed" (3:233). Her comment offers a spatial figure for the description of her own life that immediately follows: "Far away in tomorrow, stood the established, unchanging world of [the office at] Wimpole Street, linked helpfully to the lives of the prosperous classes. Just ahead, at the end of the walk home, the small isolated Tansley Street [boardinghouse] world, full of secretive people drifting about on the edge of catastrophe [. . .] In the space between these surrounding worlds was the everlasting solitude; ringing as she moved to cross the landing, with voices demanding an explanation of her presence in any one of them" (3:233).

In the novel's terms, crossing London, like crossing the hall's spaces, lets Miriam move between worlds determined by class and determining the subject—whether prosperously conventional or catastrophically poor. In this account, the price paid by moving between spaces—Miriam's difficulty accounting for herself in any sphere—is not only well worth paying for the resulting "wonder" but marks the extent to which as a subject she is no longer restricted by the terms of any local world—she is freed into a form of critical autonomy. This same logic transforms Miriam's loss of class position at the novel's opening from a disorienting social disaster to a far more enabling doubleness: both "life's stupid error" and "life's wisdom" (3:245). *Pilgrimage* imagines this loss as inaugurating the mobile subjectivity authorizing the text; loss as class movement frees Miriam from the constraints of her childhood world, allowing her both to inhabit its views and see its restrictions. Circulation between urban spaces, like that between classes, thus lets the female subject inhabit her social contexts differently in *Pilgrimage*, by figuring a way to live both within and outside them. Indeed Miriam's mobility lets her register the details of her own social immersion as a simultaneous outsider and insider; this consciousness clarifies for her the way local codes or impressions shape her identity, even as the text renders the gesture of consciousness as itself freeing Miriam from place.

With this flexibility of position, *Pilgrimage* thus proposes a complex relationship between femininity and outsiderhood, indeed between femininity and foreignness. The strains in this conjunction suggest that we need to examine the form and limits of feminine foreignness in the text more thoroughly. The conjunction is perhaps more visible because the novel juxtaposes Miriam to so many actual foreigners. For if modern woman's mobility in the text places her structurally outside any scene she enters as well as in it, never fully at home in any world, for *Pilgrimage* such mobility works in part by bringing her into formative contact with the foreigners occupying London's fluid social and intellectual circles. Set free between boardinghouses and political groups like the Lycurgans (i.e., Fabians) and the New Tolstoyans, she meets foreigners similarly detached from single contexts; their distant view of the world Miriam takes for granted helps create the double relation of her identity to its surroundings.

Foreigners are necessary in *Pilgrimage* to convince Miriam not just of her distance from her culture but more importantly of the details of her immersion in the first place—an awareness which establishes what it means to view herself as a foreigner would. Through her conversations with Michael Shatov, for instance—a Russian Jew who eventually proposes to her—she becomes conscious of the specificity of her cultural identity. "Seeing England from his point of view, was being changed; a little. The past, up to the last few moments, was a life she had lived without knowing that it was a life lived in special circumstances and from certain points of view. Now, perhaps moving away from it, these circumstances and points of view suddenly became a possession, full of fascinating interest" (3:151). Her discussions with the Italian Guerini while vacationing in Switzerland similarly render her London life visible in its particularities. "For the first time, she was seeing London as people whose secret had revealed itself during this last two weeks, and was at this moment beginning consistently to live her life there as in future it would be lived, as she had lived it, but unconsciously and only intermittently, during the past year" (4:122–23).

In both moments Miriam recognizes herself as shaped by the details of cultural place. It is in light of this recognition and her resulting double stance inside and outside culture that we should read Miriam's growing self-consciousness about the socially privileged class inflections of her own voice after traveling abroad. Her accent "was now claiming her attention for its own quality grown strange: sounding the gentle south of England [. . .] and the large-gardened, uncrowded south-western suburbs" (4:138). While this awareness of class and regional accent is not new—throughout the novel Miriam has noted and disdained voices of the "alien north [. . . which] grated even at their gentlest," and flattered herself that she "belonged to a superior, more cultivated way of being" (4:138)—her self-consciousness here about her accent's social function rather than its aesthetic essence is new. Foreignness as self-consciousness here allows Miriam to register the social details shaping her exchanges with others: she hears her voice "proclaim itself a barrier and yet the vehicle of her everlasting communion with [North London friends]; of her prevailing with them by virtue of the echo within it of the way of being from which it had come forth" (4:138).

Pilgrimage suggests that Miriam's access to a foreigner's, outsider's view of her world thus immerses her in that world more fully, because it lets her consciously see her own formation by social details and structures. But the form of foreignness available to Miriam does more than underline her connection to social patterns; this same foreign view simultaneously moves her away from the world newly recognized and into a familiar sphere of autonomy. Seeing "English prejudices" through Michael, she possesses them in an act of vision that ensures that "their removal would come; through a painless association" (3:151).[14] Seeing her London life from abroad with Guerini, she may be aware of the multiplicity of her particular identities—"she had that haunting sense of being a collection of persons living in a world of people always single and the same" (4:122)—but these same travels will allow her to unify her multiplicities and exceed her social place.

Indeed woman's foreignness is a form of that privileged feminine doubleness we have seen throughout *Pilgrimage*, and in this sense it joins her status as outsider to a more privileged stance as a universal subject. For if being between spaces—the foreignness of being a modern woman—allows the feminine subject to grasp her multiplicity by returning the conflicting details of her life to her, in Richardson's account she may, in turn, only see her own details from the stance of an underlying general identity. Inherent in modern woman's foreign stance, then, lies a potent and problematic drift from multiplicity to singleness. In particular, a voyage into the foreign may collapse the differences of cultural spaces into incarnations of the same—and of the same subjectivity.

For instance, in the following passage, Miriam, just returned from Switzerland and dining with Hypo and Alma, thinks back on the trajectory of her life that her voyage has revealed to her:

The *What am I doing here?* that had sounded from time to time during their past association [. . .] held now a promise, as if of an appointment made towards which, though all her ways seemed blocked, she was invisibly moving. [. . .] "Foreign countries," she said, [. . . wanting to share] the way one's own deep sense of being, so vibrant and so still, is never stronger or more curiously alarming than when it is confirmed by being found existing in foreign, unknown ways of being. The same way set in a different form. [. . .] "Of course there is actually no such thing as travel. So they say. There is nothing but a *Voyage autour de ma Chambre,* meaning *de tout ce que je suis,* even in a *tour du monde."* (4:166–67)

Foreign travel allows Miriam to recognize both her context and her difference from it, and she uses this recognition to frame a trajectory or plot for her life. But if contact with foreign difference has enabled Miriam's self-assessment, such enabling difference all but vanishes in her account of traveling abroad, where what she claims to have found is not difference but sameness. This sameness, in fact, is that deep model of subjectivity underpinning *Pilgrimage*'s articulation of an abstracted subject. Travel abroad reveals the same deep self everywhere, and proves that self's depth by its continuing presence across foreign cultures. Indeed the universality of the subject here is nearly literalized, and the sameness of foreign places domesticated, when travel around the world may be redefined as travel around one's room or around oneself.

The novel's definition of femininity as a provisional, partial form of foreignness thus allows the female subject to be formed by her contexts while remaining free of the most radical flux or estrangement that such formation implies. Woman's limited foreignness, we might say, makes it possible to discern a continuous plot in the discontinuous identities of social immersion. And we might mark the limits of the analogy between women and foreigners by noting the difference between an English-woman like Miriam and the actual foreigners she encounters. For while Miriam may align herself with the views of the Italian Guerini or the Russian Jew Shatov and rely upon their cultural difference, she never fully becomes foreign in the text in the way that they are. Miriam's feminine foreignness is a form of self-distancing which lets her recognize her own identities and achieve the double stance we have examined. In contrast, Guerini's and Shatov's foreignness involves no such privileged self-reflection or inhabiting of double registers. For *Pilgrimage* literal foreignness is imagined in contrast as the inability to attain a certain privileged, universalizing mobility. Foreigners like Guerini and Shatov are placed and limited by their national and racial identities; they are tied to the local and lack the enabling self-distantiation that is the primary work of foreignness for female subjectivity.

Women are thus privileged as both outsiders and insiders in *Pilgrim-age*. Their mobility and modified foreignness make them exemplary modern subjects, able to reconcile the implicit modern tensions between social particularity and universality, and thus able to offer a powerful ground for the radically modern fiction Richardson envisions. But the fact that the text is so concerned to juxtapose Miriam's version of empowered outsiderhood with that of men who are literally foreign to the English spaces in which the novel is largely set must prompt us to ask about the category of Englishness itself, which has emerged throughout the modernist texts I have been reading whenever the idea of the subject's universal status is evoked. Why does *Pilgrimage* evoke English national identity as part of a project of defining modern femininity and how does Englishness function there? How might a novel committed to the destabilizing mobility of the feminine subject even define national identity? Given the text's persistent questioning of whether identity of any sort forms contextually or exists internally, in what register might nationality itself be imagined—and why imagine it through woman?

The debate over nationality emerges in the text, I will argue, primarily as a way to ensure the privileged mobility and the representative status of Richardson's female subject. It works to safeguard her from the narrative dangers of a marriage plot that threatens to constrain both Miriam's and the novel's unconventional freedom of movement. For the marriage plot in *Pilgrimage* is simultaneously a plot about competing national identities and their nature; it appears in Miriam's courtship by the Russian Jew Michael Shatov.[15] Marriage in this text is thus also intermarriage, and it poses the threat not just that Miriam will be constrained within the single space of the home but that marriage will assimilate her into an identity not her own; it underlines the danger implied in the suggestion that Miriam may have no internal identity to resist alteration. In this context, the evolving notion of Miriam's Englishness helps ensure that her identity remains simultaneously fixed and mobile— both immune to assimilation and free from constraint.

It is hardly accidental that the dilemmas of feminine subjectivity should be rhetorically resolved by nationality in the text. Nor is it surprising that a debate over the function of female national identity should take place through the juxtaposition of Englishness and Jewishness. Debates over national identity pose questions comparable to those invoked by modern femininity—crucially the question of whether the subject's identity is internal or instead contextually formed, particularized or universal. And as critics have noted, definitions of Jewishness have long been central to Western debates over modern national identity (Cheyette; Anderson, "George Eliot"; Ragussis). For the Jews are envisioned in such debates both as a racially particularized proto-nation and as a dispersed and placeless people. In this capacity they may stand for the virtues and the dangers of differing notions of the modern nation, from the universalizing vision of civic and assimilative nationalism to the racializing accounts of Romantic nationalism. In raising the question of whether peoples, and subjects, can be assimilated to their contexts or instead possess an internal essence, the debate over the Jewish question summons a notion of race as interior identity that speaks powerfully to the shape and privilege of Richardson's modern woman.[16]

Pilgrimage's interest in articulating female subjectivity with the categories of nationality and race thus expands beyond the novel's frequently discussed question of whether woman can be reduced to her reproductive function, to ask whether modern woman is fundamentally *placed* by a national or racial identity, or whether either might instead insure her autonomy and her mobility. As we shall see, the novel will gradually redefine national identity—and specifically Englishness—as internal and racialized. But it will do so in order to construct a compatibility between nationality and mobility—place and placelessness—that echoes the reconciling powers ascribed to female subjectivity. Just as modern women may reconcile their particularity with their universality, their contextual malleability with their interior depths, so too will English national identity offer the surest route to women's mobility and universality in the text.

We can see both the uses of national identity and its shifting nature in Miriam's debates with Michael over race and English identity. For here she increasingly describes Englishness as the internal ground of who she is, indeed as the ground enabling her very theorizations of individualism and female identity. While Miriam begins by denying the validity of race, she ends by reforming it in a running debate that becomes pressing as she considers what marrying Michael would mean for her identity. She opens by dismissing race as a necessarily invalid generalization. Arguing against his rhetorical questions—"'has the race not a soul and an individuality? Greater than that of its single parts?'"—she contrasts race with the primacy of the individual subject: "'The race is nothing without individuals [. . .] the biggest thing a race does is to produce a few big individualities" (3:150). She rejects his description of her as visibly English in her belief in the law and in individualism. "'That is only my stamp'" she says. "'I can't help that. But I myself have no prejudices'" (3:151). Her rejection, however, is uncertain. Immediately afterward she moves from disclaiming Englishness to recognizing her English prejudices in the act of gaining distance from them: "the past, up to the last few moments, was a life she had lived without knowing that it was a life lived in special circumstances and from certain points of view" (3:151). Later still she begins to investigate Englishness as something substantive, seeking "the immediate truth that shone, independent of speculation, all about her in the English light" (3:239). This "deep common understanding" (4:252), "the *mystery* of being English" (3:238), necessarily diffuse as it is, she redefines as the production of individual inviolability, "something [. . .] that had offered her [. . .] a safeguard of individuality" (3:241)—as a fundamental characteristic shaping a nation of people "sure every day of the blissful solitude of the interim times" (3:241).

In effect, Miriam adopts Michael's quite conventional account of English identity as a predisposition toward individual freedom. But we must notice the way her adoption of Englishness as a valid category of identity relocates it. While she begins by denying Englishness as something external to the individual, disparaging its appearance in herself as merely her "stamp," when she accepts the category, she alters it—no longer a context around her, something that may impress itself on her, it becomes a "point of view" as well, a "common understanding," a "mystery." Englishness, in short, becomes affiliated with what the subject knows and how it sees; in effect it moves within, and perhaps as a corollary, it now preserves the subject rather than constrains it. Thus if Miriam's dispute with Shatov over the validity of race began by defining its stakes as the individual's defiance of generalization, the continuing resonances of their discussion yield another familiar set of stakes in the novel—the dilemma of whether national identity presses in on the subject from without or offers instead an internal source of subjectivity on the model of race.

Pilgrimage tests the nature and validity of national categorization in terms that largely resolve the issues in advance: the novel debates nationality's validity by invoking precisely an intrinsic racialized split between English and Jewish identities. Indeed in Miriam's arguments with Michael, the potentially objectionable nature of a racial view of the subject becomes a problematic *Jewish* view of the subject. Thus while Miriam criticizes Hypo Wilson for what she considers a masculine belief in the priority of race and the imperative that women reproduce it, she attributes Shatov's comparable belief in race to his Judaism. In a familiar cultural gesture, *Pilgrimage* casts Jewish philosophy as particularly committed to the primacy of racial categories of identity, as committed to a historical determinism that imposes a plot on the individual—through Zionism, which Miriam describes as "'that strange thing, the thing that makes you stare, in history. A sort of shape. . .'" (3:169).[17]

The frame of Jewish racial determinism versus English individualism is particularly fraught for *Pilgrimage* because of the way the novel has defined the modern feminine subject as free from the determinations of plot, and as singularly able to draw individual autonomy out of the shaping force of contexts. These stakes emerge most clearly when Miriam discusses with Michael what Jewish views on race would mean for her status as his wife. For his opinions emerge through his comments about women—whom Judaism, in this account, treats as conveyers of the race rather than as individuals. In Shatov's articulation, such treatment of women is doubly racialized—not only does it characterize Jewish thought but its value for him lies its contribution to racial viability: "'With Jews, womanhood has always been sacred. And there can be no doubt that we owe our persistence as a race largely to our laws of protection for women; *all* women. [. . .] To-day there is a very significant Jewish wit which says that women make the best wives and mothers in the world'" (3:220). For Miriam this signals Judaism's inability to see women as individuals—indeed to see them as the bearers of that complexly engaged and transcendent subjectivity *Pilgrimage* constructs and privileges. "'Christ was the first man to see women as individuals,'" she comments (3:221). Later in the novel, when Michael is about to marry her beloved Amabel, Miriam elaborates on this link between the Jewish abstraction of race and the suppression of female subjectivity.

> "The Russian in him [. . .] knew, in spite of his Jewish philosophy, something of the unfathomable depths in each individual, unique and irreplaceable [. . .] And the Jew in him so far saw Amabel only as charmingly qualified to fulfill what he still regarded as the larger aspect, the only continuing aspect of himself, his destiny as part of his 'race,' the abstraction he and his like so strangely conceived as alive, immortal, sacred, and at the same time as consisting of dead and dying particles with no depth of life in them, mere husks." (4:427)

In this way the abstraction and constraint associated with Judaism converge with the conventional masculine ideas about women embodied in the coercions of the marriage plot. In the union of these two problems, marriage to a Jew may be read as the most extreme instance of the problems Richardson locates in reproductive marriage. But we should note that Michael's courtship in turn rhetorically transposes the dangers of marriage for women into the threat of encroaching Judaism as a kind of forced assimilation. Thus when he proposes to Miriam a second time, when she may be pregnant with Hypo's child, she sees the danger as a conversion to Jewish identity, rather than as marriage: She is filled with a bitter "amusement over his failure to recognize that the refuge he offered [. . .] was a permanent prison; over his assumption that she might be scared into flight, disguised as a Jewess, from the open road, down into Judaea" (4:302–3).

Judaism's threat here is that of social immersion and potential determination—the danger that marrying a Jew may change or misrepresent Miriam's identity and thus imprison her, that female subjectivity's promise of a freeing distance from the contexts forming it will vanish. It is in response to this threat condensed in Michael Shatov's courtship that *Pilgrimage* articulates a notion of Englishness that may underwrite the unique status of its female subject and protect it from the threat of assimilative transformation hovering in marriage. The novel ultimately does so by reconstructing English identity as a form of deep, racialized identity. However this new construction paradoxically depends on absorbing an element the text has cast as ostensibly opposed to Englishness: Jewish conceptions of race. In this attempt to imagine for its protagonist an enabling racial identity, *Pilgrimage* engages in a revealing exchange of racial definitions. Both Englishness and Judaism at moments stand for assimilative (or contextual) and essential (or internal, racial) understandings of national identity; the novel envisions their contact as a way in which such affiliations may move between them, and as the precondition for forming Englishness as an intrinsic aspect of Miriam's identity— one not merely contingent and unstable. *Pilgrimage* sets in motion the transformation of Englishness from an apparently liberatory contextual identity to an essential but more freeing deep one—prompted by a contact with Judaism that transfers the problems of both modes onto Judaism and safeguards Miriam's privileged, mobile relation to these models of subjectivity.

As we saw, by late in *Pilgrimage* the danger of Miriam's marriage to Michael Shatov lay in Judaism's threatening power to assimilate her. We should note, however, that in their earlier explicit debates on racial and national identity, it was Englishness instead which assimilated, and it assimilated benevolently rather than ominously, as the very mark of its openness of identity. Assimilation here, we might almost say, signals the lack of a notion of intrinsic, racial national identity in England. Englishness amounts instead to a national commitment to the individual rather than the race at this moment, guaranteeing "the last fastness of the private English mind" and the subject's freedom (3:190). Significantly it is the presence of Jews in England that is described as putting this model to its most severe test.[18] For while Miriam endorses English tolerance and openness as a model of nationality that avoids racial exclusion and anti-Semitism—("England can assimilate anything" she says, referring to the earlier races it has absorbed, ostensibly in a benign manner)—Shatov insists that the presence of Jews will generate just that form of racial feeling, for "no nation can assimilate the Jew" (3:167). The proximity of Judaism thus endangers characteristic Englishness itself by prompting it to a more cohesively racial version of the nation. The national openness which allows immigration in service of assimilation here risks being converted to a "Jewish" notion of racial intactness through contact with the Jews. When Miriam considers Michael's contention that increased Jewish immigration may lead to "the closing of this last door" (to England), she sees him forecasting this transformation of Englishness in the nation's new desire to preserve an intact racialized identity (3:167). "'It's impossible to think of,'" says Miriam. "'It will be the end of England if we begin that sort of thing.' 'It may be the beginning of Jewish nationality,'" Shatov responds (3:168).

Jewish notions of racial identity thus condense an oddly double threat in the novel—both the power of assimilation and context to alter identity and the intractable, insular resistance of racialized subjectivity to context. Jews cannot be assimilated by England in Michael and Miriam's debate, but they can induce England, by their proximity, to be converted to them—or rather, paradoxically, assimilated to their notion of essential, unassimilable race. England only comes to insist on its Englishness in *Pilgrimage* in the presence of Jewish immigrants; the more insistent Englishness is, the less "English" it becomes in its understanding of the nature of its own identity. Cast in these terms, the debate about English and Jewish conceptions of nation and race reframes the questions about the subject's identity that are so central to *Pilgrimage* as a whole—recasting the question of whether one takes one's identity from the place one inhabits, reformulating the novel's persistent question about how fully Miriam is formed by her contact with a specific place, and how far her subjectivity might lie beneath the effects of that contact.

The novel, as we have seen, poses these questions most acutely for Miriam as questions about marriage—about the ways in which marriage may alter female identity or reveal its basis. Thus *Pilgrimage* explores the problem of Miriam's Englishness in greater depth as she considers whether marriage to Michael Shatov would change her identity, indeed considers how and whether such an identity might inhere in her. In particular, Miriam attempts to resolve her anxieties over the prospect of being assimilated into Judaism by interviewing an Englishwoman who has intermarried and converted. This meeting with Mrs. Bergstein, though it leaves Miriam dissatisfied and unable to decide whether she should marry Michael, nonetheless offers her a strategy for resolving the conceptual problem of assimilation—by continuing that reformulation of Englishness as deep identity begun hypothetically in her discussion of immigration.

Encountering in Mrs. Bergstein the figure of an Englishwoman converted and thus potentially assimilated, Miriam reacts by delineating the differences between them so that she may imagine her own identity as immune to threatening assimilation. For despite the fact that Miriam feels "a common incommunicable sense" (3:228) of Englishness between them (notably about the "'impossibil[ity] of associat[ing] with Jewish *women*'" [3:228]), she works hard to cast the other woman as different because insufficiently, inauthentically English. In the process she asserts her own Englishness as a form of intrinsic and thus permanent identity. In Miriam's account, Mrs. Bergstein has been able to convert to Judaism only because she doesn't possess a deep identity of any sort to convert from. Unitarian rather than Anglican, she is ruled by "the chill of a perpetually active *reason*," which, like masculine logic in the novel, blocks access to a deeper reality (3:227). "This woman to whom the fact of life as a thing in itself never had time to appear" thus lacks the substance of both Christian and English—indeed feminine—identity to begin with (3:225). Her marriage to a Reformed Jew, part of a movement "as much cut off from Judaism as Unitarianism from Anglicanism" is thus part of a conversion that is no conversion at all, because she has never possessed an intrinsic English identity and because she doesn't touch "real" Judaism even in marriage (3:227).

In rendering true intermarriage and assimilation impossible, Miriam thus constructs a form of intrinsic English national identity which guarantees modern woman's autonomy. Englishness becomes anything but a contextual immersion or "stamp." Its depth is confirmed by the way it exemplifies a register of "mystery" signaling the real, and by the way in which it offers Miriam a ground of identity resistant to assimilation and to the subject's utter and continuous reformation by one context after another. As a result she reimagines intermarriage as something that can only happen to women without intrinsic national identities to jeopardize. Miriam casts Amabel's ultimate marriage to Michael Shatov—discomforting enough as a union of two people she has loved—in these terms. Amabel becomes marked as a figure of unstable nationality—an amalgam of shifting affiliations. If at one moment her Irish and Welsh background makes her "'more Celtic than English,'" at another moment she may become French "'in manner and bearing [when she moves to Paris]'" (4:242). The same lack of intrinsic national identity that allows Amabel to become French enables her in this account to marry Michael—and makes her unable to understand Miriam's objections to marrying him herself.[19] For Miriam, these own objections now seem "a tide flowing freely from an immovable deep certainty which for Amabel had no existence. [. . .] Why should it be right to have no sense of nationality? Why should it be wrong to feel this sense as something whose violation would be a base betrayal? Much more than that. Something that could not be. Not merely difficult and sacrificial and yet possible. Simply impossible. With her unlocated, half-foreign being, Amabel could see nothing of the impossibility of spending one's life in Jewry" (4:292).

In the context of this intermarriage, *Pilgrimage* emphasizes the loss implied by identities like Amabel's, formed without a deep or intrinsic core; the novel stresses the way national identity—English identity—is necessary to appreciate both the specificities of cultural place and the powerful register of abstract reality beneath it. Amabel's lack of national identity, we might note, does not make her marriage to Michael a happy one. Without it, Miriam claims, Amabel has no source for registering the differences between people that the novel insists upon; she cannot understand Michael's character or its sources. In particular, she is mistaken in her "everlasting attribution to others of the width and generosity of her own nature. Taking it for granted, she believed it to exist even below the most pitifully constricted surfaces" (4:292). Miriam here suggests that intrinsic national identity is needed to register cultural specificity. But by the same gesture she imagines national identity as necessary too for reaching that region in which the novel proposes subjects as potentially the same—that universalizing arena in which "width and generosity" appear beneath the surface. In distinguishing between the sameness Amabel wrongly attributes to subjects and the universality she herself legitimately reaches, Miriam thus makes intrinsic national or racialized subjectivity—like modern female subjectivity—necessary to acknowledge and connect specificity with universality. We might say as well that deep, intrinsic Englishness becomes a precondition in the text for access to abstracting freedom. Only through such Englishness can the subject attain the freedom of individualism or contact with a universalized "reality."

This redefinition of English national identity as an intrinsic disposition to the real and the individual thus spans the same sets of terms joined by the female subject in *Pilgrimage*. Offering a way to be simultaneously enmeshed in and freed from the specificities of a culture, it maps the same anxieties: that a subject constantly moving might be endlessly reformed, or that one staying still might be imprisoned by local social convention. If modern woman's mobility lets her avoid the entrapment of home or provincialism, even as in the novel's terms it allows her to reach an abstracted reality beneath any place, the Englishness of that subject reconfirms a homelike anchor for her mobility, neutralizes the necessary risk of foreignness and the danger of endless assimilation to new contexts. The more Miriam moves beyond the constraints of place or race, the more she is confirmed as an Englishwoman; the more English she is, the less confined to specificity and place, the better attuned to mystery and the real.

To read *Pilgrimage*'s construction of a national identity enabling the mobile female subject is not to suggest, however, that the novel proposes the nation instead of an international space as the terrain it sees female subjectivity—or experimental narrative—encompassing. The striking interest of Richardson's text for a reading of modernism is the way it insists on an interdependence *between* national identity and international transcendence in a historical moment in which heightened nationalism coexists with increasing international mobility, and in which modernist experiments are as likely to draw on the claims of expatriate cultural distance as on ideas about national essence for their innovations.[20] Indeed Richardson explicitly claims an international reach for art in *Pilgrimage*. And the novel's international claims depend upon its basis in female subjectivity. Just as the female subject gains cultural power in the text through her ability to reconcile specific social detail and abstracted freedom, national identity with universal mystery, in *Pilgrimage* the art that encompasses this subject, in transcending mere convention, merges national cultural specificity with international movement.

In order to read this interdependence of national identity and the international claims of art in *Pilgrimage*—and the relation of both to the female subject who moves between specific contexts and universal depths—we must return to the novel's continuing interest in international movement and culture. We might recall that it was the sublimity of German music which led Miriam to realize both national difference and an abstracting, placeless epiphany in *Pointed Roofs*. There German music revealed the distinctions between English and German musical spirit at the same time that it lifted Miriam to a figurative freedom from any place—a freedom nonetheless marked by her immersion in English childhood memories. The moment suggests the peculiar compatibility of the national and the international for *Pilgrimage*—a mutuality made possible because the text has redefined certain national identities as giving access to both the individual and the universal.[21] Nationality, in offering intrinsic or "real" identity, becomes both a precondition and a reference point for international culture.

We should note, of course, that *Pilgrimage* limits this compatibility to a western, specifically European internationalism—a restriction which emerges in the text's scapegoating of Judaism as fundamentally alien despite its enabling function. While contact with the Jews (or in Miriam's case, courtship by Michael Shatov) prompts the formation of a substantive English identity, Judaism remains an instance of the foreign in the text, never attaining the privileged internationalism of either English individualism or German culture. Indeed the status of Jewish culture contrasts sharply with that of Russians, which appears as another national repository of reality, depth, and trans-European philosophy. The sound of Russian is "not *foreign*" to Miriam (3:43); names in Russian literature do not seem arbitrary but summon the real depth of the characters (3:60); and when Miriam hears a Russian song she both senses "the thronging golden multitudes" of the Russian folk and sees London anew: "The Bloomsbury squares were changed. It was like seeing them for the first time" (3:130). The text is in fact so committed to this logic that Miriam splits Shatov's cultural identity into two discrete halves, the European and the Jewish. "Frenchman, Russian, philosophical German-brained, he sat there white-faced, an old old Jew, immeasurably old, cut off [. . .] Why could he not be content to be a European?" she despairs (3:168).[22]

The preconditions and the privileged reach of European internationalism thus shape and are shaped by the definitions of art in *Pilgrimage*. The novel proposes that it is the function of true art to make "reality" visible, and in doing so to forge a relation between national identity and international community, as between the specificities of place and the abstractions of placeless freedom. In this, art does a kind of work in *Pilgrimage* that cannot be divided from the effects of modern female subjectivity. Richardson's newly mobile female subject mediates too between the claims of location and of abstraction, between movement and a universalizing stillness. And while I have been arguing that the novel's premises join the feminine subject to the claims of modern art conceptually, we should note that the novel's trajectory joins these terms quite concretely and thematically as well. As Miriam Henderson moves through an ever-widening range of social contexts into a discovery of an insistent, continuing "reality," she also moves toward what the text suggests may be her vocation as a writer. To produce a properly modern art, the subject must be able to span the contraries we have seen the novel exploring.

In *Pilgrimage* then, the female subject offers the central authoritative resource for modern revisions of the novel, indeed she virtually demands modernist narrative experiment to encompass her various mobilities and to give "reality" "its own say." Richardson's insistence on the importance of female subjectivity for modern narrative, and for that narrative's most ambitious claims to reconcile national and international cultures, thus both repeats and imagines an answer to the continuing questions about gender, subjectivity, and the cultural power of the novel worked out in modernist impressionism. For the distance Ford and Conrad envisioned as necessary between a female subject and narrative authority becomes in Richardson a distance intrinsic to that subject, who is always both in contexts and outside of them. Indeed in Richardson's account this internal distance or doubleness is the very mark of modern woman's unique power to mediate between specificity and abstraction, between impressionist permeability and an abstracted subject, between the construction by culture and the claim to stand apart from it. The female subject for Richardson, explicitly modern in her difference, not only answers these questions as questions about subjectivity but offers a claim for the importance of a new, modernist art, a claim only legible when it is understood as absolutely dependent on the figure of modern woman.

6 Woolf's Abstraction

The Edwardians were never interested in character in itself. . . . They were interested in something outside. . . .

[Their] tools are the wrong ones for us to use. . . . They have given us a house in the hope that we may be able to deduce the human beings who live there.

—Woolf, "Mr. Bennett and Mrs. Brown"

Two pictures hung opposite the window. . . . The man was an ancestor. He had a name. He held the rein in his hand. He had said to the painter:

"If you want my likeness, dang it sir, take it when the leaves are on the trees." There were leaves on the trees. . . .

He was a talk producer, that ancestor. But the lady was a picture. In her yellow robe, leaning, with a pillar to support her, a silver arrow in her hand, and a feather in her hair, she led the eye up, down, from the curve to the straight, through glades of greenery and shades of silver, dun and rose into silence.

—Woolf, *Between the Acts*

A study of gender and modernism heads with a kind of inevitability toward the work of Virginia Woolf. Her writing has been central to critical discussions of these issues—both because it embodies and critiques the major theoretical and literary concerns of the period and because it has so strongly shaped traditions of feminist literary criticism. Woolf's work is equally central here, for the views of impressionism and female subjectivity that I have been tracing prefigure the main questions of Woolf's writing, just as Woolf's writing in turn comments with unusual clarity on the cultural compulsions, claims, and impasses of this discourse. Her work has been canonical in raising impressionist questions about subjectivity, and in asking how they connect with the narrative possibilities of women's lives and the structures of gender. It investigates the tension between a subject dissolved and a subject interiorized, between the subject who absorbs impressions and the one who exists beneath them. It does so in part through the figure of the domestic woman, which it both critiques and recomposes—describing her as someone who creates unities outside a rigidly rational, linear, instrumental world, even as she is confined by the social terms of that feminine role. Woolf's work thus frames the period's most pressing questions about female subjectivity, asking whether it is in fact wholly defined in socially gendered terms, or whether it may give access to a realm outside the social. It investigates alternative plots for female character, even as it is concerned with a metaphoric language that promises to expand beyond the distinct terms of social plots. Her writing offers the claims of realism against those of abstraction, pits "fact" against "vision," and insists on both.[1]

The doubleness in Woolf's account of gender and the subject has long raised the critical question of how we are to read these registers together. The issue has emerged in the problem of how we assess Woolf's political stance and the forms it takes, how we weigh the force of her social critique beside her fascination with sublime aesthetic moments, and how we evaluate the import of such moments themselves.[2] The issue is frequently cast as the problem of connecting Woolf's feminism and her modernism. Do her feminist commitments create a modernism that is itself disruptive, or do these strands of her work remain at odds with one another? My discussion thus far has suggested that terms of gender can neither be divided from nor seamlessly merged with the aesthetic claims of modernism. Instead I have been examining the way the tension between these terms signals the related conflicts within each category. As a result I have been tracing the late-nineteenth- and early-twentieth-century understanding of feminine subjectivity as both socially shaped and transcendent, in order to see how this contradiction itself helps generate the political tensions of modernist impressionism. The conflicts between social specificity and abstraction, between subjective openness and enclosure, are thus inescapable for notions of femininity and modernism together.

This concluding chapter reads the connections among feminine subjectivity, abstraction, and the construction of modernist narrative authority in Woolf's work. However while most productive commentary on Woolf has cast her as the acute analyst of how gender enters an ostensibly abstracted modernism, I wish to reverse the trajectory of how we read these intersecting terms. Rather than reading Woolf for an account of gender's subversive appearance within impressionist abstraction, I wish to read her texts for their account of how abstraction works within the shared field of gender and modernist form. To do so will of course engage the question of how Woolf imagines feminine subjectivity, just as it will link the forms of gender in her work with the forms of modernism. But Woolf's presentation of these issues will serve here to frame a discussion of abstraction's work within modernism, for Woolf is both abstraction's greatest advocate and its most thorough critic.

The connection between gender and modernist literary authority underpins the question of abstraction in Woolf's work. I argue here that the often-divided terms of her literary project emerge from the double register in which she imagines modern female subjectivity. In particular, women's new urban mobility will generate a familiar ambiguity in Woolf's texts, both for the female subject and for the modernist novel. Women wander in these texts; this mobility suggests that they may move beyond their particular social places, and it also raises the possibility that feminine subjectivity offers a way outside the register of the social entirely.[3] Women thus become figures at once socially concrete and universalized. Woolf's writing will clarify the difficulties of that rhetorical doubleness, imagining ways that female subjectivity may stand for a more generalized communal consciousness, even as her texts criticize the political implications of such ostensible universality. This doubleness of feminine subjectivity in Woolf's writing offers a model for the imagined cultural power of the modern novel itself—which moves here between the registers of the social and the abstract, charting social divisions as well as more mobile metaphorical patterns of unity. We might read Woolf's work then as an explicit debate on the relative power and limits of historical specificity and abstraction, which emerges as she grounds high literary culture in feminine subjectivity.

This chapter begins by reading *Mrs. Dalloway*—the novel in which Woolf's modernism intersects most visibly with questions about the nature of feminine subjectivity and mobility. In particular I consider the necessary dilemma of placing and interpreting the central figure of Clarissa Dalloway—a character the novel types as a woman constrained by her class and her marriage, even as it uses her consciousness to measure whether impressionist subjectivity can expand beyond social place. The problem of Clarissa's rhetorical and physical expansiveness and of the narrative and social unities she may provide anchors broader questions about how Woolf imagines the function of the modernist novel itself— questions about how central a rhetoric of abstraction may be to the novel's work. I then turn to an extended reading of Woolf's most abstract novel, *The Waves*. This text sets socially concretized detail and a socially anchored reading of impressionist subjectivity against the patterning force of abstraction. Indeed the novel's self-consciously extreme narrative experiment is based in the power of abstract narrative trajectories and abstract imagery to offer a new account of the subject. But in tying the power of the modern novel's experiment to abstraction, *The Waves* also clearly envisions the limits of abstraction in supplying cultural authority. Committed to the powers of modernist abstraction, the novel nonetheless provides both the high point and the impasse of that strand of generalization I have traced throughout impressionist fiction. It may serve then to point to the cultural limits and goals of modernism's abstraction, its attempt to move from the ambiguities of gender through the patterned ambiguities of modernist narration.

Woolf is famous for her long-standing interest in the nature and depiction of subjectivity. She articulated this concern explicitly in her 1924 manifesto "Mr. Bennett and Mrs. Brown," an essay in which she places character at the center of questions about the novel: "I believe that all novels, that is to say, deal with character, and that it is to express character . . . that the form of the novels . . . has been evolved" (102). Criticizing a previous generation of writers for their failure to "catch" (94) character, indeed their lack of "interest . . . in character in itself" (105), the essay defines the goal of a new generation of writers as precisely such a capture. The question of character is joined securely and familiarly here to that of narrative form. If existing narrative conventions for evoking character—the extensive detailing of houses and rents, the histories of urban development, that she finds and criticizes in Arnold Bennett's *Hilda Lessways*—have failed, as she argues, then clearly the depiction of character "in itself" requires new narrative methods. If novels must describe the subject rather than its surroundings, narrative order too must change; it can no longer proceed carefully *around* characters.

Woolf here bases her challenge to the Edwardian commitment to character on a pointed redefinition of subjectivity. The essay's repetition of the phrase "character, in itself" places Woolf's subject, the character to be explored by modern novels, in a sphere securely separate from the houses and economics on which Bennett relies: the subject here exists "in itself" rather than in society or history. But as critics have noted, Woolf did not argue consistently or univocally for this conception of subjectivity in her writing as a whole; indeed her work often defines the subject as shaped by the presence of precisely those historical, economic, and social conventions that she walls off from character in this section of "Mr. Bennett and Mrs. Brown."[4] Most notably, in *A Room of One's Own*, by emphasizing the effect of material conditions on women and their work, and by suggesting that women writers must forge a different kind of sentence to express their minds—for "the weight, the pace, the stride of a man's mind are too unlike her own for her to lift anything substantial from him successfully" (79)—Woolf suggests that social surroundings shape character, and in particular shape men's and women's minds differently. The tension between these paradigms will inform all of Woolf's fiction; it will be particularly central to the sequence of her most canonical novels, *Mrs. Dalloway*, *To the Lighthouse*, and *The Waves*, which raise most fully the prototypically modernist question of whether art or subjective perception can locate a unifying truth of the subject beyond the sphere of social and economic conflict. These novels, however, equally interrogate the desires prompting such searches for unity and question their quite worldly effects and origins.

In investigating the doubled shape of subjectivity in Woolf and tracing its connection to patterns of gender, it is tempting to read the category of gender itself too simply as the mark of the social alone. In particular when addressing the question of feminine subjectivity in Woolf's work, we would do well to consider the potential complexities of a central category like femininity. To unravel some of its ambiguities here it may be useful to glance for a moment at those two paintings from *Between the Acts* which have hung silently over this discussion so far. For the contrast between them underlines the shifting forms of representation through which gender appears, and the varied registers to which it gives access.

These two paintings—one of them truly a work of art, a "picture," and one merely an "ancestor"—draw a range of qualities relevant to Woolf's own narrative work into opposition. The ancestor's portrait, it is clear, functions in a social field: as an "ancestor," he signifies lineage rather than "art." To possess this portrait, for instance, is a mark of family status; so too is the act of having such a portrait painted, of marking oneself as an ancestor. Further, the ancestor's identity as patriarch not only governs his conversation (he demands leaves, and he gets them) but determines too the contents of his portrait—defined by his possessions, he is depicted with them, if not nearly enough of them for his taste. To depict this "ancestor" *is* to represent the social elements that define him, rather than to reach toward an essential character that might lie beneath such elements.

Woolf's emphasis on the ancestor's externally defined identity also links the social function of his portrait to the representational mode in which it is painted. The painting is a "likeness" much in the manner of Bennett's likenesses: "'If you want my likeness, dang it sir, take it when the leaves are on the trees.' There were leaves on the trees." It represents things (like leaves) around character as its method of depicting character. This approach to character through the likeness of its surroundings as well as through social conventions is associated here with patriarchal language, and with a particularly trivializing vision of language as "talk." This ancestor speaks profusely—"he was a talk producer"—and he speaks of inconsequential things in a colloquial manner: "'If you want my likeness, dang it sir, take it when the leaves are on the trees. . . . Ain't there room for Colin as well as Buster?' Colin was his famous hound. But there was only room for Buster. It was, he seemed to say . . . a damned shame to leave out Colin whom he wished buried at his feet, in the same grave, about 1750; but that skunk the Reverend Whatshisname wouldn't allow it" (36).

On the other hand, the painting of the lady—bought for its own sake, because "[Oliver] liked that picture" (49)—is "a picture." To illustrate what being a "picture" means, the passage offers the way that, leaning on a pillar, the lady "led the eye up, down, from the curve to the straight, through glades of greenery and shades of silver, dun and rose into silence." This procession within the painting—from the artistically contrived props of pillar and arrow to "the curve" or "the straight," to "silver, dun and rose," to "silence"—mark it as a "picture" by drawing attention to those elements of painting that are not transparently representational, to the color and line which constitute the means of representation. But the painting also becomes a picture by leading the eye further and further into abstraction, away from feathers and arrows and into color, line, and ultimately—in a kind of synesthesia—silence. It is a portrait of a woman, but in order to present her, it must do so by rendering her abstractly.

The passages offer a representational opposition both clearly valued and familiarly modernist: socially coded mimesis opposes abstraction, language opposes silence, and the latter terms are privileged as art. More important for my argument, the opposition is also distinctly gendered. Femininity here gives access to the privileged terms of modernist aesthetics; modernist art is feminized. The ancestor's portrait associates masculine subjectivity with realist representation and a disparaged world of obvious cultural hierarchy, in particular with those patriarchal structures of naming and possession that here shape it so visibly. In contrast, the picture of the lady identifies femininity with art and silence, associating the feminine subject with a realm transcending the limits of language and the social. Recent critics have noted how such an opposition may work to undermine linguistic regularity as a form of patriarchal ordering, by associating femininity with a rupturing of language, with the mysteriously destabilizing world of silence.[5] But while an aesthetics of silence may indeed signal disruption in Woolf, we must also register how far this evocation of the extralinguistic also merges with the cultural claims of a deliberately ambiguous and abstract modernism (Kermode; Reed); the alternative registers provided by feminine subjectivity thus offer a form of aesthetic authority.

Earlier impressionist texts suggest that this ideal of femininity as exceeding social and linguistic orders does not sum up modernist accounts of femininity; this is particularly the case in Woolf's work. Not only do her texts imagine feminine subjects moving between abstract, ephemeral realms and the world of social categories but the distinction characteristically does not remain stable—even here. For instance, to the extent that the lady in the picture occupies abstraction because she is a "lady," she does not truly occupy abstraction at all. The portraits thus question abstraction itself as a discrete category—even as they summon its cultural power. Feminine subjectivity particularly prompts this movement in Woolf, as it has for impressionism in the period more broadly. The feminine subject will offer Woolf's texts a central site for investigating the ways in which social specificity itself can be exceeded, while it allows her to question the terms of that excess.

Mrs. Dalloway will place the question of abstraction and subjectivity explicitly within the context of domestic femininity. The novel poses a series of questions about the value of the domestic woman and her activities: How do we read the central character of Clarissa Dalloway? Is Clarissa, like the lady in the portrait above, a figure who can transcend the ordinary social language of realist representation? Can she lead from "the curve to the straight," from "shades of silver, dun and rose into silence"? Or is she, like the ancestral portrait, defined irrevocably by her relation to wealth, status, and propriety? Is she merely a rich hostess— the logical dead end of conventional domestic femininity—or can her consciousness stand for or reach something else? These questions are pivotal for the novel, which expands on this dilemma in its portrait of

Clarissa: What belongs between the covers of a book entitled *Mrs. Dalloway?* Which aspects of her character must the novel present to have depicted her fully? This is the character's question too, as she considers whether she can now be summed up as merely "Mrs Richard Dalloway; not even Clarissa any more" (11) and as she wonders how she might hold out "her life in her arms . . . a whole life, a complete life . . . [and say] 'This is what I have made of it! This!'" (43).

Mrs. Dalloway repeatedly thematizes this problem of who Clarissa Dalloway is in the linked questions of whether character can expand beyond its conventionally visible borders by contact with others, and whether it can live on after death.[6] Clarissa, for instance, asks: "did it matter that she must inevitably cease completely . . . or did it not become consoling to believe that death ended absolutely? but that somehow in the streets of London, on the ebb and flow of things, here, there, she survived . . . she being part, she was positive, of the tree at home; of the house there . . . part of people she had never met" (9). Her question is repeated near the end of the novel, as Peter recalls how they "used to explore London" (152): "But she said, sitting on the bus going up Shaftesbury Avenue, she felt herself everywhere; not 'here, here, here'; and she tapped the back of the seat; but everywhere. She waved her hand, going up Shaftesbury Avenue. She was all that. So that to know her, or anyone, one must seek out the people who complete them, even the places. Odd affinities she had with people she had never spoken to, some woman in the street, some man behind a counter" (152–53).

The connection between Clarissa's literal or imaginative travels through London and her speculations about whether she might exceed the narrow confines of being merely "Mrs. Dalloway" is an important one. For while Woolf's novel interrogates Clarissa's character as a part of evaluating domestic femininity—of considering whether the domestic work of party-giving and hospitality may have a value beyond mere convention—the novel poses this question by redefining the domestic woman here as one who also travels.[7] Like Richardson's *Pilgrimage, Mrs. Dalloway* links its concern with the reach and nature of feminine subjectivity to the specific promise of female mobility. In asking whether Clarissa can move, the novel asks whether she can be formed by the urban spaces and figures around her in such a way that she can exceed her social place. Clarissa's movement through London, her contact with others in London, thus suggests a way she may be more than merely a housewife, more indeed than a constrained or even unified subject.

As Rachel Bowlby has noted, referring in particular to Woolf's 1927 essay "Street Haunting," walking through the city offers Woolf's female subjects the opportunity to expand beyond the confines of conventional social identities ("Walking, Women, and Writing"). In "Street Haunting," for instance, the subject becomes characteristically permeable and impressionist when the door of her house shuts behind her and she ventures out onto the city streets: "The shell-like covering which our souls have excreted to house themselves, to make for themselves a shape distinct from others, is broken, and there is left of all these wrinkles and roughnesses a central oyster of perceptiveness, an enormous eye" (21–22). Wandering and window-shopping, this figure floats upon a stream of impressions offered by the city or dives deep into identification with the imagined narratives of others on the street. Urban mobility thus seems to offer the possibility that the subject may identify elsewhere, live a variable and speculative life through the fantasy world of *flânerie*—here feminized explicitly as a form of window-shopping. Of course the promise of the urban wanderer's expansive identification with others is hardly unqualified in this essay—or in *Mrs. Dalloway.* "Street Haunting" evokes the limits of such connections by suggesting the Woolfian *flâneuse*'s complementary self-enclosure through economic privilege: identification with others is a luxury much like shopping; the street haunter remains separate from the spectacles she sees: from the dwarf in a shoe store or the derelicts lying on public steps (Squier 44–51).[8]

We might read *Mrs. Dalloway* then as an investigation of the metaphorical possibilities of female *flânerie.* The novel asks whether Clarissa Dalloway's contacts in London may expand her so thoroughly that she is no longer restricted by her social place. The problem is thematized most importantly in the question of whether Clarissa can communicate with the socially marginalized figure of Septimus Smith. In one of the text's best known passages, Clarissa hears of Septimus's death while she is at her party and, withdrawing alone, relives the event vicariously: "He had killed himself—but how? Always her body went through it first, when she was told, suddenly, of an accident; her dress flamed, her body burnt. He had thrown himself from a window. . . . Death was defiance. Death was an attempt to communicate. . . . Somehow it was her disaster—her disgrace. It was her punishment to see sink and disappear here a man, there a woman, in this profound darkness, and she forced to stand here in her evening dress" (184–85). This contact with Septimus is not literally a question of street encounters. In Paterian fashion, the home here opens itself to sensations and Clarissa imagines her contact with Septimus in the heart of protected domestic space. But the potential of their contact marks the possibility that the urban connections forged across London and followed throughout the novel shape even the most intimate interior gatherings. Indeed the convergence of two physically separate characters within Clarissa's private room—as within her consciousness—echoes a powerful claim for women's simultaneous mobility and autonomy, much like the one we saw in Richardson's *Pilgrimage*. If Clarissa can identify with Septimus in his death, her consciousness not only has been rendered mobile but inhabits a realm above those class divisions that would make his disaster merely inappropriate news for her party. The inner space of feminine consciousness—aligned here with the innermost space of the home—would thus be marked as a place that is both open to the world and able to rise above that world's merely social details.

In this optimistic reading of one register of the novel, the domestic woman appears as an exemplary modern, mobile subject: both dispersed and generalized. Feminine consciousness is thus formed by urban encounters—even those it does not directly have—even as it has the power to expand and incorporate London and Londoners of different classes. To depict modern woman a novel would thus have to describe all the people and places that complete her; by the same token the modern novel might represent all of London in a portrait of Clarissa, who may stand for more than just the wealthy socialite who shops for flowers, sews dresses, and hosts the prime minister. The universalizing capacities of the modern woman are here metaphorically embodied in the act of hospitality: such hospitality allows her to host the mobile spirit of those with whom she is linked far less concretely but far more importantly.

We might well be skeptical of this reading of Clarissa Dalloway, of class, or of domestic femininity. Indeed the novel itself suggests skepticism. The contact between Septimus and Clarissa, like the characterization of Clarissa herself, is susceptible of far less sympathetic readings. Such readings emerge the more we see the text as emphasizing the social divisions shaping London and shaping subjectivity. For instance we may read the vicariousness of Clarissa's response as a sign that Septimus's death enables the pleasures of her life in a very problematic way. Indeed she acknowledges that "she felt glad that he had done it; thrown it away. . . . He made her feel the beauty; made her feel the fun" (186). It is not only possible but necessary to read Septimus's death as—at least in part—a sacrifice for the good of Clarissa's parties. In this sense it echoes the sacrifices of the war itself, in which young men (here, lower-middle-class young men) die so that hollowly conventional, class-bound ideas about England and English community may continue.

However it is not my purpose here to argue that one or the other reading triumphs in *Mrs. Dalloway*. Clarissa Dalloway continues both as a socially produced character and as a figure for how consciousness may expand and be shaped by something less tangible. The text's importance lies in the way it sustains the simultaneous pressure of both readings throughout, juxtaposing social criticism with visions of a more abstract collective unity to be found through feminine consciousness. Indeed the novel's primary effect is to examine a constant tension between the two accounts of London, of feminine subjectivity, and of the novel's cultural work itself. Can the modern novel—*Mrs. Dalloway* seems to ask—provide a space which may legitimately abstract and connect various characters and classes? Is the cultural work of the novel—to paraphrase a familiar account of modernism—the task of subsuming social details, redeeming them and a postwar community in the higher realm of the aesthetic? Or is the work of the novel social critique? What are the possible relations between the two?

My argument throughout this study has been that modernist impressionism implicitly negotiates between an understanding of the novel as historically embedded and a vision of its cultural work as uniting, abstracting, and transcending social detail. *Mrs. Dalloway* in particular proposes that the novel's function is to provide an aestheticized cultural community, while insisting that the novel register those very social divisions that make aesthetic unity inadequate. The text's modernist rhetorical strategies illustrate this doubleness. We can see this in its famously mobile narrative voice. Moving from one character's consciousness to another, usually with the shared urban setting for transitions, the narrative dips into the stream of impressions of one subject after another. The narrative thus suggests both the city's divisions—the disparity and isolation of each character—and its fundamental unity, the fleeting sights and sounds that nonetheless join the varied figures together. The consistent tone of this voice reinforces the effect: the narrative embeds differing dialects and dictions but collects them in a distinct narrative style that is not self-consciously marked as having a social place.[9] This movement through varied consciousnesses, the novel's adaptation of impressionism, thus allows the text to register both immersion and distance, a multiplicity of voices and the power of one voice to encompass all the others.

For Woolf, this narrative strategy is linked to the problematic power of metaphor to unify the text. In *Mrs. Dalloway*, repeated metaphors offer a series of images which recur across different characters' thoughts and which provide models for the shape of the subject. For instance Clarissa's image of "being laid out like a mist between the people she knew best, who lifted her on their branches" (9) echoes Septimus's more literal sensation that he is dissolving into the earth: "The earth thrilled beneath him. Red flowers grew through his flesh" (68). More pervasively still, the novel repeats a series of metaphors for the plenitude of the subject in the image of "something central which permeated" (31). This image resonates throughout the novel, elaborated in its most sensuous detail in Clarissa's orgasmic account of desire for a woman resembling a "match burning in a crocus" (32): "It was a sudden revelation, a tinge like a blush which one tried to check and then, as it spread one yielded to its expansion, and rushed to the farthest verge and there quivered and felt the world come closer" (32). The sexualized metaphor figures an expansive, nearly borderless subject—in a sense the idealized version of what both Clarissa and the narrative voice might attain (Boone, *Libidinal Currents* 172–203).

But the recurrence of such images pulls the novel's characters together in part by finding a figurative resemblance that lies beneath the details of their lives; such metaphors provide a form of sheer structure that generalizes the subject away from its particularities and defines it through a register that is less clearly social or historical. In emphasizing such imagery, and in resting the novel's cohesion in part on the unities forged by such metaphors, Woolf reiterates the modernist concern with abstraction's role in the novel. Can the register of metaphor provide a shape for the modern novel? And if so, does such a shape work by providing a form of aesthetic generalization through which the profusion of social details governing Edwardian fiction may be organized and transcended?

We may take this as a question about the power of imagery—and particularly abstract imagery—to unify the novel, subjectivity, or historical detail. The category of abstract imagery will concern Woolf throughout her career—nowhere more so than in her novel *The Waves*, which centers on the question of whether abstract patterns adequately sum up the multiple social narratives of the city. We may use Woolf's concern here as a self-conscious reprise and response to Walter Pater's strategic invocation of abstraction in "The Child in the House," in which he suggested that the impressions of the city and the city's formation of the subject might be abstracted into the sheer play of color and light.[10] For Woolf, as for the other impressionist writers I have discussed, this question is linked to the power of feminine subjectivity to interiorize and abstract the pressures of the world—a power that must be absorbed into the claims of modernist narrative experiment. And lest we forget the persistence of this domestic figure for Woolf's discussion of abstraction, we might recall the connections she will again forge in *To the Lighthouse* between the troubling angel in the house and the power of abstract art. In that novel, Lily Briscoe's ability to paint depends on her mourning, incorporating, and surpassing Mrs. Ramsay—that quintessentially double domestic woman, both a guardian of conventional family structures and the creator of sublime artistic unities. In this novel, Lily's own abstract art takes over the organizing functions of Mrs. Ramsay's dinner party, as Lily's modern, more mobile version of feminine subjectivity inherits Mrs. Ramsay's centering role. Lily's painting further offers an answer to the question modernist impressionism has repeatedly asked about its relation to domestic femininity and Victorian culture more generally. When William Bankes asks her "What did she wish to indicate by the triangular purple shape, 'just there'? . . . [she replies that] it was Mrs. Ramsay reading to James. . . . But she had made no attempt at likeness" (52). Considering her painting, Bankes, perhaps an ideal reader of impressionist abstraction, concludes that "mother and child then—objects of universal veneration . . . might be reduced . . . to a purple shadow without irreverence" (52).

The Waves offers as thorough a version of Woolf's commitment to abstraction as we are likely to find. Traditionally read as the epitome of Woolf's high modernism, the novel elaborates the vision of character and form suggested by the sublimely abstract portrait of a lady we examined in *Between the Acts* (Naremore; Fleishman; Beer, "*Waves*").[11] It is her most formally experimental novel, the work whose pattern most explicitly departs from conventional, realist, narrative structures and whose notion of character is similarly unconventional. Thus the text has for a long time seemed separate from Woolf's concern with gender and with social patterning. Indeed in many ways *The Waves* presents speakers who embody a wholly abstract notion of character. As J. W. Graham has noted, the novel's speakers do not speak according to the conventions for representing "real" or socially marked speech, but rather speak in a stylized, uncolloquial manner. All six of the novel's speakers possess similar voices and use the same diction, their consciousnesses only separated by the cluster of particular images assigned to each; and all of these characters finally merge into one at the end. The novel's structure emphasizes a related notion of character by framing the speakers' stories with the cyclical pattern of waves that, only apparently distinct, emerge from the sea to be reabsorbed into it. It is a formal structure that seems to emphasize the irrelevance of conventional, socially grounded notions of subjectivity and subjective differences by comparing its speakers metaphorically with the unstable shapes of furniture in a room, whose very borders and substance are created and altered by the light that moves over them.

Woolf's own comments on the novel reinforce the impression that

The Waves might be shaped by a wholly abstract pattern, might be entirely opposed to the conventions of realist narratives with their interest in the details of the social world. It was "to be an abstract mystical eyeless book" (134) she wrote in her diary on November 7, 1928, one in which she would "eliminate all waste, deadness, superfluity . . . this appalling narrative business of the realist: getting on from lunch to dinner: it is false, unreal, merely conventional. Why admit anything to literature that is not poetry—by which I mean saturated?" (136).[12] Woolf similarly suggests that what we might assume to be conventional "characters" in the novel are indeed not characters at all, wondering why reviewers "should praise my characters when I meant to have none" (170).

But Woolf's comments on her intentions in writing the novel—her reassertions in her diary that the significant pattern of life lies beneath conventional, social narratives and beneath the individual identities formed in these narratives—simplify the notions of character and narrative form as the novel explores them. *The Waves* presents us with seven characters in many ways distinct and socially marked. It offers the details of material life, of conventional narratives and phrases, as equally central to the truth of subjectivity and its patterning. The tension between these two methods of characterization provides the basis for Woolf's investigation of abstraction in *The Waves*. It is Woolf's abstraction—and her examination of the limits of abstraction—to which I turn my attention here.

Abstraction for Woolf is a question in the formulation of character, as well as a question of form. Characters may be rendered abstractly in *The Waves;* they may also desire the abstract, a desire in which they are persistently thwarted and critiqued. This thwarted desire, no less than Woolf's own ambiguous strategies, creates the tension between differing visions of character in the novel. Abstraction and its refusal will thus structure the terms in which *The Waves* offers its central observation about subjectivity: that the apparently unitary self is unstable—only achieved at great cost and with great effort. In actuality, the novel suggests, subjectivity is dispersed, multiple, decentered (Minow-Pinkney 157–61). Thus Rhoda—the speaker who feels her identity to be most fragile—describes this identity slipping away: "'That is my face . . . in the looking-glass behind Susan's shoulder—that face is my face. But I will duck behind her to hide it, for I am not here. I have no face. . . . I shift and change and am seen through in a second'" (43).

All of the speakers in *The Waves* describe themselves as similarly dispersed, though not all do so with Rhoda's sense of fear. Bernard, for instance, seeks out conversations with strangers to court the dissolution of boundaries that such contact brings: "'I at once wish to approach [the man entering the train compartment, he notes]; I instinctively dislike the sense of his presence, cold, unassimilated, among us. I do not believe in separation. We are not single'" (67). Bernard's habitual garrulity proceeds from his sense that he does not have one fixed identity but rather many, which emerge in response to his surroundings. "'What am I? I ask. This? No, I am that.... I am not one and simple but complex and many.... [I] have to cover the entrances and exits of several different men who alternately act their parts as Bernard'" (76). The single identities by which others know us, *The Waves* thus suggests, are fictions we carefully construct for ourselves, shapes we impose or that are imposed on us to provide us with an illusion of solidity. Louis signs his name to business papers—"'I, and again I, and again I. Clear, firm, unequivocal, there it stands, my name. Clear-cut and unequivocal am I too'" (167)—and the signature, despite his sense that "'a vast inheritance of experience is packed in me,'" renders him safely "'compact'" (167). For Louis notes that "'if I do not... out of the many men in me make one... then I shall fall like snow and be wasted'" (170).

What interests me here is the fact that *The Waves* suggests contrasting ways of understanding this fictiveness of unitary identity, and through this conflict frames its debate on the power of abstraction. The possibilities offer a divided vision of what the true nature of subjectivity might be, and they suggest as well the implications for the modernist novel's narrative form of such differing visions. Rhoda's lack of a single identity, for instance—her sense that, despite what the mirror displays, she is not "'here, [she has] no face'" (43)—implies that the alternative to the false picture in the mirror, the alternative to a single life fixed in a specific, material, culturally framed body, lies radically elsewhere, out of the cultural world, in a realm both abstract and metaphorical. Thus when she touches the rail of her bed each night in order to hold on to her precarious identity in a material world—to "'assure myself... of something hard. Now I cannot sink; cannot altogether fall through the thin sheet now'" (27)—the realm to which she drifts is mutable and abstract. "'I am above the earth now.... All is soft, and bending. Walls and cupboards whiten and bend their yellow squares on top of which a pale glass gleams. Out of me now my mind can pour'" (27).

In contrast, Bernard's experience of dispersed identity looks quite different and has different implications for the novel that would depict him. His sense, as he puts it, that "'I have to cover the entrances and exits of several different men who alternately act their parts as Bernard,'" locates the subject's multiplicity in the fact that it plays many "parts." The resistance he offers to singular identity thus does not draw on an abstract world apart from the conventional, material one, but draws instead on the multiplication of conventions that form him. Indeed one of the novel's parodies of Bernard centers on the familiarity of these conventions. For instance, in order to invent a "spontaneous" persona for himself, he imitates Byron: "'I want her to say . . . "Where did I read that? Oh, in Bernard's letter." It is the speed, the hot, molten effect, the lava flow of sentence into sentence that I need. Who am I thinking of? Byron of course. I am, in some ways like Byron. Perhaps a sip of Byron will help to put me in the vein'" (79). Neville satirizes this procession of masks: "'Once you were Tolstoi's young man; now you are Byron's young man; perhaps you will be Meredith's young man; then you will visit Paris in the Easter vacation and come back wearing a black tie, some detestable Frenchman whom nobody has ever heard of. Then I shall drop you'" (87). But while Neville may believe himself to be "'one person—myself'" (87), and claims he can find the one, real Bernard—"'Byron never made tea as you do, who fill the pot so that when you put the lid on the tea spills over. . . . that is so essentially you'" (87)—Bernard experiences this fixing as an artificial contraction. "'All semblances were rolled up, [he says] "You are not Byron; you are your self." To be contracted by another person into a single being—how strange'" (89).

The Waves repeatedly comments on this dispersal of subjectivity; the common language with which it does so forms part of the novel's antirealist, often abstracted tone. But the novel is also concerned to embed its characters' very speculations on the force of social convention within a socially concrete world. It insists, that is, that its characters are not simply abstract entities whose multiplicity or singularity must be debated, but subjects shaped by middle- and upper-class British culture. The novel's speakers find their way through proper schools to careers and identities as businessman, mother, academic, or socialite, and recognizable social conventions shape their ideas about identity, and even about escaping from it.

Such shaping appears, for instance, in the way the male characters define themselves in relation to school authorities and to embodiments of conventional heroism and athleticism such as Percival (Booker 36–41). Even their rebellion against such authority, figured, for instance, by Neville's homoerotic desire for Percival and for the series of beloved figures succeeding him, will replicate the structures of authority to be defied. Thus, proclaiming his rejection of public school values, Neville nonetheless re-creates their authoritarianism. The shaping force of authority will persist, not only in his love for Percival, who "'takes my devotion; he accepts my tremulous, no doubt abject offering'" (48), but in the rigid order of his later poetry.

A similar cultural order governs the life of the girls, framing both their accommodation to conventional identities and their imaginative construction of spaces outside them.[13] This framing is made explicit in the response of these characters to their school looking glass—an emblem of the way the school calls on them to shape themselves as presentable objects of a social gaze. Jinny characteristically moves from objecting to the mirror—"'it cuts off our heads'" (41)—to accepting its definition of her body and absorbing it as an organic image: "'[In front of the long glass] I see myself entire. . . . Look, when I move my head I ripple all down my narrow body; even my thin legs ripple like a stalk in the wind'" (41–42). But the rebellious alternatives imagined by the other female characters are no less framed by the glass. Most importantly, Rhoda's self-dissolving movement away from identity and the material world that we observed earlier is generated precisely by a recognition of her identity in culture: "'*That is my face in the looking-glass . . . that face is my face.* But I will duck behind her to hide it, for I am not here. I have no face'" (43, my emphasis).

The Waves thus begins to suggest that subjects cannot escape the terms of a material and social world, even in their most deliberate attempts to find spaces wholly free of it. The novel will devote considerable attention to the terms in which characters imagine these alternatives—and in particular to the language of abstraction in which they do so—in order to ask what function this language serves. The question is central to the problem of abstraction and generalization we have seen Woolf—and modernist impressionism—address elsewhere. Indeed we might rephrase it as a question that applies to Woolf's project in *The Waves* as well as to the motivation of characters within it: What is the work of an imagined realm that is sheerly abstract?

The Waves takes up this question by considering the abstract imagery so central to its characters' and its own representations of an alternative world. The imagery is most marked in Rhoda's repeated descriptions of an alternative space. Fleeing the torment of social gatherings, for instance, she imagines landscapes where human bodies and faces become abstract and featureless. There she "'see[s] a shape, white, but not of stone. . . . When the white arm rests upon the knee it is a triangle; now it is upright—a column; now a fountain, falling. It makes no sign, it does not beckon, it does not see us'" (139).

The novel explores such flights—and their language—further when it narrates Rhoda's trip to a music hall to seek consolation for a world in which Percival has just died, and to escape from the press of crowds and commerce in Oxford Street. The music seems to transport her far away; when the violinists play, "'there is ripple and laughter like the dance of olive trees and their myriad-tongued grey leaves'" (161), and Rhoda seems to see "'the thing that lies beneath the semblance of the thing'" (163). In figuring this mysterious element that Rhoda seeks beneath semblances, the novel shows her vision once again turning to abstraction, in a passage whose tensions bear investigating. "'There is a square; there is an oblong. The players take the square and place it upon the oblong. They place it very accurately; they make a perfect dwelling-place. Very little is left outside. The structure is now visible; what is inchoate is here stated. . . . This is our triumph; this is our consolation'" (163).

While Rhoda's images promise relief, it is notable how quickly the novel unravels their promise (Naremore 182–83). It does so precisely by unraveling their abstraction. The squares and oblongs are hardly transcendent; they are manipulated like building blocks—an action which seems to require a great deal of material effort. "'The players come again. But they are mopping their faces. They are no longer so spruce or so debonair'" (163). The value of the apparently abstract structure thus built is further qualified by the modified language of the passage: The placement is "very" accurate; the dwelling-place is "perfect"; "very little" is left outside. This diminution of the square and oblong and their capacity to stand for transcendent refuge will be reinforced later, when these same images are associated with an English political past. Visiting Hampton Court with the others, Rhoda notes that "'Wren's palace, like the quartet played to the dry and stranded people in the stalls, makes an oblong. A square is stood upon the oblong and we say, "This is our dwelling place. The structure is now visible. Very little is left outside"'" (228). And as Bernard notes, the past evoked by such palaces is more trivial than transcendent: "'Our English past'" he says, "'—one inch of light. Then people put teapots on their heads and say, "I am a King!"'" (227).

With passages such as Rhoda's, *The Waves* casts doubt on the opposition between an abstract world and the marketplace it is designed to oppose. The square and the oblong are meant to protect Rhoda from the rush of people and commerce on London's streets: "'As we lurch down Regent Street, and I am flung upon this woman, upon this man, I am not injured, I am not outraged by the collision. A square stands upon an oblong. Here are mean streets where chaffering goes on in street markets, and every sort of iron rod, bolt and screw is laid out, and people swarm off the pavement, pinching raw meat with thick fingers. The structure is visible. We have made a dwelling place'" (163–64). And yet the passage reveals the connections between abstraction and the market far more than their division. "The structure is visible . . . a dwelling-place" might oppose the swarming market, or it might just as easily refer to the market itself, since what is bought and sold in this market is just a concrete version of Rhoda's square and oblong—iron rods, bolts, and screws. Rhoda's concern to escape from a conventional, material world is thus a form of class anxiety as much as a desire for transcendence. After all, the novel offers a pointed satire of the very music hall within which Rhoda seeks "the thing beneath the semblance of the thing." Here music is placed fully within the life of an all-too-material, all-too-social world. The hall is a place "'where one pays money and goes in'" (162). Its audience is identified by its propriety ("'white hair waved under our hats; slim shoes; little bags . . . here and there a military moustache'") and by a grotesque materiality: "'somnolent people who have come here after lunch on a hot afternoon,'" who have "'eaten beef and pudding enough to live for a week without tasting food,'" who "'cluster like maggots on the back of something that will carry us on'" (162). In this parodic context, we must reread the music hall as a site of attempted social distinction rather than as a sheer escape from the social.

What we see in *The Waves*, then, is a consistent questioning of the power of abstraction, reembedding it in the social terms it claims to transcend. This strategy—as Rhoda's turn to the music hall may begin to suggest—has important implications for the workings of art, implications which will be particularly resonant for the question of modernist form in Woolf's text itself. For the complications visible in Rhoda's turn to abstract imagery suggest that abstraction may be a problematic category for the modernist novel and a problematic solution to the dilemmas of the subject.

The Waves is quite explicit about the difficulties of abstract art, difficulties it introduces through the question of abstract imagery I have been examining. The novel explores these problems thematically in part by focusing on visual art in a scene in which Bernard visits the National Gallery after Percival's death to separate himself from the narratives of ordinary life—to "'submit [him]self to the influence of minds like [his] outside the sequence'" (155) and to find comfort in something explicitly abstract—that is, nonreferential. He goes looking for pictures like Rhoda's shapes that "'[do] not beckon,'" pictures that "'make no reference . . . do not nudge . . . do not point'" (156).[14] Needless to say, this turn toward abstraction proves neither simple nor wholly successful. In part this is because Bernard turns, curiously, to referential art: to paintings of "'gardens; and Venus among her flowers . . . saints and blue madonnas'" (156).

As this last phrase suggests, abstraction can certainly be found here—in the "blue madonnas"—but it will be difficult to disentangle from reference, and certainly will not solve the troubles that reference evokes.

In fact it is the paintings' abstract quality itself—which appears most often as their color—that compromises claims for the transcendence of abstraction. Color pulls Bernard back to the material world, rather than away from it, by producing sensation like that which first fleshed the world for him as a child. Looking at a painting he observes "'The ruffled crimson against the green lining; the march of pillars; the orange light behind the black, pricked ears of the olive trees. Arrows of sensation strike from my spine, but without order'" (157).[15] Indeed these paintings do not offer a world apart because they cannot be divided from Bernard's emotions: "'Behold then, the blue madonna streaked with tears'" (157). Even the color of the paintings and the visual movement of their design will lead Bernard to place them within a kind of realist narrative—a narrative that recasts abstract color as the product of a human painter's story, even as it suggests that emotion may find adequate expression in color itself. "'Yet that crimson must have burnt in Titian's gizzard [he comments]. No doubt he rose with the great arms holding the cornucopia, and fell, in that descent'" (157).

When Bernard tries to sum up what he has gained from this journey into abstraction, he produces an image quite divided in its assessment of the transcendent image of reality, the "thing beneath the semblance of the thing" that abstraction seems to offer. "'Yet something is added to my interpretation [he notes]. Something lies deeply buried. For one moment I thought to grasp it. But bury it, bury it; let it breed, hidden in the depths of my mind some day to fructify. After a long lifetime, loosely, in a moment of revelation, I may lay hands on it, but now the idea breaks in my hand. Ideas break a thousand times for once that they globe themselves entire. They break, they fall over me'" (157–58).

We might take Bernard's image as an emblem of the problem of artistic abstraction and its promise to offer a deep reality beneath the detailed narratives of representational art. Such a submerged and abstracted reality cannot be "grasped" in isolation; more often the attempt to separate out "the idea" merely breaks it; and its fall over him, echoing the image of his falling bathwater, suggests a return to the realm of sensation. Still more significant is Bernard's decision to "bury it, bury it," to return it to the earth where, like a seed or animal, it will "breed" and "fructify"—words which undermine the abstraction of the idea, linking it with fertility and the earth, and marking as unfruitful the very attempt to abstract out the "thing that lies beneath the semblance of the thing."

And when Bernard tries to theorize his idea abstractly, he soon gives up: "'Line and colours, they survive, therefore . . . '" he begins; then he yawns, he grows numb, and he hails a taxi (158).

The Waves thus thematizes the problems of abstract art very explicitly. Indeed much of the novel's anti-realism comes from this foregrounding of debates about abstraction, about art, and about character which mark the novel as metafiction. This metafictional quality is all the stronger because the novel's narrative is so clearly patterned to explore the relation of abstract form to conventional social narratives played out in the novel's debates, to test the power of abstract patterning. One important element of this formal patterning is the novel's rise to a collective epiphanic moment halfway through the novel, as its characters gather to celebrate the departure of Percival for India. Again we might read this moment as an emblem of the questions the novel poses about abstraction and narrative patterning. For its status as a centering epiphany will allow the novel to question the shaping power of modernist epiphany itself—with its claim to organize both life and art.

Here the connection between abstraction and epiphany is importantly linked to the mysterious character of Percival. Percival, with his peculiarly double function in *The Waves*, embodies most pointedly the novel's doubled structure of characterization. He is at once the most conventional of imperial heroes and the most purely abstract of characters, existing only as a structuring absence uniting the others. If Percival himself importantly concentrates the novel's debates over character, his force in this moment also comes from the way the novel's characters use his presence here to try to formulate an alternative, abstract, and non-narrative model for the vision of subjectivity he seems to promise. This alternative in turn illuminates the novel's considerations of its own form, elucidating both the appeal and the implications of abstraction for modernist narrative.

Percival is the figure who most often allows the speakers in *The Waves* to perceive the limits of their conventional identities; his presence moves them to reimagine these identities as surfaces, semblances, hiding the truth beneath. Louis, for instance, points out that "'it is Percival . . . sitting silent . . . who makes us aware that these attempts to say "I am this, I am that," . . . are false. . . . We have tried to accentuate differences. . . . But there is a chain whirling round, round, in a steel-blue circle beneath'" (137). Here, most obviously, Percival exposes the falsehood of separate individual identity as it is formed by language. Disrupting the narrative line of an individual life with images of depth, he allows the others to realize instead that there is a coherent wholeness, the unity of a "circle beneath." Similarly, his silence throughout the novel—never speaking, only spoken of—stands opposed to other characters' talk, and to the conventional stories and the identities with which that talk is associated.

This "unity beneath" conventional identity promised by Percival will be embodied in the moment constructed at his dinner party, where the characters are united, their separate selves forged into a single general identity: "'we, who . . . loved Percival'" (147), "'a seven-sided flower'" (127). This unity is possible only within the confines of an epiphanic moment standing apart from the characters' conventionally plotted lives and the discretely divided identities in which they live them, and like many such moments in modernism, it seems to promise a view of a truth beyond conventional vision. Unlike the world it transcends, for instance, the moment of unity is all-inclusive, leaving nothing out. As though to illustrate this, characters begin (almost parodically) to catalogue everything the moment encloses: "'Forests and far countries on the other side of the world,' said Rhoda, 'are in it; seas and jungles. . . .' 'Happiness is in it,' said Neville, 'and the quiet of ordinary things. A table, a chair, a book with a paper-knife stuck between the pages. . . .' 'Week-days are in it,' said Susan, 'Monday, Tuesday, Wednesday'" (145–46).

But just as important as this encyclopedic completion is the moment's existence as a coherent whole whose unity comes from its primarily (if convolutedly) spatial nature. The moment appears as a globe: "'Let us hold it for one moment,' said Jinny; 'love, hatred, by whatever name we call it, this globe whose walls are made of Percival, of youth and beauty, and something so deep sunk within us that we shall perhaps never make this moment out of one man again'" (145). The logistics of this moment are complex, if not impossible, and the dynamics are both spatial and abstract: intangible qualities imagined as interior—"Percival . . . youth and beauty, and something . . . deep sunk within us"—themselves form the outer edge of a globe (logically still further within), which paradoxically can be held as if in the palm of a hand. To attempt to imagine this moment is to figure out a spatial knot; its involutions halt the flow of narrative for the reader, reenacting and reconfirming the moment's separation from linear narrative, marking it in the atemporality of a different—visual, spatial, and abstract—register.[16] The moment Percival inspires thus unites a cluster of privileged values linked with abstraction—unity, completion, spatial abstraction, silence, poetry (Louis's "steel-blue circle" of unity appears elsewhere as a "'steel ring of clear poetry that shall connect'" [128])—and binds them to a notion of time that stands against linear and socially particularized narrative.

This moment of unity offers a paradigm of modernist epiphany and its promise: it is part of a timeless whole, in which collective identity promises to generalize away the local details of character, of class, or of history. But in a pattern that will have become familiar, Woolf's text complicates such a moment in various ways: by the doubleness of Percival's characterization in the novel as well as by the desires with which the characters invest it. For Percival of course is the novel's most conventional, most thoroughly class-marked, and parodied, figure. As public school hero and aspiring imperial administrator, he becomes the central target of the novel's fierce satire of those public school ideals and imperial fantasies shaping the lives of its speakers. In childhood one of the "'boasting boys . . . [who] leave butterflies trembling with their wings pinched off'" (46–47), Percival will become an administrator of English justice in India, solving Indian problems "'by applying the standards of the West, by using the violent language that is natural to him'" (136).

And if the novel's speakers characterize their shared moment at the dinner party as a transcendence of conventional identities and plots, the ideological weight of such an escape becomes clear in the way that it takes shape against an inevitable flow of narrative and age. The speakers use the occasion of Percival's triumphal departure for India as an opportunity to imagine their own youth as a heroic form of power and possession. "'How proudly we sit here,' said Jinny, 'we who are not yet twenty-five. . . . Beauty rides our brows. . . . Days and days are to come; . . . we have scarcely broken into our hoard'" (141). The vision offered by such a moment of unity promises the same control, a power imperial in its scope: "'Look [says Rhoda]—the outermost parts of the earth—pale shadows on the utmost horizon, India for instance, rise into our purview. The world that had been shrivelled, rounds itself; . . . we see muddy roads, twisted jungle, swarms of men and the vulture that feeds on some bloated carcass as within our scope, part of our proud and splendid province'" (137). The universal vision of the epiphanic moment is thus itself a metaphorical form of global empowerment; it converts the precariousness of the speakers' lives into a moment of imperial control and vision.

And yet, despite such important qualifications, this moment uniting the speakers offers a powerful paradigm for the novel's attempts to work through the problems of modernist literary form. In proposing in her diary that *The Waves* be affiliated not only with abstraction but with poetry, rather than with that "appalling narrative business of the realist" (136), Woolf suggests that some alternate, poetic, form shapes her novel, and shapes the complex interrogation of subjectivity it sustains. The epiphanic moment, with its links to poetry as well as abstraction, establishes one such potential model for *The Waves* itself within the context of the speakers' narratives; the rise toward unity and subsequent dispersal suggested by such a moment may encircle and shape the multiple, interweaving stories of its characters' everyday, conventional lives.

In considering the potency of such an encircling and shaping form, *The Waves* investigates the implications of the poetry which provides its literary model. The novel's evocations of poetry are voiced mainly by Louis, who wishes "'to make a steel ring of clear poetry that shall connect the gulls and the women with bad teeth'" (128); to take that which "'hint[s] at some other order, and better, which makes a reason everlastingly . . . [and] fix [it] in words, to forge in a ring of steel, though Percival destroys it. . . . [Yet] it is Percival who inspires poetry'" (40). Louis's language here connects poetry with those images of circularity and depth (the ring, the circle, the globe) associated with the transcendent moment. And it reinforces the connection such images make between the values of unity and totality and the transcendent supraworldliness claimed for the moment. But poetry's unity sounds coercive and ominous. Poetry has "'binding'" (95) power for Louis; it "'ropes you in'" (95) to create its unity. Poetry, with its encircling order, here resembles nothing so much as Neville's insistence on the singularity of character; poetry, rather than encompassing, begins to contract. Related images of order and circularity in the novel reinforce this sense of their entrapping nature; circularity itself, we should note, is often figured as a "'chain'" (137), "'steel-blue'" (137). Thus Bernard's engagement, for instance, prompts in the others the sense that "'something irrevocable has happened. A circle has been cast on the waters; a chain is imposed. We shall never flow freely again.' 'For one moment only,' said Louis. 'Before the chain breaks, before disorder returns, see us fixed, see us displayed, see us held in a vice'" (142).

Like Rhoda's squares and oblongs, poetry's unifying power is socially motivated. Louis's concern to enclose the world with poetry is linked to his status as the novel's perpetual outsider, an Australian forever excluded from the unity of the English world. His reestablishment of a new unity in poetry appears less a perception of a truth beneath society's trivial divisions than an order determined by his particular sense of exclusion. Further, this new unity will repeat the social unities and exclusions he justly resents, and which this image of poetry is designed to oppose.[17] Just a moment before invoking this "binding ring," Louis feels himself outside another "unbroken" circle, at his eating-house: "'The circle is unbroken; the harmony complete. Here is the central rhythm; here the common mainspring. I watch it expand, contract; and then expand again. Yet I am not included'"(94). If poetry here, like abstraction elsewhere,

proves more coercive than illuminating, its unities false and compensa-
tory, to what other options can the novel turn?

Against these ever more qualified powers of poetry to encompass the
patterns of subjectivity, the tenuous order of life, *The Waves* will turn
for a model of literary innovation, paradoxically enough—to narrative,
centrally through Bernard, with his stories and phrases. Bernard's little
stories, though they are conventional and thus, we might expect, restricted and restricting, in fact appear in *The Waves* as instances, not of conventional closure but of incompletion and escape (Booker 47). These stories have no closure in part because Bernard never seems to finish them;
Neville speaks of them as "'tail[ing] off absurdly'" (51), and describes
Bernard as being, like his stories, "'a dangling wire'" (19), always trail-
ing off in a new direction. But Bernard's inability to complete a story is
not mere personal idiosyncrasy; this incompletion also offers a kind of
proliferation or excess that the novel will take seriously as a possible
pattern for new narrative structures. More a collection of ever-emerging
images than a plot, these stories promise escape rather than contraction.
When Bernard talks, "'burbl[ing] on'" (37), Neville comments: "'up they
bubble—images. "Like a camel," . . . "a vulture." The camel is a vulture;
the vulture is a camel; for Bernard is a dangling wire, loose, but seductive. Yes, for when he talks, when he makes his foolish comparisons, a
lightness comes over one. One floats, too, as if one were that bubble; one
is freed; I have escaped, one feels'" (38).

The bubbling up, the proliferation of images, like the proliferation
of Bernard's stories in the novel as a whole, links this storytelling to the
fertility we found in Bernard's buried globe of an idea at the National
Gallery. Bernard's images are enormously generative: "'Images breed instantly. I am embarrassed by my own fertility. . . . To speak . . . is to bring
about an explosion. Up goes the rocket. Its golden grain falls, fertilizing,
upon the rich soil of my imagination'" (117). Despite the evident parody
of this ejaculatory imagery, I think we may see in this kind of storytelling a formal correlative to that self-consciously multiple, fictional subjectivity found in Bernard's masquerades, a form quite unlike the coercive encircling of "'complete integration'" that gradually becomes linked
to Louis and his poetry (39), and to the false closure and transcendence
of an aesthetics of the moment.

With Bernard's stories, *The Waves* imagines an alternative narrative
form that may oppose closure and unity with the values of profusion and
excess, values that may construct a subject and a story without recourse
to abstraction. We must recognize here an alternative that speaks directly
to the issues of form and abstraction that Woolf's own text grapples with

narratively as well as thematically. For in critiquing the poetry privileged by Woolf's diaries, and in setting by its side the potential of those narratives against which poetry, unity, and abstraction are defined, *The Waves* rearticulates the problems of the abstract moment in terms that shape its own formal design. Indeed the structure of *The Waves* may be seen as a debate between the pressure of abstraction on narrative and characterization, and the counterpressure of a narrative form that shapes story around the trajectories of socially shaped subjects.

For on the one hand the overarching shape of the novel furthers the aesthetic values associated with the moment, and contributes to the abstracted vision of character associated with those values. The novel frames the soliloquies of its speakers, as they proceed from childhood to death, with italicized interludes describing both the sea and a house with its garden during the course of one day. These interludes provide a metaphorical frame for the lives of the text's characters, offering the cyclical structure of an implicitly recurring day as a governing metaphor, indeed claiming the power of metaphor to unify characters and encompass a character's life. In doing so, the interludes suggest that the conventional, socially detailed narrative elements of a character's life are inessential; that fiction can more fully describe subjectivity by abstracting away from such details. The vision of the waves and the house offered in these sections reinforces the notion that social distinctions—or any distinctions—between characters are illusory, for the subject's identifying boundaries are only apparent. The metaphor of the waves, for instance, frames the particularity of any one wave as merely temporary. And the description of household objects in these interludes similarly establishes their borderlessness: their identifying shapes are malleable; they are wholly altered, indeed made, by the changing light: "*The light touched something green in the window corner and made it a lump of emerald, a cave of pure green like stoneless fruit. It sharpened the edges of chairs and tables*" (29). "*Then shapes took on mass and edge. Here was the boss of a chair; here the bulk of a cupboard*" (110).

The narrative of the characters' lives that is contained between these interludes is thus framed by their pattern and by the abstracting metaphorical pressure of what they portray. The speakers' narratives themselves participate in this same pattern to some extent, as I have already suggested: in rising to an apparently epiphanic moment at its center they suggest a nonlinear, indeed nonsocial pattern to their lives. These narratives will also echo the interludes when all the characters merge into Bernard at the end—when Bernard's sense that he is "'not one person,'"—"'I am many people; I do not altogether know who I am—Jinny, Susan,

Neville, Rhoda, or Louis: or how to distinguish my life from theirs'"
(276)—becomes literal at last: "'Here on my brow is the blow I got when
Percival fell. Here on the nape of my neck is the kiss Jinny gave Louis.
My eyes fill with Susan's tears'" (289).

But while *The Waves* thus presents its characters' lives as framed,
merged, made spatial rather than linear, metaphoric rather than socially
detailed, the novel extends its critique of abstraction by clarifying this
model's limits, by formally intertwining one model with another. Indeed
the two organizations might be better described as standing in perpetual
tension in the novel. For the shape of narrative in *The Waves*, despite its
emphatically centering moment, is equally formed by the trajectories of
the characters' roles—tracing their paths from childhood through densely
culturally specified lives to death—and the novel as a whole takes much
of its momentum from these paths (Fleishman 155). Indeed the very
merging of characters in Bernard at the end may yield the linear sense of
a climactic ending.[18]

Still more importantly though, the novel ends less in the triumph of
one set of narrative terms than in a moment fueled by their conflict.
Bernard's assertion of climactic victory at the moment of his death is
indeed undermined by the novel's closing reassertion of death as a reab-
sorption of the waves into the sea—a reassertion of cyclical organization
and generic, transpersonal unity.[19] But the contradictions of this climax
prevent our sense of easy closure; instead they reveal the unresolvable
tension between Woolf's two models of narrative form—and between the
languages for describing subjectivity which accompany them. For the
momentum of Bernard's soliloquy and of the path of his life as he sees it
at this concluding moment derives from a rhetoric that is anything but
abstract: "'It is death against whom I ride with my spear couched and my
hair flying back like a young man's, like Percival's, when he galloped in
India. I strike spurs into my horse. Against you I will fling myself, un-
vanquished and unyielding, O Death!'" (297). His rhetoric—the conventional language of imperial heroism—may be inadequate here, but it is
only through its rhetorical pressure that the novel's final line—*"The
waves broke on the shore"* (297)—attains its conclusive, containing, and
abstracting force.

The Waves is bound to this conflict, and in this sense it offers a suggestive epitome and endpoint for impressionist modernism. Endlessly
fascinated by the abstract moment and the abstracted subject, by metaphorically patterned forms as well as by their perpetual unraveling, *The
Waves* manages its critique through the deadlocked embrace of both
positions. In this it not only suggests the centrality of abstraction to

modernist fiction but simultaneously traces the political complexity of that abstraction's production. The persistent doubleness of characterization and form in *The Waves*, then, provides a self-conscious inquiry into the force and adequacy of abstract design to narrate permeable subjects. In shaping its speakers by multiple cultural narratives and examining the escape from those identities and stories that abstraction promises, *The Waves* makes clear the allure of abstraction so central to modernist impressionism. It clarifies abstraction's promise of a world contained and transcended by the novel and clarifies too abstraction's dependence on the most constraining of ideologies. It is an appeal, and a critique, that Woolf pursued throughout her work, considering in novel after novel, from *Mrs. Dalloway* through *The Waves*, the potential for an abstract, unifying order to give shape and meaning to visibly restricting social plots. If *The Waves* is a central focus for this investigation and critique in both its stylistic extremity and the stark insistence of its structural interconnection, it also offered Woolf and the modernist novel a way of moving past the coercive promise of abstraction as the central method of reimagining cultural stories, and in particular reimagining cultural stories for women. In her subsequent novels, *The Years* and *Between the Acts*, for instance, Woolf shapes her narratives more fully through gaps and dispersals rather than the unity provisionally ordering *The Waves*; she turns to proliferating, overlapping narratives much like Bernard's stories, displacing or disrupting the image of family homes and domestic spaces and questioning the subject's formation by refracting it through a multiplicity of protagonists and stories (DuPlessis 164). It is a shift of view made possible by—indeed inherent in—the negotiation with modernist abstraction performed by *The Waves* and by modernist impressionism more generally.

The doubled registers of subjectivity and form in both *Mrs. Dalloway* and *The Waves*—in which abstraction is both central and precarious—should remind us that the categories of the social and the abstract, indeed the gendered and the abstract, cannot be simply distinguished as cultural opposites in modernism. Arising from a shared historical context, one gives rise to the other, and reemerges through it. The mystical and abstract imagery of *The Waves* emerges from a long tradition of imagining feminized private consciousness and domestic difference in modernity as a whole and at the turn of the century in particular; we might say that it is no coincidence that the recurrent universalizing, metaphorical space in *The Waves* which provides a formal frame for the narrative is that of a house. Nor perhaps should we be surprised that in earlier drafts Woolf considered figuring the novel's impersonal voice as the voice of a woman (*A*

Writer's Diary 140). In this connection between feminine interiority and the possibilities of an abstract and impersonal subject, between the home and the abstracting space of metaphor, we may read the mark of gender even in its apparent disappearance. Thus Woolf's work as a whole recapitulates questions that have been pivotal for the trajectory of modernist impressionism: what is the shape of feminine subjectivity, what is the place of social specificity in the novel, what are the possibilities of abstraction? The category of femininity has no single position in this discussion; rather its movements between the material and the transcendent, the worldly and the unworldly, place it at the center of those continuing debates that shape modernism and its notions of art.

Epilogue

I have been suggesting throughout this study that to read the narrative experiments and the narrative politics of modernism we must recognize the ways that feminine subjectivity centers one of its most important strands, impressionist fiction. In emphasizing the importance of the feminine subject and the work it does in grounding modernist innovation and authority, I have sought to complicate a series of oppositions that frame our understanding of this literary movement. I have argued, that is, for the difficulty of disentangling those aspects of modernism that acknowledge its debt to history and those that try to efface it; those aspects of modernism that register the intractable specificity of place and those that seek a universalizing transcendence; the aesthetic form that aims for subversive effect and the one that consolidates authority; a modernism that rejects an ostensibly feminized modern world and one that embraces it. By reading the feminine subject as modernism's central figure for subjectivity—by showing how this historically imagined figure might join literature's historical reference to its formal innovation, might create fantasies of interiority as well as fantasies of openness, ideals of cultural authority as well as hindrances to it—I have sought to rework our account of modernist canons as well as the critical paradigms we use to approach this movement.

Clearly one of my purposes in insisting on the importance of femininity to a movement so long canonically defined as masculine has been to emphasize, as other recent feminist critics have done, that our revisionist readings of modernism cannot leave intact the idea of a core movement whose texts concern masculinity but not femininity, male authors but not female authors. Such an approach, as others have pointed out, relegates female writers and the category of feminine subjectivity itself to a marginal or alternative space that does not touch the central texts they seem to oppose (Lyon, "Militant Discourse"). This is one evident reason that I have read male and female writers together and, more importantly, read together ideas about masculine and feminine subjectivity—often finding that their relation is less one of opposition than of uneasy identity, overlap, and dependence. This is also the reason I have been concerned to trace the links between ideas of feminine subjectivity and those of literary authority. To register this subject's importance requires that we attend to the ways modern femininity helps shape modernism's fantasies of aesthetic autonomy and abstraction just as much as it unravels them.

While I have worked out my argument through an analysis of a strand of modernism—impressionism—that I find central, self-conscious, and important, my goal has not been to substitute a new modernist canon for an old one. The historical, thematic, and formal convergences I have traced here shape a much broader range of texts in the period. If they influence the canonical work of Joyce and Eliot, as I suggested in my introduction, they reach no less to the work of less-canonized writers such as Jean Rhys or Katherine Mansfield—both of whom trace the precarious status of the private sphere and consider how the predicaments of modern femininity reshape the borders of the subject, redefining fiction and the work of its form. For that matter, while I have focused in part on the way impressionist fictions define their narrative strategies as forms of high culture, the problems I have discussed reveal useful commonalities with popular fiction of the period. Michael Arlen's best-selling novel *The Green Hat*, for instance, would tell us much about the way feminine mystery and obscurity, pressed in service of masculine narrative authority, can contribute to the popularization of ambiguous style. Similarly, Dorothy Sayers's *Gaudy Night* underlines the critically noted resemblance between modernism and detective fiction while connecting these forms explicitly to problems of modern women's narrative and professional authority (McHale 9). Thus to take feminine subjectivity as a pivot for both narrative and historical questions may reveal links between texts that have seemed to occupy different cultural terrains, canonical and noncanonical, popular and obscure, mass-produced and defiantly undistributed.

Indeed by reading the experiments of modernist narrative as part of broader attempts at the turn of the century to think through what it means to be a modern subject—to grapple with the British empire and its decline, to engage with modern women as they move into public spaces—this book seeks to suggest some of the tensions of a category like modernism itself. One of my central concerns has been to understand literary experiment as simultaneously a social category and a formal one, and to see the forms of impressionist subjectivity traditionally imagined as the domain of literature also threading through cultural texts ranging from Victorian panegyrics on the home to Boy Scout training manuals. In analyzing the social space literary texts tried rhetorically to carve out for themselves and the specific forms of cultural authority they asserted, I have read such work as part of a larger set of questions about British culture at the turn of the century. As recent studies of this culture have underlined, questions about the status of the subject, about new narrative genres, and about women's role in making these genres persuasive shaped a range of social discourses that extended beyond aesthetic and literary debates—to questions of suffrage, national revival, and empire among others (Green; Light; Lynch). Thus, though I have focused my argument through a particular modernist formal technique, I hope that my conclusions may echo beyond modernism. Were I to imagine the directions in which these issues could be pursued further, I might be looking at a field in which the borders sometimes implied by modernism had faded beyond recognition.

In the case of modernism, this general point must resonate as more than the critical truism that literature takes its meaning from a broader social field. Modernism as the name for an area of study has long categorized its objects through a stylistic, thematic, or aesthetic lens. In this sense the term may raise questions about the relation of high-cultural and other texts more acutely than other definitions might. However modernism as a field also intrinsically selects certain kinds of texts written in the late nineteenth and early twentieth centuries as relevant for inclusion and study, and has done so far more restrictively than fields grouped by a period of time do—though the boundaries of periodization of course set terms of inclusion and exclusion too. And while much recent criticism has pulled against the cultural hierarchy this has traditionally suggested and worked against the accompanying association of modernism with a formally based aesthetic, the term "modernism" pulls back. Thus criticism that seeks to expand what we read in the period nonetheless often suggests inadvertently that to merit examination, an early-twentieth-century text must be defined as modernist. Such revisions do not necessarily keep a familiar modernism; they open our view by redefining modernism as a concern with the new, or with technology, or with a spirit of the age (T. Armstrong). But it is telling that the category of modernism persists to characterize varied concerns that might surely be described persuasively through entirely other terms.

This persistence must raise the question of just how the category of modernism works and what it does. In its most problematic incarnations, it may isolate certain works as the only worthy emblems of their age; it also may let critics praise or damn a set of texts with a label that sets neat boundaries and produces a narrative of clean literary ruptures. We can think here not only of advocates of modernism who claimed its absolute difference from a Victorian past but also of those early critical advocates of postmodernism who used modernism as a straw-figure against which to frame the possibilities of a later fiction (Hassan 91–92). But the effects of a term like modernism have also been more productive and more complex than this warning indicates. Astradur Eysteinsson has written about the varied ways the concept of modernism has been a subject for debate, centering arguments about the social conditions of the aesthetic, and of institutional, avant-garde and commercial writing. It is ultimately the historical persistence of these debates that I think signals the continuing importance of a term like modernism. For while we would do well to be skeptical about the uses of the term to define which texts can represent a period and which cannot, we need to register the way modernism as a field of critical discussion has come to name an important cluster of questions about what art does and where and how it does it. Modernism can productively work as a name for some of modernity's most pressing debates—precisely because it has historically done so already—debates about what art might have to do with the modern subject, with public and private spheres, with our versions of history. Using modernism as a category, we need not ignore the fact that such debates spread beyond particular literary texts, that they equally emerge under other rubrics, nor that they draw upon dynamics of modernity that exceed the confines of a brief historical moment. Rather the term, properly read, would register the very difficulties of such divisions.

In investigating the close relation of modernism and femininity, I have sought to consider the way modernism speaks about the impossibility of these divisions, and offers a history for how we speak about them now. By taking up the tensions of the modern female subject, modernist debate links even its most traditional qualities—formal innovation, the ideal of high culture—to a series of questions that unravel familiar literary unities. Feminine subjectivity and modernism together point toward both aesthetic autonomy and the aesthetic realm's implication in the social; they point toward specific cultural details and to universalism; they point toward cultural resistance and appropriation. Recognizing the way modernism talked about all of these problems may clarify the history of our own critical debates, which modernism—and impressionism—have helped to shape.

Notes

Introduction

1. Lewis's distinction may be aligned with the gap between what have been termed the "subjectivist" and "objectivist" strands of modernism. As Levenson notes, "modernism was individualist before it was anti-individualist" (*Genealogy* 79). However this shift does not support the claim sometimes made that the anti-individualist tendency—as Lewis certainly would have it—was more truly modernist. See, for instance, Jay. Levenson discusses the connections between these premises in *Genealogy*.

2. Nicholls's work reveals one problem of this divide for a broad definition of modernism. His survey characterizes a cluster of male-authored modernisms through the lens of Baudelaire's "'elimination' of the feminine"; as a result it ends by imagining even plural "modernisms" without room for the work of Barnes, Loy, or Woolf (4). Gendered configurations other than the masculinist thus seem to stand "outside 'modernism,' effecting as they do such a fundamental break with [what is here cast as] the gendered aesthetics of the various avant-gardes" (222).

3. Some of the critics who have established the importance of female writers for modernism include Benstock; DeKoven; DuPlessis; Friedman and Fuchs; S. Friedman, *Penelope's Web*; S. Kaplan; B. Scott, *Refiguring Modernism*.

4. In "'Beyond' Gynocriticism," S. Friedman analyzes the limits of these models of analysis, which she groups through Elaine Showalter's terms, gynocriticism and gynesis. See also Lyon, "Militant Discourse."

5. On the historical links between modern femininity and conservatism in the period, see Light; Lynch.

6. Throughout this study I have drawn on recent work that poses women as central subjects of modernity; see Felski; N. Armstrong; Bowlby, *Just Looking*.

7. Doane has also shown how the association of instability with woman may restabilize the discourses of cinema, psychoanalysis, and philosophy.

8. As Levenson shows, Ford's search for new sources of authority claimed for impressionism both a greater subjectivity and a greater objectivity (*Genealogy* 105–20).

9. Critics have on occasion defined these techniques more strictly, separating impressionism proper from stream-of-consciousness narration or interior monologue. See for instance M. Friedman. For a narratological account of related distinctions, see Cohn.

10. Indeed the idea of rupture is a rhetorical commonplace in modernist texts, from Pound's injunction to "make it new" through Woolf's proposal that "on or about December 1910 human character changed." For commentary on critical and literary narratives of modernist rupture, see Levenson, *Genealogy* ix–x; Lyon, "Militant Discourse"; Marx.

11. My project is indebted throughout to Jameson's analysis of the work of modernist form. The association of modernism with a politically retrograde solipsism, however, is widely held. See for instance Howe; Hassan 91–92. For a discussion of interiority in modernist fiction, see Levenson's *Genealogy* and *Modernism and the Fate of Individuality*.

12. Useful accounts of modernist impressionism have been offered by Levenson (*Genealogy* 103–20); Matz; Meisel, *Absent Father*; Schwartz; Watt. Eysteinsson summarizes critical approaches to the problem (26–49).

13. P. Smith analyzes related contradictions of the subject in discourses of the human sciences. Pecora discusses a similar tension in the subject of modernity and modernist fiction—between its instrumentalization and its apparent freedom. For a history of ideas of the subject in Western philosophy, see Taylor.

14. For an opposed reading of modernist uncertainty as the mark of epistemological challenge, see P. Armstrong, *Challenge*.

15. The complexity of this attention to women has been noted most fully in reference to Freud. See for instance Kofman; S. Friedman, "Hysteria"; Hertz 122–43; Bernheimer and Kahane.

16. Altieri's analyses of Flaubert (112–22), Duchamp, and Matisse (15–23) point—albeit indirectly—to the role femininity plays in prompting the gesture of abstraction. On modernist abstraction, see also Cascardi; Lukács, "Ideology"; Schwartz. On the abstraction and universalization of the subject more generally, see P. Smith; S. Smith 1–23. On abstraction and authorship, see S. Marcus, "Profession."

17. I also refer, most obviously, to Stephen Dedalus's desire to fly by the nets of "nationality, language, religion" in *Portrait* (220)—a desire whose simultaneous importance and impossibility are central subjects of Joyce's work. Also see Forster's version of this aspiration, in which he envisions the history of English novelists "seated together in a room, a circular room, a sort of British Museum reading room—all writing their novels simultaneously" (9).

18. Kenner here suggests that modernism proper liberates words from the details of their local historical usage. In a gesture characterizing much criti-

cism of modernism until the 1980s, the frame of his text contrasts such mobile and liberated words to the less important "talk" of "young women," which has not survived (*Pound Era* 5). See also Nicholls on how artists of high modernism, like "the men of 1914" reacted against the interior of subjectivity, "restoring art to the public sphere" (251).

19. This project reads a specific strand of modernism; however my analysis has benefited from critical work on other modernists as well. Recent analysis of Joyce, for instance, has begun persuasively to trace the import of identifying with the feminine. See Froula and the essays collected in Pearce.

Chapter 1: Pater's Domestic Subject

1. For instance, domesticity provides a historically specific lens through which to read Pater's much-noted attraction to the power of place; see Shuter 16–38; E. Frank 15–49.

2. Pater's comment appears on a scrap of paper found among his manuscripts; see Evans xxix.

3. Felski discusses this double-edged identification and distancing in aestheticist texts more generally (91–114); see Adams on the interrelation of Victorian masculinity and cultural feminization.

4. Critics have debated whether these definitions in fact represent Pater's own thought; see for instance Inman; Meisel, *Absent Father* 111–17; C. Williams 14–25; Wollheim. However Pater's consistent attempts to negotiate between these positions suggest to me that he found the dilemmas compelling enough to address, whether or not he presents them as his own.

5. For accounts of the influence of nineteenth-century science on these views, see Hill's notes to Pater's *The Renaissance* 452–55; Inman; Small. On the influence of Hegel and German idealism, see McGrath 118–31; Ward 43–77.

6. Pater often defined art as possessing the power to bridge this gap; see Iser 29–32; Meisel, *Absent Father* 139–44.

7. I draw the term "generic" from Pater's essay "Coleridge," in which he describes that writer's thinking as participating in the "absolute" spirit of "[a]ncient philosophy [which] sought to arrest every object in an eternal outline, to fix thought in a necessary formula, and the varieties of life in a classification by 'kinds' or genera" (66). Pater anticipates much of my argument here by noting critically that a classification by genera outlines and thus encloses that which it defines.

8. See Loesberg; Dellamora, "Critical Impressionism"; C. Williams. I am particularly indebted to Williams's analysis of the movement between generality and historical specificity in Pater's work, although I read the relation between them less as a dialectical synthesis than as a culturally motivated contradiction. On the long tradition of gendering specificity, see Schor.

9. My discussion of Victorian ideas about the home and its relation to self and society draws broadly on the work of N. Armstrong; Davidoff and Hall; Gallagher; Langland; Poovey; and Riley.

10. Riley discusses the related way the nineteenth-century sphere of the "social" grouped questions about poverty under the category of women's familial concerns and removed such issues from the realm of the "properly" political or governmental (47–51).

11. This insistence makes Pater's declared cultural relativism unstable. A longer excerpt from the essay highlights the contradiction, "out of so many possible conditions, just this for you and that for me, brings ever the unmistakeable realisation of the delightful *chez soi;* this for the Englishman . . . that, quite other, for the wandering Arab. . . . With Florian then the sense of home became singularly intense, his good fortune being that the special character of his home was in itself so essentially homelike. . . . I have come to fancy that some parts of Surrey and Kent are, for Englishmen, the true landscape, true home-counties . . . so I think that the sort of house I have described . . . is for Englishmen at least typically homelife [*sic*]" (5).

12. This double function of the house in shaping the child—metonymically, as context, and metaphorically—thus unites two strands of Pater's argument in the essay: his assertion of the influence of "environment" (4) on the child's mind, and his emphasis on the importance of the "sensible vehicle" (9) of Florian's thought.

13. See Sharon Marcus's *Apartment Stories* on the link between the mid-nineteenth-century ghost story and domestic ideology in England (83–132).

14. Newfield discusses the way that male feminization and suffering may themselves reinforce masculine hegemony.

15. Pater links metaphor to the dispersal of subjectivity elsewhere in his work. In "Style," for instance, figuration incarnates a dilemma about the unity of the writer. There, the mind's "unity, [its] identity with itself," shapes and is shaped by the "laws of good writing," which also give "the phrase, the sentence . . . unity with its subject and with itself" (22). But, predictably, both writer and reader in "Style" must be perpetually on guard against "vagrant" language and sympathy (25). Pater urges that the writer in particular "must be fully aware . . . of all that latent figurative texture in speech. . . . [and] scrupulously [exact] of it ['vague, lazy, half-formed personification'] . . . its exact value" (20–21).

J. Hillis Miller has commented on the way figuration is a generalized problematic in Pater's work ("Walter Pater"). In "Critical Impressionism," Richard Dellamora astutely comments on the political problem of discussing figurative language as a general category.

16. On Pater's use of types, see C. Williams 123–29, 194–97. Williams defines the type as a dialectical synthesis of the specific and the abstract, rather than as a pure abstraction. However in the context of this essay, when Pater turns to types he moves away from the sensory and the actual, and they thus have the rhetorical effect of abstracting.

17. The androgyny evoked by Florian's association with the home thus maintains rather than disrupts a normative division between genders, even as it broadens available definitions of masculinity. Both Felski (91–114) and J. Marcus ("Still Practice") have made this point about fin-de-siècle androgyny more generally. For an opposing view, see Dellamora, *Masculine Desire*.

Chapter 2: The New Woman and the Modern Girl

1. For sources on the New Woman, see Ardis; Boumelha 63–97; J. E. Miller; Pykett; Rubinstein; Showalter, *Sexual Anarchy*. While my argument diverges from Ardis's reading of the New Woman's subversion of domestic ideology and the public/private divide, I have found her account of the range of New Woman writings and her bibliography of contemporary commentary especially valuable. For a discussion of women's increasing power to shape public discourses from the 1880s, see Walkowitz, *City*; for a discussion of women's movement into the professions, see Vicinus. On the naming of the New Woman, see Rubinstein 12–23; Jordan.

My discussion refers to the "New Woman" as well as to the less clearly defined categories of the modern girl or young woman. Critics have sometimes distinguished between the New Woman and related figures such as the "independent woman" or the "odd woman" on the basis of the New Woman's more explicit rebellion against social categories and hierarchies (see for instance Ardis 16–17; Showalter, *Sexual Anarchy* 38). The strands of debate I discuss here address concerns which apply to girls or women construed more generally as well as to the openly defiant New Women—even as these debates were importantly conditioned by the challenges of those explicitly identified as New Women. Thus James's Maisie, clearly not a New Woman herself, is nevertheless imagined in relation to a debate about young girls' vulnerability in a sexualized and commodified world, and she responds to the formulations of subjectivity shaped in that debate.

2. George Egerton, for instance, whose stories made sexuality central to the female subject, has often seemed divided from the "purity school" of writers, whose criticism of marriage stressed the corrupting nature of male sexuality and the virtues of female chastity (Cunningham).

3. On turn-of-the-century feminist debates over female sexuality see Ardis 83–114; Bland; Ledger. On Egerton, eugenics, and primitivism see Chrisman. The association between an anthropologically imagined savagery and the mind's interior has been much discussed in modernism, where the classic instance for analysis is usually Conrad's *Heart of Darkness*. See for instance, C. Butler 89–131; Torgovnick.

4. Indeed in introducing the category of Ego, "The Apple and the Ego of Woman" comments that "as it is a moot point whether there is sex in mind or not, we wish to use a neuter gender" (374). In a rhetorical gesture familiar from Pater, femininity thus provides the basis for a definition of subjectivity, even as the subject is generalized away from women.

5. For a history of the idea of degeneration in European biology and social science, see Pick. On the association between the New Woman and degeneration, a link often affiliating the New Woman with male homosexuality and aestheticism, see Dowling, "The Decadent and the New Woman"; Siegel.

6. For "The Revolt of the Daughters," see Crackanthorpe, "Revolt" and "Revolt: A Last Word"; Harrison; Haweis; Cuffe; A. Smith; Jeune; Hemery; and Amos. See Rubinstein for commentary (12–15).

"The Tree of Knowledge," by Besant et al., collects comments by a series of writers. Further references will cite the writers individually in the text. The figure of the tree of knowledge reappears frequently in this period as a way of addressing the issue of women and their potentially threatening knowledge.

7. Discussions of venereal disease had been prominent since controversy over the Contagious Diseases Acts in the 1870s and they extended through the early-twentieth-century suffrage movement, defining the disease's social meaning and effects differently at different moments. For discussion, see Showalter, "Syphilis"; Walkowitz, *Prostitution*.

8. Thomas Hardy, alone among the essayists in "Tree of Knowledge," questions the adequacy of marriage. However, other discussions of marriage at the time—both by and about New Women—did criticize the institution; such critiques often echo the terms here, most prominently the description of marriage as a debased commercial contract or a form of prostitution. See Boumelha 83–85; Rubinstein for discussions (38–50).

9. Predictably enough, the two most conservative contributors in "Tree of Knowledge," Elizabeth Linton and Mrs. Edmund Gosse, use the language of domestic privacy to refrain from comment, "deprecat[ing] the public discussion of the whole subject . . . as indecent and unnecessary" (Linton in Besant et al. 682) and as an indelicate exposure of "intimate and domestic" matters best left in home's privacy (Gosse in Besant et al. 681).

10. The novel couples its criticism of Edith's inwardness with objections to the Catholicism that tinges her religious pictures. The novel associates Catholicism with Edith's sensual and irrational religious ecstasies, which resemble the unthinking education she has had as a girl. The sensual (and in one instance sadomasochistic) resonances of Edith's religiosity—the "ghastly [picture of the] Crucifixion too painful to be endured" on the wall (158), the "perfect stupor of ecstatic contemplation" into which she falls when she worships at her picture of Christ" (169)—foreshadow her coming madness.

11. On the importance of the fallen woman in Victorian discussions of the subject's agency, see Anderson, *Tainted Souls*.

12. The central example of this openness is the way Evadne absorbs and judges her father's inconsistent teachings, remaining true to his general principle that "to know the facts of life exactly is a positive duty" (4), while using his precepts only as "matches . . . which fired whole trains of reflection, and lighted her to conclusions quite other than those at which he had arrived himself" (5). Most notably, his contradictory comments on women's lack of ability prompt her own "inquiry into the condition and capacity of women, and made her, in the end of the nineteenth century, essentially herself" (13). Mangum discusses the importance of women's reading and education in the novel, noting Evadne's revision of her father's views (85–143).

13. Mangum surveys critical accounts of this narrative shift (116–18).

14. Jacobson (120–38) and Jones (x–xvii) discuss James's debt to New Woman fiction in *The Awkward Age*; Jacobson notes that James included a bemused aside on Grand's classical allusions in *The Heavenly Twins* in one of

his columns on London (132). James's affinity for female protagonists has long been noted. Veeder and Habegger relate this interest to his family history; critics who discuss the position of women in his fiction more broadly include Rowe, *Theoretical Dimensions;* Allen. I have found particularly interesting several articles that place James's concern with female characters within cultural discourses linking women with the erosion of the private sphere and with shifts in contemporary culture: see Wardley; Blair; Fleissner. Also see Rowe's productive discussion of gender instability in *Maisie;* my reading differs from his in seeing a legitimate connection between James's formal, aesthetic, and narrative strategies and the social disruptions sketched in the novel (*Other Henry James* 120–54).

15. James's account of the private realm is complex in both texts; while the collapse of private into public seems to threaten vulgar commercialism on the one hand (we might note the pervasive danger of the manager-husband in both), the novels nevertheless place advocacy of marriage as woman's proper role in the voice of possessive and problematic suitors. For a reading of these issues in *The Bostonians*, see Wardley.

Throughout the 1880s and early 1890s James's stories and short novels addressed the nexus of issues clustered around public women and redemptive girls that I discuss here. His stories about writers of the period considered public women (notoriously in "Greville Fane"'s deluded, commercial female writer, but also in the young woman at the telegraphic exchange in "In the Cage"). For discussion see Anesko 88. Echoing the issues of *Maisie* and *The Awkward Age,* James wrote a series of works in the period which he would later collect into volume 10 of the New York Edition: *The Spoils of Poynton* (1896), "A London Life" (1889) and "The Chaperon" (1893). His preface to the volume introduces these works by describing the power of a young girl to offer an elevating "appreciation" which may potentially redeem family entanglements and corruption (xiv).

16. Seltzer has discussed the omnipresence of power in James's novels, as well as the oppositions by which forms of power disguise themselves. Posnock describes how thoroughly James refuses his subjects autonomy when he reveals them as socially shaped (*Trial*). While I agree with this reading of the subject in James, I disagree with Posnock's conclusion that James thus rejects rather than reaches for authority, transcendence, or mastery. I argue instead that James's desire for literary authority grows out of the paradoxical ground of his critique, rather than being disabled by it. One register of this movement is the way that the "bewilderment" Posnock praises as James's decentered, vulnerable stance reappears in the preface to *Maisie* as the quality that redeems her from her vulgar setting (238). Also see Cameron's discussion of the way that thought and knowledge in James's work are not anchored in individual subjects or consciousnesses, but increasingly float between or above them. For a reading that historically situates the conflicting logics of identity in the novel, see Tucker.

17. We might think of the way Nanda's mother exposes her for helping to circulate a French novel, and of the way Maisie's mother Ida rejects her each

time Maisie fails to discuss Ida's place in a circuit of exchanging lovers as though no such circulation occurred.

18. Carolyn Steedman discusses a related cultural dynamic in *Strange Dislocations*, analyzing the way that nineteenth-century English culture associated the child with an interiorized history of the adult while indulging in a fascination with the way adults violently shape or deform children's bodies.

19. This in some ways resembles the traditional idea that James redefined virtue as heightened consciousness, the knowledge of good and evil (Brooks 165).

20. The ideal of alternate knowledge has often been taken up by critics who see Maisie as representing the triumphs of the Jamesian "imagination" or as an example of a phenomenological vision of the subject's power. Such readings tend to offer her as proof of the triumph of literary imagination in general over the constraints of historical context, rather than as a historically specified place for imagining social authority. See for instance J. H. Miller, *Versions of Pygmalion* 76–77; P. Armstrong, *Phenomenology*.

21. Earlier in the novel James emphasizes the risk that we cannot be sure repetition is repetition with a difference. In a famous passage, Maisie reproduces her relationship to her mother with her doll Lisette: "She [Maisie] could only pass on her lessons and study to produce on Lisette the impression of having mysteries in her life, wondering the while whether she succeeded in the air of shading off, like her mother, into the unknowable. . . . There was an occasion when, on her [Lisette] being particularly indiscreet, Maisie replied to her—and precisely about the motive of a disappearance—as she, Maisie, had once been replied to by Mrs. Farange: 'Find out for yourself!' She mimicked her mother's sharpness, but she was rather ashamed afterwards, though as to whether of the sharpness or of the mimicry was not quite clear" (33). The unclear referent of Maisie's shame underlines the difficulty of placing this moment as either Maisie's satire of her mother or a reproduction of her.

22. See White for a discussion of the social value of James's ambiguity and obscurity (130–62).

23. For a discussion of how James's prefaces construct and deconstruct authority, see Blair; Posnock, "Breaking the Aura." Cameron discusses the way the prefaces revise the accounts of subjectivity offered in the novels (32–82). For readings of the relation between James and Maisie in the preface, see Hertz; Kaston 123; Teahan 38–67.

24. The presence of monetary language in James's assessments of literary value has been much noted; see Posnock, *Trial* 327–28 n. 21.

25. Cameron notes Maisie's exemplary status here: "In the Preface . . . not-knowing is a general case, only epitomized in the child" (64). However she reads the text wholly in light of this generality, setting aside a reading of Maisie's limited consciousness in the more culturally specific "terms of the child's sentimentalized innocence" (65).

Chapter 3: "One of Us"

1. The connection implied here between James and Conrad—which I trace in terms of impressionism's gendered implications—has long been noted as an issue of literary technique. See Nettels for discussion.

2. On Conrad's obscurity as a strategy of literary authority, see White 108–29. For an oppposed reading of the politics of difficulty, see P. Armstrong, *Challenge* 109–48.

3. The famous phrase, of course, comes from Conrad's *Heart of Darkness* 84. For a more complex reading of women's simultaneous absence and centrality in that text, see London, "Reading Race."

4. For historical overviews see Hobsbawm 56–141 and 192–218; Dangerfield; Showalter, *Sexual Anarchy*. On the New Imperialism and its writings, see Bongie; Brantlinger 19–45; Bristow; McClintock 232–57. On masculinity and the expansion of an urban petty bourgeoisie, see Boscagli 55–91.

5. Samuel Hynes cites a 1902 article by Army General Frederick Maurice which claimed that 60 percent of Englishmen were unfit for service, a government committee investigation (which disproved the figure, though this was generally ignored), and the popular pamphlet *The Decline and Fall of the British Empire* (*Edwardian Turn* 22–26). In reading related debates in American culture, Lears describes this turn toward the individual to solve social problems as the period's characteristically "therapeutic" strategy (47–58).

6. In line with this vision of the Scout as free from self and devoted to a higher purpose, Baden-Powell elsewhere compares steamship engines to Boy Scouts: "It is indeed an impressive sight to stand below these great monsters of steel and watch them faithfully and untiringly pounding out their work, all in order and exactly in agreement with each other . . . doing their duty with an energetic goodwill which makes them seem almost human—almost like gigantic Boy Scouts" (qtd. in Rosenthal 124).

7. Associations of the crowd with contagion and the sapping of individual autonomy are common in the period; the most influential is Gustave LeBon's 1895 *Psychology of the Crowd*. For commentary see Boscagli 55–91; Tratner 21–33; and in relation to Conrad, Bongie 151–72. For Baden-Powell, various aspects of mass behavior testify to the subject's dangerous susceptibility to influence, smoking in particular: he says elsewhere that "no boy ever began smoking because he liked it, but because he thought it made him look like a grown-up man" (28).

8. The figure on the left has also been aligned with class-based physiognomies; Bristow describes him as a "working class oaf" (192); the character's hair and foolish expression also match Baden-Powell's description of dissolute overprivileged boys.

9. Critics of Kipling's *Kim* differ over whether the text reconsolidates British identity quite so firmly after this identification with others; see Lane 38–44; Mohanty 21–40. For my argument, it matters more that Baden-Powell thought it did.

10. Jameson's account—which has influenced most subsequent readings of the novel, including my own—does see a cohesive social field in which impressionist strategy and visible historical content unite as signs of an underlying whole. But because this whole is stratified for Jameson between access to a historical real and formal displacements of it, narrative strategy is defined against the text's representation of imperialism and labor. One signal of this difficulty is Jameson's inability to link the narrator to any of the text's central values. Like Bongie, Gikandi reads the bewildered uncertainty of narration in *Heart of Darkness* as signaling a breakdown of securely mapped imperial knowledge (156–89). On knowledge and uncertainty in British conceptions of empire, see Richards; Suleri. Readings of gender in Conrad such as McCracken's have begun more persuasively to align Marlow's uncertain narration with the structures of colonialism.

11. Watt gives a history of interpretations of the passage (325–31).

12. Sprinker and Rader have debated whether Brown and Jim are individuated or universal figures in the text; their argument extends to whether the novel should be read as an expression of imperial ideology (in which individuation works as an alibi for imperial structures) or as a representation of a universal existential dilemma.

13. I do not directly address the moments in which Marlow's friends take on Jim as a surrogate son while referring to him as """blush[ing] like a girl""" (185). As my discussion of Marlow will make clear, I think that the text more centrally casts such attachments through a rhetoric of masculine sameness.

14. McCracken, for instance, notes that Marlow claims an explicitly masculine authority through his reflective stance.

15. Said and J. H. Miller (*Fiction and Repetition* 126–74) emphasize this proliferation of stories as the novel's foregrounding of textuality and link it to the instability of meaning. Jameson draws on these critics when he claims the novel embodies a postmodern *écriture* (*Political Unconscious* 223). In contrast Watt reads the shifts as shaping a bildungsroman about Marlow—as the sign of his evolving judgment (300). My account reads the text as joining these interpretations but ultimately privileging Marlow as a character.

16. Although White discusses the obscurity of objects of knowledge in Conrad's texts, his comment that this enigma is feminized has a bearing on the related point I will be making here—that the position of the *subject* who cannot know lies close to the feminine. My account of the authority of "not knowing" in Conrad—and in James and Ford as well—draws on Sedgwick's analysis of the links between epistemology, power, and the contradictions of homo/heterosexual definition.

17. This stance is endorsed by more than Marlow; the novel's first, unmarked narrator comments that Jim had never been tested by "those events of the sea that show in the light of day the inner worth of a man . . . that reveal the quality of his resistance and the secret truth of his pretences" (50). See Harpham's commentary, in which he reads the sea as a privileged space of unfathomable contradiction in Conrad—a space that ruptures the subject along with ideals of mastery and authority (71–136). I argue that this invoca-

tion of an unplaceable "beyond" in fact offers a characteristically modernist definition of mastery.

18. Harpham reads the desire between Marlow and Jim as an incorporation of the "feminine" and a dissolution of the self (119–37). My account of this desire draws instead on Sedgwick's proposal that the famous modernist trope of doubling covers over masculine desire, thus blurring solipsism and intersubjectivity. We might recast her formulation slightly: instead of saying "I do not *love* him; I *am* him," Conrad's text might be imagined to say "I love him *because* I am him" (164). For a psychoanalytic reading of the relation between identification and desire in imperial texts, see Lane.

19. My reading here differs from Rosemary George's account of the power of home, which situates home securely in England in the text (81–83). Despite the novel's brief invocations of that home, I think it is more fully devoted to considering which intimacies might offer a "mobile" home—one that evokes the powerful properties of that space while apparently transcending its limited place.

20. Seeley offers a similar structural analysis of the novel, arguing that as Marlow improves on Jim's understanding of romance, so the novel's understanding improves on Marlow's. Her point—that better versions of romance comprehend the necessity of failure—accords with my reading of the text's courting of unknowing.

Chapter 4: Ford, Femininity, and Unreliable Narration

1. There has been much critical debate over whether the novel's narrator is indeed unreliable. I discuss this important issue at length later in this chapter. As will be evident throughout, I read Dowell as unreliable because of the pattern in which information appears in his tale, and because of the text's thematization of the problem of knowledge.

2. Levenson has elaborated the two different versions of character that follow from these notions: the first, a character explained and constructed by social systems, the second, which he describes as more characteristically modernist, one that stands in opposition to society; see his *Modernism and the Fate of Individuality* 102–8. My argument draws upon his insight by taking literally the spatial logic of these models, in preparation for showing how these understandings are gendered in the period. The related observation that the novel concerns the conflict between Convention and Passion is a traditional one; these particular terms were set out by Samuel Hynes in "The Epistemology of *The Good Soldier*."

3. This lack of a distinct interior in Edward is suggested again by the passage that immediately follows: If Dowell "ever penetrated into his private room" and saw Ashburnham standing "with his coat and waistcoat off," he would discover "the immensely long line of his perfectly elegant trousers from waist to boot heel" (31). The description links him to the line-drawn Leonora; the profusion of pigskin cases Edward opens and closes in this scene will come later in the novel to function as symbols of the expensive but empty

case of the Ashburnhams' marriage; at this moment, however, their main effect is to present a series of surfaces "stamped with his initials, E.F.A.," within his private room (31).

4. The use of the word splendid here must be contrasted with its more clearly ironic use earlier in the novel, when Dowell associates Edward's being a "splendid fellow" with his "public character" rather than his private passion (89). Leonora deflates the term, opening a discussion about the value of "public character" which Dowell fails to understand: "I asked her whether her husband was not really a splendid fellow—along at least the lines of his public functions. . . . 'Didn't you know?' she asked. 'If I come to think of it there is not a more splendid fellow in any three counties, pick them where you will—along those lines'" (91).

5. Saunders argues that the novel remains far more critical of Ashburnham, citing what he sees as the suggestion of incest—potentially literal—between Ashburnham and Nancy (422).

6. Although these comments refer to a moment at the novel's first setting of Nauheim, Leonora's abandonment of reserve occurs most fully later at Branshaw. However the more relevant transition in the novel's representation of interiority and talk lies less between the events at Nauheim and Branshaw than between early and late moments in Dowell's narration.

7. Sale links Dowell's scapegoating of women to Ford's belief that he was himself unjustly tormented by Violet Hunt and his wife Elsie Hueffer (55–61). Also see Cassell, "Notes" 167, 173.

8. As Mizener notes, Edward's feudalism expresses—and parodies, albeit very gently—Ford's own Tory-radical dreams about an ideal English community, an ideal that relies upon a reciprocal social bond between landed gentry and local peasants and artisans (263, 271).

9. Characteristically, La Dolciquita—a courtesan—lacks any passion and views their affair as a business deal. Edward is overwhelmed by desire and considers the money incidental; further, he feels a tie of honor to a woman with whom he has had an affair.

10. Florence's knowledge, predictably, embodies the worst of both private and public; it is both too secret and too promiscuous. Dowell faults her for the shallow publicity and abundance of her knowledge. "A graduate of Poughkeepsie" and a "queer, chattery person," she reels off lists of unrelated facts acquired from books (19). Her superficial unrootedness in any particular culture contrasts with Leonora's knowledge. "It really worried poor Florence that she couldn't, in matters of culture, ever get the better of Leonora. . . . [who] gave, somehow, the impression of really knowing what poor Florence gave the impression of having only picked up" (43).

11. In contrast Paul Armstrong reads bewilderment as unsettling narrative authority in the novel (*Challenge* 189–224).

12. Donoghue points out that the verb "to know" appears seven times in the first paragraph alone; he also notes that Dowell expresses doubt about his own knowledge in order to give himself more credibility as a narrator, observing that his "trope of ignorance" "keep[s] him immune to his subject, or

superior to it" (48). Also see Ford's advice that you should "always consider that the first impression with which you present [the reader] will be so strong that it will be all that you can ever do to efface it, to alter it or even quite slightly to modify it" ("On Impressionism, I" 172).

13. Ford termed this gradual buildup of information, which accelerates the narrative for the reader, the *progression d'effet*. For a discussion of the technique see Cassell, "Notes" 160–75.

14. Donoghue (45) notes that Dowell distances himself and emphasizes his own innocence when he casts himself as the tale's auditor rather than its narrator; Dowell calls the tale "the saddest story I have ever heard" (11) rather than the saddest story he has ever told or known.

15. Dowell notes quite early in part 4 that he has "been writing away at this story now for six months" (167–68); he mentions that Edward has "cut his throat" (177) as part of "bring[ing the story] up to date" (178) in the first section of part 4.

16. For a survey of opinions on Dowell's reliability, see Wiesenfarth. For commentary see Snitow 165; Mizener 113, 115.

17. Recent essays that attempt to avoid the deadlock of this debate do so by concentrating on the social effects of impressionism, or on the frame of storytelling that produces the effect of truth and its impossibility. See for instance Brian May's productive reading of how "Fordian impressionism depoliticizes as fully as it disaffects" (92); also see Donoghue; Bailin.

18. Levenson has noted the way Ford casts himself as a child against the background of such figures, briefly commenting on Dowell's childlikeness in *The Good Soldier* (*Genealogy* 54–59).

19. Showalter has noted the frequency with which writers at the turn of the century defined themselves in relation to the figure of George Eliot (*Sexual Anarchy* 59–75).

Chapter 5: Pilgrimage

1. The individual installments of *Pilgrimage*—"chapters," as Richardson called them—were originally published as follows: *Pointed Roofs* (1915); *Backwater* (1916); *Honeycomb* (1917); *The Tunnel* (1919); *Interim* (1919); *Deadlock* (1921); *Revolving Lights* (1923); *The Trap* (1925); *Oberland* (1927); *Dawn's Left Hand* (1931); *Clear Horizon* (1935). *Dimple Hill* appeared in the four-volume Dent Collected Edition of 1938; *March Moonlight* (not necessarily completed) appeared in the posthumous reprint of the Collected Edition in 1967. My citations refer to the volumes of the 1967 edition.

I cite here protagonist Miriam Henderson's comments on her own writing project as continuous with Richardson's, although the relation between implied authorial stance and the character's stance is complicated in the novel. Later I discuss more fully the much-debated problem of how we are to read Miriam's views. Here I wish simply to note, without oversimplifying the central question of narrative distance in the novel, that Miriam's aesthetic views overlap with opinions Richardson herself offered elsewhere, and that precise narrative distance is hard to detect in moments when Miriam artic-ulates these views later in the novel.

2. My account in the following three paragraphs draws on the many dis-cussions of Richardson's notion of feminine identity and feminine writing practice—a topic which has centered most readings of the novel since her rediscovery as an obscured presence in modernist and feminist literary ex-periment. In addition to articles by Friedman and Hanscombe cited above, see for instance Bluemel, *Experimenting;* DuPlessis; Heath; Radford, *Dorothy Richardson.* I have found Radford's and Heath's accounts the most produc-tive for my argument.

3. Richardson thus continues Egerton's (and James's) ambiguous privileg-ing of woman as enigma, a role whose highly problematic implications for a tradition of representation have been explored extensively by psychoanalyt-ic accounts of the figure of woman. Heath has described Richardson's stance as a "radical edge to what effectively becomes the stock reference to 'the fem-inine'" (143). I agree with the terms of his reading although I believe the text's movement to dismantle representational coherence is reconsolidated by its claims about feminine narrative privilege. My aim here is to explore the his-torically specific terms in which Richardson imagines such disruption and consolidation.

4. A fuller version of this passage amplifies the point: "'whereas a few men here and there are creators, originators, *artists,* women are this all the time. [. . .] But the point is, there's no emancipation to be done. Women are eman-cipated [. . .] Through their preeminence in an art. The art of making atmo-spheres. It's as big an art as any other. Most women can exercise it, for rea-sons, by fits and starts. The best women work at it the whole of the time. Not one man in a million is aware of it. It's like air within the air. [. . .] Be-cause the thing I mean goes through everything. A woman's way of "being" can be discovered in the way she pours out tea'" (3:256–57).

5. Both Heath (130, 134) and Radford (*Dorothy Richardson* 118–19) have also noted the contradiction between Miriam's status as dispersed subject and her alternate formulation as a whole one beneath the flow of impressions, though neither focuses on the import of the doubleness. Gevirtz and Felber discuss the way *Pilgrimage* tries to reconcile linguistic deferral and a pleni-tude of meaning—terms related to the models of subjectivity I discuss.

6. Richardson often uses ellipses in *Pilgrimage* to indicate pauses, block-ages, or transitions in Miriam's thoughts. Unless bracketed, all ellipses in quoted passages are Richardson's.

7. The complexity of syntax here rivals Pater's and similarly indicates the subject's ambiguous borders. The full sentence reads: "Then, presently, a lonely, impersonal joy in whatever it was that had brought that adventuring forth, from her heart's depth, of love and devotion that glowed like the rosy fire and seemed at once the inmost essence of her being and yet not herself; but something that through her, and in unaccustomed words, was address-ing the self she knew, making her both speaker and listener, making her, to herself, as strange and as mysterious as, in the shaded lamplight, was the darkness behind the glowing fire" (4:281).

8. Thus in *March Moonlight* Miriam loves Jean in part because her engagement with others occurs in the realm of the transfigured rather than the ordinary or social: "[Jean] lives in a world she sees transfigurable. Already, for her, transfigured. What comes to others only at moments is with her always" (4:579).

9. In contrast, Hanscombe in "Dorothy Richardson versus the Novvle" declares that the novel has no ironic distance between character and narrator (86), though her book-length study, *The Art of Life,* discusses Miriam's restricted consciousness as a structural problem for Richardson's identification with the character. Despite Hanscombe's commitment here to identifying author and character, she notes helpfully that the difficulty of authorizing Miriam—and thus implicitly bringing character and narrative voice together—is the problem of establishing the generality of her views (*Art of Life* 51, 121–22).

10. Richardson wrote that she intended narrative distance from the young Miriam, noting that the discontinuous nature of *Interim* resulted from trying to convey the "'fragmentary' world of an adolescent" (125) and that *Deadlock*'s increased lucidity occurred because Miriam was now "articulate" where before she had been "vague" (139) (qtd. in Fromm). The passage I mention offers a moment at which the novel seems separate from Miriam's class-based presumptions. However these same opinions—the antiprovincialism, the disdain for the suburban—linger elsewhere, uncertainly distanced by the text. Such ironies become increasingly unstable. For instance Miriam's generalizations about the "Russian" qualities of an interlocutor may be disrupted when the text reveals him as Italian (4:74–75), but the text elsewhere demands a similar distinctness of foreign views.

11. On Richardson's account of middle-class women's professionalization, their movement out of both the home and "domestic" professions such as teaching, see Levy. On the expansion and feminization of clerical work, see Zimmeck; Holcombe; Silverstone. As Elizabeth Wilson has noted, the turn of the century saw increasing numbers of urban public spaces hospitable to middle-class women, including department stores, restaurants, and tearooms.

12. Among the many central texts on the *flâneur,* see those by Baudelaire; Benjamin; Buck-Morss; and the essays collected in Tester's *The Flâneur.* For discussions of gender and *flânerie,* see Wilson; Wolff; Green.

13. On the importance of the figure of the prostitute in modernism and urban modernity, see Buck-Morss; Teal; and Scholes.

14. Or, if they are not fully removed, they are reframed in a whole that impersonalizes their detail: "he would be there [. . .] drawing her [. . .] away from personal experiences, into a world going on independently of them; unaware of the many scattered interests waiting for her beyond this shabby room, and yet making them shine as he talked, newly alight with rich superfluous impersonal fascination, no longer isolated but vivid parts of a whole" (3:77).

15. For a reading of Miriam's relationship with Shatov, which interprets it—more optimistically than I do here—as an evolving response to the work of Otto Weininger, see Radford, "The Woman and the Jew."

16. On the function of Zionism and Jewish identity in the novel, see Jacqueline Rose, who argues that the figure of the Jew as outsider reveals limits to Richardson's definition of women as outsiders themselves. My reading elaborates on Rose's account, but differs over what it means to link feminist autonomy with outsider status in a text that complicates the formation of identity. See Egger on race in Richardson's film writing; for a related discussion of empire, see Bluemel, "'Civilization.'" Garrity details the perplexing intersections between feminine privilege, Englishness, and nationalism in "'Neither English Nor Civilized.'"

17. Miriam's attitude to Zionism actually imagines it as more than a false external abstraction, since she praises Zionism as not meaning "'fatalism [. . . but rather recognizing that] there is something *in* things'" (3:169). Here, as in the passages I will discuss shortly, racialized identity—as exemplified by the Jews and transferred to the English—becomes not extrinsic constraint but immanent nature.

18. As J. Rose notes, Richardson, writing after these historical shifts, nonetheless temporally places Michael and Miriam's debate so that it foreshadows the rise of both British Zionism and an increasingly codified, virulent English anti-Semitism marked by the passage of the Anti-Alien Bill (127).

19. We might note here that *Pilgrimage* also offers a scene in which Amabel impersonates an Englishwoman by dressing as one (4:311–15); the novel's ambiguous view of such masquerades—both admiring and disturbed—centers in its depiction of Amabel's concern with finding the proper pose. "'For every one,' she comments, 'one must have some kind of pose'" (4:314). I do not wish to argue, however, that Amabel can be reduced to this single register of the unanchored; elsewhere Miriam affiliates her with the thematics of depth and self-presence here joined to national identity.

20. The claims for modernism's (specifically Western) internationalism are long-standing and come from critics of a variety of political positions. See for instance R. Williams; Kenner, *Colder Eye.* More recent claims about the connections between forms of nationalism and modernism include that of W. B. Michaels, although here nativist modernism is problematically divided off from alternative, international, movements.

21. This structure also informs Miriam's comments on the task of translation, where texts in different languages are wholly contained within the specificity of their different languages and yet point toward a register in which they are the same. The challenge of translation is "the revelation of mutually enclosed unexpandable meanings, insoluble antagonisms of thought and experience, flowing upon the surface of a stream where both were one" (3:142).

22. Also recall the passage cited earlier: "The Russian in him believed it, knew, in spite of his Jewish philosophy, something of the unfathomable depths in each individual, unique and irreplaceable [. . .] And the Jew in him so far saw Amabel only as charmingly qualified to fulfil [. . .] his destiny as a part of his 'race'" (4:427).

Chapter 6: Woolf's Abstraction

1. The terms are Woolf's; they have been explored further in Kelley.
2. There is a large body of critical commentary on these issues. For discussion of the way these terms stand in tension or may be reconciled, see for instance Barrett; Caughie; Minow-Pinkney 1–8. For accounts of Woolf's feminism, see J. Marcus, *Virginia Woolf*; Zwerdling 9–37. For an acute reading of Woolf's importance to American academic feminism in the 1970s and 1980s, see London, "Guerrilla in Petticoats."
3. On women and walking in Woolf, see Bowlby, "Walking, Women, and Writing." For a related reading of the female professional in Woolf, which sees this newly mobile figure supplanting the angel in the house, see Cucullu; on the association of professional authorship and abstraction, see S. Marcus, "Profession."
4. See, most explicitly, the comments of Barrett; J. Marcus, *Virginia Woolf*; Zwerdling. Indeed as Bowlby notes in *Virginia Woolf: Feminist Destinations*, the essay goes on to imagine the possibilities of modern fiction by evoking possible stories for Mrs. Brown, using the social details of dress and the railway carriage in which she travels as a basis (1–16).
5. On the association between women and silence in Woolf, see Garrity, "'I Do Not Understand Phrases'"; Laurence. On the disruptions of language and the symbolic order, see Minow-Pinkney; Eisenberg; B. Scott 2:1–70.
6. For a discussion of this dilemma, and of the tension between subject and community, "I" and "we," see Beer, "The Body of the People."
7. While critics have sometimes contrasted Clarissa's limited journeys through the West End with her daughter Elizabeth's more adventurous trips, the figure of travel through London still shapes Clarissa's accounts of her identity.
8. On Bloomsbury's equation of consumption and modern consciousness, see Wicke. For an analysis of the class differentiations visible in shopping in *Mrs. Dalloway*, see Abbot.
9. I am not arguing here that we cannot stand outside the text in order to read this style as socially placed ourselves: critics of Woolf's class position often refer to the marked gentility of her diction; see for instance London, "Guerrilla in Petticoats" 27. I would argue, however, that the novel itself does not self-consciously foreground this quality. In "Reification and Utopia," Fredric Jameson describes this creation of a distinct aesthetic style as one of the strategies by which modernist high culture carves out private languages in response to the commodity system of late capitalism (16–17).
10. On the relation between Woolf and Pater, see Meisel, *Absent Father*.
11. More recently, attention has turned to the novel's critique of empire and gender formation. See Booker; J. Marcus, "Britannia Rules *The Waves*"; McGee.
12. Woolf's diaries do suggest briefly that some other view of form and character stands against and satirizes the abstraction she proposes more con-

sistently. Writing in her diary on May 28, 1928, of the central figure imagined for an early draft of the novel, she comments: "But who is she? I am very anxious that she should have no name. I don't want a Lavinia or a Penelope: I want 'she.' But that becomes arty, Liberty greenery yallery somehow: symbolic in loose robes" (140).

13. See Booker; Garrity, "'I Do Not Understand Phrases'"; Sypher; especially Garrity's and Sypher's discussions of the girls' relation to language. Woolf's attention to the delusory nature of trying to redefine woman "beyond" the domain of the social resembles a range of recent feminist critiques; one of the most influential versions appears in J. Butler 1–34.

14. A consistent pattern in the novel links abstraction with depth, as in Rhoda's vision of the "thing that lies beneath the semblance of the thing": here Bernard, who has been envisioning images whose referentiality troubles him (Percival's "'bandaged head, the men with ropes'" [156]) wants to find something "'unvisual beneath'" (156). The invocation of the "unvisual" may seem to contradict my association of abstraction with images, but the relevant distinction here is that between an image as a picture of life, and an "image" which exists in itself, nonmimetically, and thus is in a way abstract.

15. As a child, Bernard describes his bath: "'Water pours down the runnel of my spine. Bright arrows of sensation shoot on either side. I am covered with warm flesh'" (26).

16. I draw here on Joseph Frank's influential definition of the spatial. Although he uses the term to describe the overarching shape of a work, I think it can be usefully applied to moments that operate spatially as well.

17. The novel also compares the order of poetry to the order Louis imposes in his business: "'With letters and cables and brief but courteous demands . . . I have fused my many lives into one; I have helped by my assiduity and decision to score those lines on the map there by which the different parts of the world are laced together'" (167–68). The novel connects Louis's concern with power and order in his career with his perpetual sense of exclusion as an Australian. Echoing the effects of his poetic ordering, his career tightens the imperial network which has branded him as merely colonial.

18. The choice of Bernard as an encompassing voice also lends weight to the authority of storytelling. Significantly, his one impulse to describe his life spatially is phrased as an artificial contraction: "'Now to sum up. . . . The illusion is upon me that something adheres for a moment, has roundness, weight, depth, is completed. . . . If it were possible, I would hand it you entire . . . I would say, "Take it. This is my life". . . . this globe, full of figures'" (238).

19. On the tensions of the novel's ending, see DeKoven 205–6; DiBattista 188–89.

Works Cited

Abbot, Reginald. "What Miss Kilman's Petticoat Means: Virginia Woolf, Shopping, and Spectacle." *Modern Fiction Studies* 38 (1992): 193–216.

Adams, James Eli. "Gentleman, Dandy, Priest: Manliness and Social Authority in Pater's Aestheticism." *ELH* 59 (1992): 441–66.

Allen, Elizabeth. *A Woman's Place in the Novels of Henry James.* New York: St. Martin's Press, 1984.

Althusser, Louis. "Ideology and Ideological State Apparatuses." *Lenin and Philosophy, and Other Essays.* Trans. Ben Brewster. New York: Monthly Review Press, 1971. 127–86.

Altieri, Charles. *Painterly Abstraction in Modern American Poetry.* Cambridge: Cambridge University Press, 1989.

Amos, Sarah M. "The Evolution of the Daughters." *Contemporary Review* 65 (1894): 515–20.

Anderson, Amanda. "George Eliot and the Jewish Question." *Yale Journal of Criticism* 10 (1997): 39–61.

———. *Tainted Souls and Painted Faces: The Rhetoric of Fallenness in Victorian Culture.* Ithaca: Cornell University Press, 1993.

Anesko, Michael. *"Friction with the Market": Henry James and the Profession of Authorship.* New York: Oxford University Press, 1986.

"The Apple and the Ego of Woman." *Westminster Review* 131 (1889): 374–82.

Ardis, Ann. *New Women, New Novels: Feminism and Early Modernism.* New Brunswick: Rutgers University Press, 1991.

Armstrong, Nancy. *Desire and Domestic Fiction: A Political History of the Novel.* New York: Oxford University Press, 1987.

Armstrong, Paul. *The Challenge of Bewilderment: Understanding and Representation in James, Conrad, and Ford.* Ithaca: Cornell University Press, 1987.

———. *The Phenomenology of Henry James.* Chapel Hill: University of North Carolina Press, 1983.

Armstrong, Tim. *Modernism, Technology and the Body.* Cambridge: Cambridge University Press, 1998.

B[aden].-P[owell]. [Sir Robert Stephenson Smyth Baden-Powell]. *Scouting for Boys.* 1908. London: C. Arthur Pearson, 1957.

Bailin, Miriam. "'An Extraordinarily Safe Castle': Aesthetics as Refuge in *The Good Soldier.*" In Cassell 68–81.

Barrett, Michèle. Introduction. *Women and Writing.* By Virginia Woolf. New York: Harvest Books, 1979. 1–39.

Baudelaire, Charles. "The Painter of Modern Life." In *The Painter of Modern Life and Other Essays.* Trans. and ed. Jonathan Mayne. 1863. New York: Phaidon/Da Capo Press, 1964. 1–40.

Beer, Gillian. "The Body of the People: *Mrs Dalloway* to *The Waves.*" In *Virginia Woolf: The Common Ground* 48–73.

———. *Virginia Woolf: The Common Ground.* Ann Arbor: University of Michigan Press, 1996.

———. "*The Waves:* 'The Life of Anybody.'" In *Virginia Woolf: The Common Ground* 74–91.

Benjamin, Walter. *Charles Baudelaire: A Lyric Poet in the Era of High Capitalism.* 1935–39. Trans. Harry Zohn. London: Verso, 1997.

Benstock, Shari. *Women of the Left Bank: Paris, 1900–1940.* Austin: University of Texas Press, 1986.

Bernheimer, Charles, and Claire Kahane, eds. *In Dora's Case: Freud—Hysteria—Feminism.* New York: Columbia University Press, 1985.

Besant, Walter, et al. "The Tree of Knowledge." *New Review* 10 (1894): 675–90.

Bjorhovde, Gerd. *Rebellious Structures: Women Writers and the Crisis of the Novel, 1880–1900.* Oslo: Norwegian University Press, 1987.

Blair, Sara. "In the House of Fiction: Henry James and the Engendering of Literary Mastery." In McWhirter 58–73.

Blake, Caesar. *Dorothy Richardson.* Ann Arbor: University of Michigan Press, 1960.

Bland, Lucy. "Marriage Laid Bare: Middle-Class Women and Marital Sex, 1880s–1914." In *Labour and Love: Women's Experience of Home and Family, 1850–1940.* Ed. Jane Lewis. Oxford: Basil Blackwell, 1986. 123–46.

Bluemel, Kristin. "'Civilization Is Based upon the Stability of Molars': Dorothy Richardson and Imperialist Dentistry." In *Modernism, Gender, and Culture: A Cultural Studies Approach.* Ed. Lisa Rado. New York: Garland Press, 1997. 301–18.

———. *Experimenting on the Borders of Modernism: Dorothy Richardson's Pilgrimage.* Athens: University of Georgia Press, 1997.

Bongie, Chris. *Exotic Memories: Literature, Colonialism, and the Fin de Siècle.* Stanford: Stanford University Press, 1991.

Booker, M. Keith. "Tradition, Authority, and Subjectivity: Narrative Constitution of the Self in *The Waves.*" *Lit: Literature, Interpretation, Theory* 3 (1991): 33–55.

Boone, Joseph. *Libidinal Currents: Sexuality and the Shaping of Modernism.* Chicago: University of Chicago Press, 1998.

———. *Tradition Counter Tradition: Love and the Form of Fiction.* Chicago: University of Chicago Press, 1987.

Boscagli, Maurizia. *Eye on the Flesh: Fashions of Masculinity in the Early Twentieth Century.* New York: Westview Press, 1996.

Boumelha, Penny. *Thomas Hardy and Women: Sexual Ideology and Narrative Form.* Sussex: Harvester Press, 1982.

Bowlby, Rachel. *Just Looking: Consumer Culture in Dreiser, Gissing, and Zola.* New York: Methuen, 1985.

———. "Walking, Women, and Writing: Virginia Woolf as *Flâneuse.*" In *Still Crazy after All These Years: Women, Writing and Psychoanalysis.* London: Routledge, 1992. 1–33.

———. *Virginia Woolf: Feminist Destinations.* Oxford: Basil Blackwell, 1988.

Brantlinger, Patrick. *Rule of Darkness: British Literature and Imperialism, 1830–1914.* Ithaca: Cornell University Press, 1988.

Bristow, Joseph. *Empire Boys: Adventures in a Man's World.* London: HarperCollins Academic, 1991.

Brooks, Peter. *The Melodramatic Imagination: Balzac, Henry James, Melodrama, and the Mode of Excess.* New Haven: Yale University Press, 1976.

Buck-Morss, Susan. "The *Flâneur*, the Sandwichman and the Whore: The Politics of Loitering." *New German Critique* 39 (1986): 99–140.

Butler, Christopher. *Early Modernism: Literature, Music, and Painting in Europe, 1900–1916.* New York: Oxford University Press-Clarendon Press, 1994.

Butler, Judith. *Gender Trouble: Feminism and the Subversion of Identity.* New York: Routledge, 1990.

Calinescu, Matei. *Five Faces of Modernity: Modernism, Avant-Garde, Decadence, Kitsch, Postmodernism.* Durham: Duke University Press, 1987.

Cameron, Sharon. *Thinking in Henry James.* Chicago: University of Chicago Press, 1989.

Cascardi, Anthony J. "The Ethics of Abstraction." In Dettmar 117–35.

Cassell, Richard A., ed. *Critical Essays on Ford Madox Ford.* Boston: G. K. Hall, 1987.

———. "Notes on the Labyrinth of Design in *The Good Soldier.*" In *Modern British Fiction.* Ed. Mark Schorer. New York: Oxford University Press, 1961. 160–75.

Caughie, Pamela L. *Virginia Woolf and Postmodernism: Literature in Quest and Question of Itself.* Urbana: University of Illinois Press, 1991.

Cheyette, Bryan. *Constructions of "the Jew" in English Literature and Society: Racial Representations, 1875–1945.* Cambridge: Cambridge University Press, 1993.

Chrisman, Laura. "Empire, 'Race' and Feminism and the *Fin de Siècle:* The Work of George Egerton and Olive Schreiner." In Ledger and McCracken 45–65.

Cohn, Dorrit. *Transparent Minds: Narrative Modes for Presenting Consciousness in Fiction.* Princeton: Princeton University Press, 1978.

Conrad, Joseph. *Chance.* 1913. New York: Doubleday, Page & Co., 1914.

———. *Heart of Darkness.* 1899. Harmondsworth: Penguin, 1973.

———. *Lord Jim.* 1900. Harmondsworth: Penguin, 1986.

———. Preface. *The Nigger of the "Narcissus."* By Conrad. 1897. Garden City: Doubleday, Page & Company, 1926. xi–xvi.

Crackanthorpe, B. A. "The Revolt of the Daughters." *Nineteenth Century* 35 (1894): 23–31.

———. "The Revolt of the Daughters I: A Last Word on 'The Revolt.'" *Nineteenth Century* 35 (1894): 424–29.

Cucullu, Lois. "Retailing the Female Intellectual." *Differences* 9.2 (1998): 25–68.

Cuffe, Kathleen. "A Reply from the Daughters I." *Nineteenth Century* 35 (1894): 437–42.

Cunningham, Gail. *The New Woman and the Victorian Novel.* New York: Macmillan, 1978.

Dangerfield, George. *The Strange Death of Liberal England, 1910–1914.* 1935. New York: Perigee, 1980.

Davidoff, Leonore, and Catherine Hall. *Family Fortunes: Men and Women of the English Middle Class, 1780–1850.* Chicago: University of Chicago Press, 1987.

DeKoven, Marianne. *Rich and Strange: Gender, History, Modernism.* Princeton: Princeton University Press, 1991.

Dellamora, Richard. "Critical Impressionism as Anti-Phallogocentric Strategy." In *Pater in the 1990s.* Ed. Laurel Brake and Ian Small. 1880–1920 British Authors Series, 6. Greensboro: ELT Press, 1991. 127–42.

———. *Masculine Desire: The Sexual Politics of Victorian Aestheticism.* Chapel Hill: University of North Carolina Press, 1990.

Dettmar, Kevin J. H., ed. *Rereading the New: A Backward Glance at Modernism.* Ann Arbor: University of Michigan Press, 1992.

DiBattista, Maria. *Virginia Woolf's Major Novels: The Fables of Anon.* New Haven: Yale University Press, 1980.

Doane, Mary Ann. *Femmes Fatales: Feminism, Film Theory, Psychoanalysis.* New York: Routledge, 1991.

Donoghue, Denis. "Listening to the Saddest Story." In Stang 44–54.

Douglas, Ann. *Terrible Honesty: Mongrel Manhattan in the 1920s.* New York: Farrar, Straus & Giroux, 1995.

Dowling, Linda. "The Decadent and the New Woman in the 1890s." *Nineteenth-Century Fiction* 33 (1979): 434–53.

———. *Hellenism and Homosexuality in Victorian Oxford.* Ithaca: Cornell University Press, 1994.

DuPlessis, Rachel Blau. *Writing beyond the Ending: Narrative Strategies of Twentieth-Century Women Writers.* Bloomington: Indiana University Press, 1985.

Dyos, H. J., and D. A. Reeder. "Slums and Suburbs." In *The Victorian City: Image and Reality.* Ed. H. J. Dyos and Michael Wolff. Vol. 1. London: Routledge and Kegan Paul, 1973. 369–71.

Egerton, George. "A Keynote to *Keynotes.*" In *Ten Contemporaries: Notes toward Their Definitive Bibliography.* Ed. John Gawsworth [Terence I. F. Armstrong]. London: Ernest Benn, 1932. 57–61.

———. *Keynotes.* 1893. London: Elkin Mathews and John Lane, 1894.

Egger, Rebecca. "Deaf Ears and Dark Continents: Dorothy Richardson's Cinematic Epistemology." *Camera Obscura* 30 (1992): 5–33.

Eisenberg, Nora. "Virginia Woolf's Last Words on Words: *Between the Acts* and 'Anon.'" In *New Feminist Essays on Virginia Woolf.* Ed. Jane Marcus. Lincoln: University of Nebraska Press, 1981. 253–66.

Eliot, T. S. "Tradition and the Individual Talent." *The Sacred Wood: Essays on Poetry and Criticism.* London: Methuen, 1920. 42–53.

Elliott, Bridget, and Jo-Ann Wallace. *Women Artists and Writers: Modernist (im)positionings.* London: Routledge, 1994.

Evans, Lawrence, ed. *The Letters of Walter Pater.* Oxford: Clarendon Press, 1970.

Eysteinsson, Astradur. *The Concept of Modernism.* Ithaca: Cornell University Press, 1990.

Felber, Lynette. *Gender and Genre in Novels without End: The British Roman-Fleuve.* Gainesville: University of Florida Press, 1995.

Felski, Rita. *The Gender of Modernity.* Cambridge: Harvard University Press, 1995.

Fleishman, Avrom. *Virginia Woolf: A Critical Reading.* Baltimore: Johns Hopkins University Press, 1975.

Fleissner, Jennifer. "Dictation Anxiety: The Stenographer's Stake in *Dracula.*" *Nineteenth-Century Contexts* (forthcoming).

Fogel, Aaron. *Coercion to Speak: Conrad's Poetics of Dialogue.* Cambridge: Harvard University Press, 1985.

Ford, Ford Madox. *The Critical Attitude.* London: Duckworth, 1911.

———. "English Literature of To-day—I." In *The Critical Attitude* 55–78.

———. "English Literature of To-day—II." In *The Critical Attitude* 79–110.

———. *The Good Soldier: A Tale of Passion.* 1915. Harmondsworth: Penguin, 1946.

———. "On the Function of the Arts in the Republic." In *The Critical Attitude* 25–51.

———. "On Impressionism, I." *Poetry and Drama* 2 (1914): 167–75.

———. "On Impressionism, II." *Poetry and Drama* 2 (1914): 323–34.

———. "The Passing of the Great Figure." In *The Critical Attitude* 113–29.

———. "Women and Men, I." *Little Review.* 4.9 (January 1918): 17–31.

———. "Women and Men, II." *Little Review.* 4.11 (March 1918): 36–51.

———. "Women and Men, III." *Little Review.* 4.12 (April 1918): 54–65.

———. "Women and Men, IV." *Little Review.* 5.1 (May 1918): 56–62.

———. "Women and Men, V." *Little Review.* 5.3 (July 1918): 49–54.

———. "Women and Men, VI." *Little Review.* 5.5 (September 1918): 54–59.

Forster, E. M. *Aspects of the Novel.* 1927. New York: Harcourt, Brace & World, 1954.

Frank, Ellen Eve. *Literary Architecture: Essays toward a Tradition—Walter*

Pater, Gerard Manley Hopkins, Marcel Proust, Henry James. Berkeley: University of California Press, 1979.

Frank, Joseph. "Spatial Form in Modern Literature." *The Widening Gyre: Crisis and Mastery in Modern Literature.* 1945. Bloomington: Indiana University Press, 1963. 3–62.

Freedman, Jonathan. *Professions of Taste: Henry James, British Aestheticism and Commodity Culture.* Stanford: Stanford University Press, 1990.

Freud, Sigmund. "The Uncanny." 1919. Trans. Alix Strachey. *Studies in Parapsychology.* Ed. Philip Rieff. New York: Collier Books, 1963. 19–60.

Friedman, Ellen G. "'Utterly Other Discourse': The Anticanon of Experimental Women Writers from Dorothy Richardson to Christine Brooke-Rose." *Modern Fiction Studies* 34 (1988): 353–70.

Friedman, Ellen G., and Miriam Fuchs, eds. *Breaking the Sequence: Women's Experimental Fiction.* Princeton: Princeton University Press, 1989.

Friedman, Melvin. *Stream of Consciousness: A Study in Literary Method.* New Haven: Yale University Press, 1955.

Friedman, Susan Stanford. "'Beyond' Gynocriticism and Gynesis: The Geographics of Identity and the Future of Feminist Criticism." *Tulsa Studies in Women's Literature* 15 (1996): 13–40.

———. "Hysteria, Dreams, and Modernity: A Reading of the Origins of Psychoanalysis in Freud's Early Corpus." In Dettmar 41–71.

———. *Penelope's Web: Gender, Modernity, H.D.'s Fiction.* Cambridge: Cambridge University Press, 1990.

Fromm, Gloria G. *Dorothy Richardson: A Biography.* Urbana: University of Illinois Press, 1977.

Froula, Christine. *Modernism's Body: Sex, Culture, and Joyce.* New York: Columbia University Press, 1996.

Gallagher, Catherine. *The Industrial Reformation of English Fiction, 1832–1867.* Chicago: University of Chicago Press, 1985.

Garrity, Jane. "'I Do Not Understand Phrases': Sexuality and Signification in *The Waves.*" Paper delivered at the Third Annual Virginia Woolf Conference, Jefferson City, Mo., June 15, 1993.

———. "'Neither English nor Civilized': Dorothy Richardson's Spectatrix and the Feminine Crusade for Global Intervention." Unpublished essay.

George, Rosemary Marangoly. *The Politics of Home: Postcolonial Relocations and Twentieth-Century Fiction.* Cambridge: Cambridge University Press, 1996.

Gevirtz, Susan. *Narrative's Journey: The Fiction and Film Writing of Dorothy Richardson.* New York: Peter Lang, 1996.

Gikandi, Simon. *Maps of Englishness: Writing Identity in the Culture of Colonialism.* New York: Columbia University Press, 1996.

Gilbert, Sandra, and Susan Gubar. *Sexchanges.* Vol. 2 of *No Man's Land: The Place of the Woman Writer in the Twentieth Century.* New Haven: Yale University Press, 1989.

———. *The War of the Words.* Vol. 1 of *No Man's Land: The Place of the Woman Writer in the Twentieth Century.* New Haven: Yale University Press, 1988.

Girouard, Mark. *Life in the English Country House: A Social and Architectural History.* New Haven: Yale University Press, 1978.

———. *Sweetness and Light: The "Queen Anne" Movement, 1860–1900.* New Haven: Yale University Press, 1984.

Goode, John, ed. *The Air of Reality: New Essays on Henry James.* London: Methuen, 1972.

Graham, J. W. "Point of View in *The Waves:* Some Services of the Style." *University of Toronto Quarterly* 30 (1970): 193–211.

Grand, Sarah. *The Heavenly Twins.* 1893. Ann Arbor: University of Michigan Press, 1992.

———. "The Modern Girl." *North American Review* 158 (June 1894): 706–14.

Green, Barbara. "From Visible *Flâneuse* to Spectacular Suffragette: The Prison, the Street, and the Sites of Suffrage." *Discourse* 17.2 (1994–95): 67–97.

Guerard, Albert. *Conrad the Novelist.* Cambridge: Harvard University Press, 1958.

Habegger, Alfred. *Henry James and the "Woman Business."* Cambridge: Cambridge University Press, 1989.

Hall, Catherine. "The Sweet Delights of Home." In *From the Fires of Revolution to the Great War.* Ed. Michelle Perrot. Vol. 4 of *A History of Private Life.* Gen. eds. Phillipe Ariès and Georges Duby. 5 vols. Cambridge: Harvard University Press, 1990. 47–93.

Hanscombe, Gillian E. *The Art of Life: Dorothy Richardson and the Development of Feminist Consciousness.* Athens: Ohio University Press, 1983.

———. "Dorothy Richardson versus the Novvle." In Friedman and Fuchs 85–98.

Harpham, Geoffrey Galt. *One of Us: The Mastery of Joseph Conrad.* Chicago: University of Chicago Press, 1996.

Harris, Wendell V. "Egerton: Forgotten Realist." *Victorian Newsletter* 33 (1968): 31–35.

Harrison, E. B. "Mothers and Daughters." *Nineteenth Century* 35 (1894): 313–22.

Hassan, Ihab. *The Postmodern Turn: Essays in Postmodern Theory and Culture.* Columbus: Ohio State University Press, 1987.

Haweis, M. E. "The Revolt of the Daughters II: Daughters and Mothers." *Nineteenth Century* 35 (1894): 430–36.

Heath, Stephen. "Writing for Silence: Dorothy Richardson and the Novel." In *Teaching the Text.* Ed. Susanne Kappeler and Norman Bryson. London: Routledge & Kegan Paul, 1983. 126–47.

Heller, Lee E. "The Paradox of Individual Triumph: Instrumentality and the Family in *What Maisie Knew.*" *South Atlantic Review* 53.4 (1988): 77–85.

Helsinger, Elizabeth K., Robin Lauterbach Sheets, and William Veeder. *Defining Voices.* Vol. 1 of *The Woman Question: Society and Literature in Britain and America, 1837–1883.* 3 vols. Chicago: University of Chicago Press, 1983.

Hemery, Gertrude. "The Revolt of the Daughters. An Answer—by One of Them." *Westminster Review* 141 (1894): 679–81.

Hertz, Neil. *The End of the Line: Essays on Psychoanalysis and the Sublime.* New York: Columbia University Press, 1985.

Hidalgo, Pilar. "Female *Flânerie* in Dorothy Richardson's *Pilgrimage.*" *Revista Alicantina de Estudios Ingleses* 6 (1993): 93–98.

Hill, Donald L. Critical and explanatory notes. *The Renaissance: Studies in Art and Poetry.* By Walter Pater. Ed. Hill. Berkeley: University of California Press, 1980.

Hobsbawm, Eric. *The Age of Empire, 1875–1914.* New York: Vintage Books, 1987.

Hogarth, Janet. "Literary Degenerates." *Fortnightly Review* 63 (1895): 586–92.

Holcombe, Lee. *Victorian Ladies at Work: Middle-Class Working Women in England and Wales, 1850–1914.* Hamden, Conn.: Archon Books, 1973.

Howe, Irving. "The Idea of the Modern." *The Idea of the Modern in Literature and the Arts.* New York: Horizon Press, 1967. 11–40.

Huyssen, Andreas. *After the Great Divide: Modernism, Mass Culture, Postmodernism.* Bloomington: Indiana University Press, 1986.

Hynes, Joseph A. "The Middle Way of Miss Farange: A Study of James's *Maisie.*" *ELH* 32 (1965): 528–53.

Hynes, Samuel. *The Edwardian Turn of Mind.* Princeton: Princeton University Press, 1968.

———. "The Epistemology of *The Good Soldier.*" In Cassell 49–56.

Inman, Billie Andrew. "The Intellectual Context of Walter Pater's 'Conclusion.'" *Prose Studies* 4 (1981): 12–30.

Iser, Wolfgang. *Walter Pater: The Aesthetic Moment.* Trans. David Henry Wilson. Cambridge: Cambridge University Press, 1987.

Isle, Walter. *Experiments in Form: Henry James's Novels, 1896–1901.* Cambridge: Harvard University Press, 1968.

Jacobson, Marcia. *Henry James and the Mass Market.* University: University of Alabama Press, 1983.

Jahn, Michael. "Suburban Development in Outer West London, 1850–1900." In *The Rise of Suburbia.* Ed. F. M. L. Thompson. Leicester: Leicester University Press, 1982. 94–156.

James, Henry. *The Awkward Age.* 1899. Oxford: Oxford University Press, 1984.

———. Preface. *The Awkward Age.* By James. 1908. Oxford: Oxford University Press, 1984. xxix–xlvii.

———. Preface. *The Novels and Tales of Henry James.* By James. Vol. 10. New York: Charles Scribner's Sons, 1908. v–xxiv.

———. Preface. *What Maisie Knew.* By James. 1908. Oxford: Oxford University Press, 1966. 1–10.

———. *What Maisie Knew.* 1897. Rev. ed. 1908. Oxford: Oxford University Press, 1966.

Jameson, Fredric. *Fables of Aggression: Wyndham Lewis, the Modernist as Fascist.* Berkeley: University of California Press, 1979.

———. *The Political Unconscious: Narrative as a Socially Symbolic Act.* Ithaca: Cornell University Press, 1981.

———. "Reification and Utopia in Mass Culture." *Signatures of the Visible.* New York: Routledge, 1992. 9–34.

Jardine, Alice A. *Gynesis: Configurations of Woman and Modernity.* Ithaca: Cornell University Press, 1985.

Jay, Martin. "Modernism and the Specter of Psychologism." *Modernism/Modernity* 3.2 (1996): 93–111.

Jeal, Tim. *The Boy-Man: The Life of Lord Baden-Powell.* New York: William Morrow, 1990.

Jeune, Ma[r]y. "The Revolt of the Daughters." *Fortnightly Review* 61 (1894): 267–76.

Jones, Vivien. Introduction. *The Awkward Age.* By Henry James. Oxford: Oxford University Press, 1984. x–xvii.

Jordan, Ellen. "The Christening of the New Woman: May 1894." *Victorian Newsletter* 63 (1983): 19–21.

Joyce, James. *A Portrait of the Artist as a Young Man.* 1916. New York: Penguin, 1993.

Kaplan, Caren. *Questions of Travel: Postmodern Discourses of Displacement.* Durham: Duke University Press, 1996.

Kaplan, Sydney Janet. *Feminine Consciousness in the Modern British Novel.* Urbana: University of Illinois Press, 1975.

Kaston, Carren. *Imagination and Desire in the Novels of Henry James.* New Brunswick: Rutgers University Press, 1984.

Kelley, Alice van Buren. *The Novels of Virginia Woolf: Fact and Vision.* Chicago: University of Chicago Press, 1971.

Kenner, Hugh. *A Colder Eye: The Modern Irish Writers.* New York: Alfred A. Knopf, 1983.

———. *The Pound Era.* Berkeley: University of California Press, 1971.

Kermode, Frank. *Romantic Image.* 1957. London: Routledge & Kegan Paul, 1986.

Kofman, Sarah. *The Enigma of Woman: Woman in Freud's Writings.* Trans. Catherine Porter. Ithaca: Cornell University Press, 1985.

Lane, Christopher. *The Ruling Passion: British Colonial Allegory and the Paradox of Homosexual Desire.* Durham: Duke University Press, 1995.

Langland, Elizabeth. *Nobody's Angels: Middle-Class Women and Domestic Ideology in Victorian Culture.* Ithaca: Cornell University Press, 1995.

Laurence, Patricia Ondek. *The Reading of Silence: Virginia Woolf in the English Tradition.* Stanford: Stanford University Press, 1991.

Lears, T. J. Jackson. *No Place of Grace: Antimodernism and the Transformation of American Culture, 1880–1920.* New York: Pantheon Books, 1981.

Leavis, F. R. *The Great Tradition: George Eliot, Henry James, Joseph Conrad.* 1948. London: Penguin, 1993.

Ledger, Sally. "The New Woman and the Crisis of Victorianism." In Ledger and McCracken 22–44.

Ledger, Sally, and Scott McCracken, eds. *Cultural Politics at the Fin de Siècle.* Cambridge: Cambridge University Press, 1995.

Levenson, Michael. *A Genealogy of Modernism: A Study of English Literary Doctrine, 1908–1922.* Cambridge: Cambridge University Press, 1984.

———. *Modernism and the Fate of Individuality: Character and Novelistic Form from Conrad to Woolf.* Cambridge: Cambridge University Press, 1991.

Levey, Michael. *The Case of Walter Pater.* London: Thames and Hudson, 1978.

Levy, Anita. "Gendered Labor, the Woman Writer and Dorothy Richardson." *Novel: A Forum on Fiction* 25 (1991): 50–70.

Lewis, Sarah. *Woman's Mission.* London, 1839.

Lewis, Wyndham. *Men without Art.* 1934. Santa Rosa: Black Sparrow Press, 1987.

Light, Alison. *Forever England: Femininity, Literature and Conservatism between the Wars.* London: Routledge, 1991.

Linton, Elizabeth Lynn. "The Wild Women as Social Insurgents." *Nineteenth Century* 30 (1891): 596–605.

Loesberg, Jonathan. *Aestheticism and Deconstruction: Pater, Derrida, and De Man.* Princeton: Princeton University Press, 1991.

London, Bette. *The Appropriated Voice: Narrative Authority in Conrad, Forster, and Woolf.* Ann Arbor: University of Michigan Press, 1990.

———. "Guerilla in Petticoats or Sans-Culotte? Virginia Woolf and the Future of Feminist Criticism." *Diacritics* 21.2–3 (1991): 11–42.

———. "Reading Race and Gender in Conrad's Dark Continent." *Criticism* 31 (1989): 235–52.

Lukács, Georg. "The Ideology of Modernism." *The Lukács Reader.* Ed. Arpad Kadarkay. 1964. Oxford: Basil Blackwell, 1995. 187–209.

———. "Narrate or Describe?" *Writer and Critic.* Trans. A. D. Kahn. 1936. New York: Grosset & Dunlap, 197. 110–48.

Lynch, Diedre. "At Home with Jane Austen." In *Cultural Institutions of the Novel.* Ed. Diedre Lynch and William Warner. Durham: Duke University Press, 1996. 159–92.

Lyon, Janet. "Women Demonstrating Modernism." *Discourse* 17.2 (1994–95): 6–25.

———. "Militant Discourse, Strange Bedfellows: Suffragettes and Vorticists before the War." *Differences* 4.2 (1992): 100–133.

MacKenzie, John M. *Propaganda and Empire: The Manipulation of British Public Opinion, 1880–1960.* Manchester: Manchester University Press, 1984.

Mangum, Teresa. *Married, Middlebrow, and Militant: Sarah Grand and the New Woman Novel.* Ann Arbor: University of Michigan Press, 1998.

Marcus, Jane. "Britannia Rules *The Waves.*" In *Decolonizing Tradition: New Views of Twentieth-Century "British" Literary Canons.* Ed. Karen R. Lawrence. Urbana: University of Illinois Press, 1992. 136–62.

———. "Still Practice, A/Wrested Alphabet: Toward a Feminist Aesthetic." *Tulsa Studies in Women's Literature* 3 (1984): 79–97.

———. *Virginia Woolf and the Languages of Patriarchy.* Bloomington: Indiana University Press, 1987.

Marcus, Sharon. *Apartment Stories: City and Home in Nineteenth-Century Paris and London.* Berkeley: University of California Press, 1999.

———. "The Profession of the Author: Abstraction, Advertising, and *Jane Eyre.*" *PMLA* 110 (1995): 206–19.

Marx, John. "Conrad's Gout." *Modernism/Modernity* 6.1 (1999): 91–114.

Matz, Jesse. "Pater's Literary Impression." *Modern Language Quarterly* 56 (1995): 433–56.

May, Brian. "Ford Madox Ford and the Politics of Impressionism." *Essays in Literature* 21 (1994): 82–96.

McClintock, Anne. *Imperial Leather: Race, Gender, and Sexuality in the Colonial Conquest.* New York: Routledge, 1995.

McCracken, Scott. "'A Hard and Absolute Condition of Existence': Reading Masculinity in *Lord Jim*." In Roberts 17–38.

McGee, Patrick. "The Politics of Modernist Form: or, Who Rules *The Waves?*" *Modern Fiction Studies* 38 (1992): 631–50.

McGrath, F. C. *The Sensible Spirit: Walter Pater and the Modernist Paradigm.* Tampa: University of South Florida Press, 1986.

McHale, Brian. *Postmodernist Fiction.* New York: Methuen, 1987.

McWhirter, David, ed. *Henry James's New York Edition: The Construction of Authorship.* Stanford: Stanford University Press, 1995.

Meisel, Perry. *The Absent Father: Virginia Woolf and Walter Pater.* New Haven: Yale University Press, 1981.

———. *The Myth of the Modern: A Study in British Literature and Criticism after 1850.* New Haven: Yale University Press, 1987.

Mezei, Kathy, ed. *Ambiguous Discourse: Feminist Narratology and British Women Writers.* Chapel Hill: University of North Carolina Press, 1996.

Michaels, Walter Benn. *Our America: Nativism, Modernism, and Pluralism.* Durham: Duke University Press, 1995.

Miller, J. Hillis. *Fiction and Repetition: Seven English Novels.* Cambridge: Harvard University Press, 1982.

———. *Versions of Pygmalion.* Cambridge: Harvard University Press, 1990.

———. "Walter Pater: A Partial Portrait." *Daedalus* 105.1 (1976): 97–113.

Miller, Jane Eldridge. *Rebel Women: Feminism, Modernism, and the Edwardian Novel.* Chicago: University of Chicago Press, 1994.

Minow-Pinkney, Makiko. *Virginia Woolf and the Problem of the Subject: Feminine Writing in the Major Novels.* New Brunswick: Rutgers University Press, 1987.

Mitchell, Juliet. "*What Maisie Knew:* Portrait of the Artist as a Young Girl." In Goode 168–89.

Mizener, Arthur. *The Saddest Story: A Biography of Ford Madox Ford.* New York: World Publishers, 1971.

Mohanty, S. P. "Kipling's Children and the Colour Line." *Race and Class* 31.1 (1989): 21–40.

Mongia, Padmini. "Empire, Narrative and the Feminine in *Lord Jim* and *Heart of Darkness*." In *Contexts for Conrad.* Ed. Keith Carabine, Owen Knowles, and Wieslaw Krajka. East European Monographs Series, 370. Boulder: East European Monographs, 1993. 135–50.

———. "'Ghosts of the Gothic': Spectral Women and Colonized Spaces in *Lord Jim*." In Roberts 1–16.

Naremore, James. *The World without a Self: Virginia Woolf and the Novel.* New Haven: Yale University Press, 1973.

Nelson, Claudia. *Boys Will Be Girls: The Feminine Ethic and British Children's Fiction, 1857–1917.* New Brunswick: Rutgers University Press, 1991.

Nettels, Elsa. *James and Conrad.* Athens: University of Georgia Press, 1977.

Newfield, Christopher. "The Politics of Male Suffering: Masochism and Hegemony in the American Renaissance." *Differences* 1.3 (1989): 55–87.

Nicholls, Peter. *Modernisms: A Literary Guide.* Berkeley: University of California Press, 1995.

Noble, James Ashcroft. "The Fiction of Sexuality." *Contemporary Review* 67 (1895): 490–98.

Nordau, Max. *Degeneration.* 1892. Trans. 1895. Lincoln: University of Nebraska Press, 1993.

North, Michael. *The Dialect of Modernism: Race, Language, and Twentieth-Century Literature.* New York: Oxford University Press, 1994.

Pater, Walter. *Appreciations, with an Essay on Style.* 1889. Evanston: Northwestern University Press, 1987.

———. "The Child in the House." *Selected Writings of Walter Pater.* 1878. Ed. Harold Bloom. New York: New American Library, 1974. 1–16.

———. "Coleridge." In *Appreciations* 65–104.

———. "Postscript." In *Appreciations* 241–61.

———. *Marius the Epicurean.* 1885. Oxford: Oxford University Press, 1986.

———. *The Renaissance: Studies in Art and Poetry.* 1873. Ed. Donald L. Hill. Berkeley: University of California Press, 1980.

———. "Style." 1888. In *Appreciations* 103–25.

Pearce, Richard, ed. *Molly Blooms: A Polylogue on "Penelope" and Cultural Studies.* Madison: University of Wisconsin Press, 1994.

Pecora, Vincent. *Self and Form in Modern Literature.* Baltimore: Johns Hopkins University Press, 1989.

Phelan, James, ed. *Reading Narrative: Form, Ethics, Ideology.* Columbus: Ohio State University Press, 1989.

Pick, Daniel. *Faces of Degeneration: A European Disorder, c. 1848–c. 1918.* New York: Cambridge University Press, 1989.

Poovey, Mary. *Uneven Developments: The Ideological Work of Gender in Mid-Victorian England.* Chicago: University of Chicago Press, 1988.

Posnock, Ross. "Breaking the Aura of Henry James." In McWhirter 23–38.

———. *The Trial of Curiosity: Henry James, William James, and the Challenge of Modernity.* New York: Oxford University Press, 1991.

Powys, John Cowper. *Dorothy Richardson.* London: Joiner and Steele, 1931.

Psomiades, Kathy Alexis. *Beauty's Body: Femininity and Representation in British Aestheticism.* Stanford: Stanford University Press, 1997.

Pykett, Lyn. *The "Improper" Feminine: The Woman's Sensation Novel and the New Woman Writing.* London: Routledge, 1992.

Rader, Ralph. "Lord Jim and the Formal Development of the English Novel." In Phelan 220–35.

Radford, Jean. *Dorothy Richardson.* Key Women Writers Series. Bloomington: Indiana University Press, 1991.

———. "The Woman and the Jew: Sex and Modernity." In *Modernity, Culture, and "The Jew."* Ed. Bryan Cheyette and Laura Marcus. Stanford: Stanford University Press, 1998. 91–104.

Ragussis, Michael. *Figures of Conversion: "The Jewish Question" and English National Identity.* Durham: Duke University Press, 1995.

Reed, Christopher. "Through Formalism: Feminism and Virginia Woolf's Relation to Bloomsbury Aesthetics." *Twentieth Century Literature* 38 (1992): 20–43.

Richards, Thomas. *The Imperial Archive: Knowledge and the Fantasy of Empire.* New York: Verso, 1993.

Richardson, Dorothy. *Pilgrimage.* 1915–67. London: J. M. Dent & Sons, 1967. 4 vols.

———. "Women and the Future." 1924. In *The Gender of Modernism.* Ed. Bonnie Kime Scott. Bloomington: Indiana University Press, 1990. 412–13.

Riley, Denise. *"Am I That Name?" Feminism and the Category of 'Women' in History.* Minneapolis: University of Minnesota Press, 1988.

Roberts, Andrew Michael, ed. *The Conradian: Conrad and Gender.* Amsterdam: Rodopi, 1993.

Rose, Jacqueline. "Dorothy Richardson and the Jew." *States of Fantasy.* New York: Oxford University Press, 1996. 117–32.

Rose, Shirley. "The Unmoving Center: Consciousness in Dorothy Richardson's *Pilgrimage.*" *Contemporary Literature* 10 (1969): 366–82.

Rosenthal, Michael. *The Character Factory: Baden-Powell and the Origins of the Boy Scout Movement.* New York: Pantheon, 1986.

Rowe, John Carlos. *The Other Henry James.* Durham: Duke University Press, 1998.

———. *The Theoretical Dimensions of Henry James.* Madison: University of Wisconsin Press, 1984.

Rubinstein, David. *Before the Suffragettes: Women's Emancipation in the 1890s.* New York: St. Martin's Press, 1986.

Ruskin, John. "Of Queens' Gardens." *Sesame and Lilies.* 1865. Ed. Agnes Spofford Cook. New York: Silver, Burdett and Company, 1900. 72–105.

Said, Edward. "Conrad: The Presentation of Narrative." *Novel* 7 (1974): 116–32.

Sale, Roger. "Ford's Coming of Age: *The Good Soldier* and *Parade's End.*" In Stang 55–76.

Saunders, Max. *Ford Madox Ford: A Dual Life.* Vol. 1. Oxford: Oxford University Press, 1996.

Scholes, Robert. "In the Brothel of Modernism: Picasso and Joyce." *In Search of James Joyce.* Urbana: University of Illinois Press, 1992. 178–207.

Schor, Naomi. *Reading in Detail: Aesthetics and the Feminine.* New York: Methuen, 1987.

Schorer, Mark. Introduction. *The Good Soldier.* By Ford Madox Ford. New York: Vintage, 1951. v–xv.

Schwartz, Sanford. *The Matrix of Modernism: Pound, Eliot, and Early 20th Century Thought.* Princeton: Princeton University Press, 1985.

Scott, Bonnie Kime. *Refiguring Modernism.* 2 vols. Bloomington: Indiana University Press, 1995.

Scott, Joan. "Universalism and the History of Feminism." *Differences* 7.1 (1995): 1–14.

Sedgwick, Eve Kosofsky. *Epistemology of the Closet.* Berkeley: University of California Press, 1990.

Seeley, Tracy. "Conrad's Modernist Romance: *Lord Jim.*" *ELH* 59 (1992): 495–511.

Seltzer, Mark. *Henry James and the Art of Power.* Ithaca: Cornell University Press, 1984.

Showalter, Elaine. *Sexual Anarchy: Gender and Culture at the Fin de Siècle.* New York: Viking 1990.

———. "Syphilis, Sexuality, and the Fiction of the Fin de Siècle." In *Sex, Politics, and Science in the Nineteenth Century: Selected Papers from the English Institute, 1983–84.* Ed. Ruth Bernard Yeazell. Baltimore: Johns Hopkins University Press, 1986. 88–115.

Shuter, William F. *Rereading Walter Pater.* Cambridge: Cambridge University Press, 1997.

Siegel, Sandra. "Literature and Degeneration: The Representation of 'Decadence.'" In *Degeneration: The Dark Side of Progress.* Ed. J. Edward Chamberlin and Sander Gilman. New York: Columbia University Press, 1985. 199–219.

Silverstone, Rosalie. "Office Work for Women: An Historical Review." *Business History* 18.1 (1976): 98–110.

Small, I. C. "The Vocabulary of Pater's Criticism and the Psychology of Aesthetics." *British Journal of Aesthetics* 18 (978): 81–87.

Smith, Alys W. Pearsall. "A Reply from the Daughters II." *Nineteenth Century* 35 (1894): 443–50.

Smith, Paul. *Discerning the Subject.* Minneapolis: University of Minnesota Press, 1988.

Smith, Sidonie. *Subjectivity, Identity, and the Body: Women's Autobiographical Practices in the Twentieth Century.* Bloomington: Indiana University Press, 1993.

Snitow, Ann Barr. *Ford Madox Ford and the Voice of Uncertainty.* Baton Rouge: Louisiana State University Press, 1984.

Sprinker, Michael. "Fiction and Ideology: *Lord Jim* and the Problem of Literary History." In Phelan 236–49.

Squier, Susan M. *Virginia Woolf and London: The Sexual Politics of the City.* Chapel Hill: University of North Carolina Press, 1985.

Stallybrass, Peter, and Allon White. *The Politics and Poetics of Transgression.* Ithaca: Cornell University Press, 1986.

Stang, Sondra, ed. *The Presence of Ford Madox Ford: A Memorial Volume of Essays, Poems, and Memoirs.* Philadelphia: University of Pennsylvania Press, 1981.

Steedman, Carolyn. *Strange Dislocations: Childhood and the Idea of Human Interiority, 1780–1930.* Cambridge: Harvard University Press, 1995.

Straus, Nina Pelikan. "The Exclusion of the Intended from Secret Sharing in Conrad's *Heart of Darkness.*" *Novel* 20 (1987): 123–48.

Stutfield, Hugh E. M. "The Psychology of Feminism." *Blackwood's Edinburgh Magazine* 161 (1897): 104–17.

———. "Tommyrotics." *Blackwood's Edinburgh Magazine* 157 (1895): 833–45.

Suleri, Sara. *The Rhetoric of English India.* Chicago: University of Chicago Press, 1992.

Sussman, Herbert. *Victorian Masculinities: Manhood and Masculine Poetics in Early Victorian Literature and Art.* Cambridge: Cambridge University Press, 1995.

Sypher, Eileen B. "*The Waves:* A Utopia of Androgyny?" In *Virginia Woolf: Centennial Essays.* Ed. Elaine K. Ginsberg and Laura Moss Gottlieb. Troy, N.Y.: Whitson Publishers, 1983. 187–213.

Taylor, Charles. *Sources of the Self: The Making of Modern Identity.* Cambridge: Harvard University Press, 1989.

Teahan, Sheila. *The Rhetorical Logic of Henry James.* Baton Rouge: Louisiana State University Press, 1995.

Teal, Laurie. "The Hollow Women: Modernism, the Prostitute, and Commodity Aesthetics." *Differences* 7.3 (1995): 80–108.

Tester, Keith, ed. *The Flâneur.* New York: Routledge, 1994.

Tickner, Lisa. "Men's Work: Masculinity and Modernism." *Differences* 4.3 (1992): 1–37.

Torgovnick, Marianna. *Gone Primitive: Savage Intellects, Modern Lives.* Chicago: University of Chicago Press, 1990.

Tratner, Michael. *Modernism and Mass Politics: Joyce, Woolf, Eliot, Yeats.* Stanford: Stanford University Press, 1995.

Tucker, Irene. "What Maisie Promised: Realism, Liberalism and the Ends of Contract." *Yale Journal of Criticism* 11 (1998): 335–64.

Veeder, William. "Henry James and the Uses of the Feminine." In *Out of Bounds: Male Writers and Gender(ed) Criticism.* Ed. Laura Claridge and Elizabeth Langland. Amherst: University of Massachusetts Press, 1990. 219–51.

Vicinus, Martha. *Independent Women — Work and Community for Single Women, 1850–1920.* Chicago: University of Chicago Press, 1985.

Walkowitz, Judith R. *City of Dreadful Delight: Narratives of Sexual Danger in Late-Victorian London.* Chicago: University of Chicago Press, 1992.

———. *Prostitution and Victorian Society: Women, Class, and the State.* Cambridge: Cambridge University Press, 1980.

Walters, Margaret. "Keeping the Place Tidy for the Young Female Mind: *The Awkward Age.*" In Goode 190–218.

Ward, Anthony. *Walter Pater: The Idea in Nature.* Worcester: MacGibbon and Keel, 1966.

Wardley, Lynn. "Woman's Voice, Democracy's Body, and *The Bostonians.*" *ELH* 56 (1989): 639–65.

Warren, Allen. "Citizens of the Empire: Baden-Powell, Scouts and Guides, and an Imperial Ideal." In *Imperialism and Popular Culture.* Ed. John M. MacKenzie. Manchester: Manchester University Press, 1986. 232–56.

———. "Popular Manliness: Baden-Powell, Scouting and the Development of Manly Character." In *Manliness and Morality: Middle-class Masculinity in Britain and America, 1800–1940.* Ed. J. A. Mangan and James Walvin. Manchester: Manchester University Press, 1987. 199–219.

Watt, Ian. *Conrad in the Nineteenth Century.* Berkeley: University of California Press, 1979.

Weinstein, Philip M. *Henry James and the Requirements of the Imagination.* Cambridge: Harvard University Press, 1971.

White, Allon. *The Uses of Obscurity: The Fiction of Early Modernism.* London: Routledge & Kegan Paul, 1981.

Wicke, Jennifer. "Coterie Consumption: Bloomsbury, Keynes, and Modernism as Marketing." In *Marketing Modernisms: Self-Promotion, Canonization, and Rereading.* Ed. Kevin J. H. Dettmar and Stephen Watt. Ann Arbor: University of Michigan Press, 1996. 109–32.

Wiesenfarth, Joseph, FSC. "Criticism and the Semiosis of *The Good Soldier."* *Modern Fiction Studies* 9 (1963): 39–49.

Williams, Carolyn. *Transfigured World: Walter Pater's Aesthetic Historicism.* Ithaca: Cornell University Press, 1989.

Williams, Raymond. "When Was Modernism?" *The Politics of Modernism: Against the New Conformists.* London: Verso, 1989. 31–35.

Wilson, Elizabeth. "The Invisible *Flâneur."* *New Left Review* 191 (1992): 90–110.

Winner, Anthony. *Culture and Irony: Studies in Conrad's Major Novels.* Charlottesville: University Press of Virginia, 1988.

Wolff, Janet. "The Invisible *Flâneuse:* Women and the Literature of Modernity." *Feminine Sentences: Essays on Women and Culture.* 1985. Cambridge: Polity Press, 1990. 34–50.

Wollaeger, Mark A. *Joseph Conrad and the Fictions of Skepticism.* Stanford: Stanford University Press, 1990.

Wollheim, Richard. *On Art and the Mind.* Cambridge: Harvard University Press, 1974.

Woolf, Virginia. *Between the Acts.* New York: Harcourt Brace Jovanovich, 1941.

———. "Mr. Bennett and Mrs. Brown." *The Captain's Death Bed and Other Essays.* 1924. New York: Harcourt Brace Jovanovich, 1950. 94–119.

———. *Mrs. Dalloway.* 1925. New York: Harcourt Brace Jovanovich, 1981.

———. *A Room of One's Own.* 1929. New York: Harcourt Brace Jovanovich, 1957.

———. "Street Haunting." *The Death of the Moth.* 1927. New York: Harcourt, Brace, 1942. 20–36.

———. *To the Lighthouse.* 1927. New York: Harcourt Brace Jovanovich, 1981.

———. *The Waves.* New York: Harcourt Brace Jovanovich, 1931.

———. *A Writer's Diary.* Ed. Leonard Woolf. New York: Harcourt Brace Jovanovich, 1953.

Zimmeck, Meta. "Jobs for the Girls: The Expansion of Clerical Work for Women, 1850–1914." In *Unequal Opportunities: Women's Employment in England, 1800–1918*. Ed. Angela V. John. Oxford: Basil Blackwell, 1986. 153–77.

Zwerdling, Alex. *Virginia Woolf and the Real World*. Berkeley: University of California Press, 1986.

Index

TAMAR KATZ is an associate professor of English at Brown University. She teaches twentieth-century literature and literary theory, and she is currently working on a book about modernism, the city, and the public sphere.

Typeset in 9.5/12.5 Trump Mediaeval
with Trump Mediaeval display
Composed by Jim Proefrock
at the University of Illinois Press
Manufactured by Maple-Vail
Book Manufacturing Group

University of Illinois Press
1325 South Oak Street
Champaign, IL 61820-6903
www.press.uillinois.edu